Popular Music Genres

Popular Music Genres

An Introduction

Stuart Borthwick and Ron Moy

LOVE THE PANTS
MATE!

Edinburgh University Press

© Stuart Borthwick and Ron Moy, 2004

Edinburgh University Press Ltd
22 George Square, Edinburgh

Typeset in Ehrhardt
by Hewer Text Ltd, Edinburgh, and
printed and bound in Great Britain by
The Cromwell Press, Trowbridge, Wilts

A CIP record for this book is available from the British Library

ISBN 0 7486 1744 2 (hardback)
ISBN 0 7486 1745 0 (paperback)

The right of Stuart Borthwick and Ron Moy
to be identified as authors of this work
has been asserted in accordance with
the Copyright, Designs and Patents Act 1988.

Contents

Illustrations

Acknowledgements

Ron Moy would like to thank – my parents and my brother and sister, Virginia and Nick, for their part in encouraging an unhealthy fixation with popular music from a very early age. Other members of my extended family, particularly my cousins Alan and Vanessa, also did much to foster an awareness in the power and potential of pop. A number of long-standing musical friendships have been very influential: I would like to particularly thank David Buckley, Brian Dunne, Ian Runeckles and Brian Sharp. Many of my colleagues at Liverpool John Moores University have helped encourage my teaching and research in the subject field, including Phil Markey and Nickianne Moody. I would also like to thank the contributions made by countless students taking popular music modules since 1992. Mike Brocken brought his great archival expertise to bear, particularly with regard to the chapters dealing with soul and psychedelia, and helped improve my knowledge. I would also like to thank Sheena Streather, the Media librarian at Liverpool John Moores University, and the staff of Northwich public library for their assistance with research sources. My final thanks go to my partner, Anne, and our children, Byron and Elena, for indulging my musical obsessions, and latterly actively contributing to an environment that denies me the opportunity to fall back on tired ageist clichés relating to the nature of contemporary music and 'the good old days'.

Stuart Borthwick would like to thank – Rachel Tolhurst, for support beyond the call of love or duty, particularly while ill during the completion of this book – 'Keep that breathless charm' my sweetheart. My mother and father for supporting my endeavours in higher education, both morally and financially. Colleagues at Liverpool John Moores University for their help, assistance and guidance, especially the Media and Cultural Studies teaching team. My line managers – Phil Markey, Nickianne Moody and Tamsin Spargo. All those students who have contributed, unwittingly or not, to my ideas around music. Mike Brocken, Mike Holderness, Paul Meme, Twist and John Eden for comments on early drafts. Hillegonda Rietveld for her continuing support. Everyone at www.uk-dance.org for their continued support, friendship and inspiration (especially the Raya crew). Those in the Liverpool music industry who have offered me their advice, especially Jules and Danny at Invicta HiFi/Liquidation. Jamie Reid and his management. The Merseyside Music Development Agency. Staff at the Institute of Popular Music at the University of Liverpool for early inspiration. Phil and Neil at The Picket venue (long may it continue). A final special thanks must also go to Dexy's Midnight Runners for their tour of 2003. These astounding gigs gave me a lifetime's inspiration in a few precious hours. Don't stop the burning. SAP!

Introduction

In the past ten years, there has been a significant expansion in the provision of academic programmes and units (discrete courses within modular degrees) that deal with the study of popular music. This expanded area of study encompasses work at undergraduate and post-graduate level within disciplines as diverse as sociology, media studies, cultural studies, marketing, English and literary studies, history, and musicology. Despite this expansion (or possibly because of it), no single discipline has managed to claim 'ownership' of the field, and the study of popular music relies upon theoretical perspectives and methodological tools that are often seen as being contradictory.

What this contradictory situation tells us is that there is no correct or true method of examining popular music. However, within this hetero-geneity of approaches, there are methodological positions that can be rejected. A purely musicological approach will tell us a great deal about the 'inner meanings' of particular pieces of popular music, but due to the 'textualism' of this approach, traditional musicology cannot tell us much about the relationship between musical texts and the cultures and societies in which they are situated. Equally, an approach that draws exclusively upon a historical method can tell us a great deal about the position of popular music in the societies in which it is situated, but it cannot tell us much about what individual pieces of music or specific musical genres actually mean.

This book rejects such a 'unidisciplinary' approach to the study of popular music and promotes an examination that is situated in the interdisciplinary space between a range of separate academic fields of enquiry. By using theoretical positions and methodological tools drawn from a range of disciplines, our approach becomes contextual, rather than textual or intertexual. While we are interested in musical texts, this interest is framed by an examination of the relationship between musical texts and their social, cultural, political and economic contexts. We firmly believe that an examination of the relationship between musical texts and their various contexts tells us far more about music and its importance to the societies in which it is situated than a purely musicological approach. Equally, we believe that the story of popular music cannot be told through charts and statistical data, and we also believe that one should not be overly reliant upon music press hyperbole for source material. While charts and statistics avoid the analysis of how ideological domination and power are reproduced through and in the consumption of music, to be overly reliant upon the music press for source material would be to make us complicit in the reproduction of those ideological discourses that the music press relies upon.

Our approach is therefore dialectical, critical and discursive. It is dialectical because it is rooted in the belief that the meaning of popular music is to be found in the interrelationship between text and context. It is also dialectical because it addresses issues related to the reproduction of social relations. Our approach is critical because it employs theoretical positions that enable the academic to move beyond the mere description of musical phenomena, towards an examination of why and how music means what it does. Our approach is discursive because of our belief that music is a language system where texts are 'made to mean' through the use of representational techniques that predate the production of in-dividual texts. Our approach also addresses contemporary debates con-cerning discourse, in that our method is informed by the belief that meaning systems such as music 'are and always have been subjected to the historical developments and conflicts of social relations in general' (Hartley 1994: 93), and that 'the potentially infinite senses any language system is capable of producing are always limited and fixed by the structure of social relations which prevails in a given time and place, and which is itself represented through various discourses' (94).

While suggesting that our approach is contextual, dialectical, critical and discursive rather than textual or musicological, we are aware of the potential dangers of such an approach. One such long-standing danger, originally highlighted by Simon Frith in 1983, is that the analysis of context is completed at the expense of textual analysis (Frith 1983: 13). Roy Shuker agrees, suggesting that this problem is not limited to academics, but can also be found in more general criticism: 'Rock critics remain essentially preoccupied with sociology rather than sound, and there has been too ready a willingness to dismiss musicology as having little relevance to the study of rock' (Shuker 1994: 136). In our approach to the study of eleven music genres, we do find time to focus on musical texts themselves. However, this textual analysis is tempered by analyses of historical roots and antecedents, social and political contexts, visual aesthetics and generic developments. In rigidly applying this analytical formula we are not suggesting that this is the 'correct' way of examining a musical genre, merely that examining these areas can lead to an appropriate balance between the study of text and context, thereby providing an analysis of the production, distribution and consumption of texts in specific social, cultural, political and economic contexts. We feel that this approach is particularly suited to the interdisciplinary nature of the undergraduate study of popular music.

Key to all these contexts, and key to the relationship between text and context, is the notion of genre, and it is this concept that sits at the centre of this book. In using the term genre, we are attempting to categorise musical styles within certain broad textual and extra-textual parameters. Of course, this approach is schematic and not without its limitations. Our assignation of generic terms to certain key works and movements will not be definitive or beyond dispute. Indeed, dispute is central to genre-based study. For instance, one of the most commonly employed generic terms in contemporary usage is R&B. However, if we look at the disparity of musical performers and styles all included under this heading, the term ceases to have any clear definition.

In examining genre, we would argue that such an analysis must be historically grounded and tightly categorised. Whereas 'overarching' metagenres such as rock or pop transcend historical epochs, others, such as progressive rock or Britpop, do not. Such genres (or subgenres) are intrinsically tied to an era, a mode of production, a *Zeitgeist* and a set of social circumstances that effectively ensures their demise, or at least mutation into other forms. Genres have a degree of elasticity, but there invariably comes a point when they split under the pressure of some force or another – be it musical, technological, commercial or social. Within each of the chapters that follow we will trace the roots and antecedents of each of our chosen genres, their defining characteristics, and how the genre develops and shifts once a split – sometimes rapid and cataclysmic, sometimes organic and almost imperceptible – occurs.

Having made the above points concerning methodology, this book is not intended to be an overview of the different approaches that can be taken in studying popular music. Other writers have produced more suitable works that introduce students to a variety of different ways of studying pop (most notably Frith 1996, Longhurst 1995, Middleton 1990, Negus 1996, Shuker 1994 and Shuker 1998). This book should not be used as a substitute for reading these theoretically rigorous tomes. First and foremost, this book is concerned with analysing eleven specific popular music genres, rather than reflecting critically upon the different approaches that can be taken to study these genres. Our book is intended to serve as an introduction to the study of soul music, funk, psychedelia, progressive rock, punk rock, reggae, synthpop, heavy metal, indie, rap and jungle. While we engage with key terms and concepts that can be applied to these genres, our approach is not wholly inclusive and should only serve as an introduction to the study of these genres.

Further reading

Frith, S. (1983) *Sound Effects: Youth, Leisure and the Politics of Rock 'n' Roll.* London: Constable.

Frith, S. (1996) *Performing Rites: Evaluating Popular Music.* Oxford: Oxford University Press.

Longhurst, B. (1995) *Popular Music and Society.* London: Polity Press.

Middleton, R. (1990) *Studying Popular Music.* Milton Keynes: Open University Press.

Negus, K. (1996) *Popular Music in Theory: An Introduction.* London: Polity Press.

Shuker, R. (1994) *Understanding Popular Music.* London: Routledge.

Shuker, R. (1998) *Key Concepts in Popular Music.* London: Routledge.

CHAPTER 1

Soul: from gospel to groove

An overview of the genre

In commercial terms, the genre that by the early 1960s became known as soul was the most successful of all the 'crossover' styles until its partial eclipse by disco in the mid-1970s. Developing from styles largely aimed at (but not necessarily consumed by) the African-American community, such as gospel, jazz and blues, soul succeeded in breaking through into the mainstream pop market in both the US and Europe. In the main but not exclusively an African-American phenomenon, soul's success was as much due to a number of labels, so-called 'house sounds', and little-known studio bands, as it was to specific performers or songwriters.

The most successful and high profile of all the soul labels was a collection of titles that we can gather under the name Tamla Motown and were most closely associated with its founder Berry Gordy Jnr (see Abbott 2001) Although Motown achieved its international breakthrough once it signed a distribution deal with EMI in the UK in 1963, its degree of creative autonomy throughout the 1960s does bolster its claim to be thought of as an independent label. Indeed, Motown was the most successful independent label of any era, if we look at its international profile, its sales and the ratio of hits to misses (Ward 2001: 47).

Before the great soul labels of the 1960s became established, important groundwork had been laid by performers such as Ray Charles (Ray Charles Robinson) and Sam Cooke. Charles had his greatest period of success between the mid-1950s and mid-1960s, working in areas as diverse as jazz, blues, gospel, soul and country. In common with so many in the soul field, Cooke came from a gospel background. After leaving his group, The Soul Stirrers, in 1956, Cooke crossed over into the secular market, achieving a string of pop hits between 1957 and 1964, the year of his early death. More importantly, he set the tone for both the autonomous creative artist and the smooth 'lover man' persona and performance style later adopted by the likes of Marvin Gaye (Marvin Pentz Gay), Al Green, Teddy Pendergrass and Alexander O'Neill.

At around the same time that Motown was emerging in the industrial heartlands of Detroit, Jim Stewart was launching Stax records in Memphis. In 1959, the Atlantic organisation – long associated with jazz and R&B – began its long and fruitful distribution relationship with Stax. This was later bolstered by having Atlantic artists such as Aretha Franklin and Wilson Pickett recording in the deep south with Stax musicians and local house session musicians such as Booker T and the M.G.'s, the Muscle Shoals, and the Mar-Keys rhythm section. From 1965 to 1968, the Stax/Atlantic combination was responsible for what many considered the perfect 'rootsy', rural antidote to the 'showbiz' trapping of Motown soul, although it is significant that what became known as the subgenre of southern soul was far more racially mixed than its northern counterpart. Crucial contributions to the sound were made by the likes of white musicians such as Steve Cropper, Donald 'Duck' Dunn and Spooner Oldham, and white producers such as Jerry Wexler and Tom Dowd. As Robert Palmer has stated, these anomalies and ironies included

> The 'blackest' of singers – with a whiteface mask of Alabama dust. The funkiest kind of down-home dance record – with a backing band of white southern crackers. These are the sort of ironies that virtually defined the soul-music era – and, arguably, the entire history of rock and roll. The issue of race seems so evident and straightforward, so close to the surface in rock and roll, and particularly soul music; but things are not always what they seem. (Palmer 1995: 80–1)

In 1967, Otis Redding Jr was voted top male singer by the most prestigious British popular music journal, *Melody Maker*, in its readers' poll. This was the first time in a decade that Elvis Presley (Elvis Aaron Presley) had not won the award and showed the huge amount of international acclaim being afforded soul music by that period.

In opposition to the working processes of Stax in Memphis – dubbed 'Soulsville USA' – Gordy, utilising production line methods of management, promotion and quality control, oversaw a label he dubbed 'The Sound of Young America', based in a small studio that bore the logo 'Hitsville USA'. It was one that in tone and delivery was unthreatening to mainstream white society, and one that had crossed over from R&B/black charts into the pop charts by 1964. It was also significant that by 1970, half of Motown's vice presidents were white (Brown 1982: 701). Motown artists were among the few American chart-based artists to thrive during the Beatles/British beat invasion of 1964–6. Indeed, The Supremes in particular had huge success in Britain at the height of Beatlemania.

Towards the end of the 1960s, Gordy's autocratic style and the perceived inequalities regarding royalties and credits led the organisation to fragment. Many artists and writers left the label, including the Isley Brothers and Holland, Dozier and Holland. In addition, Gordy's decision to relocate to California in the early 1970s, together with his largely unsuccessful attempt to promote Diana Ross (Diane Ross) as a major film star at the expense of record releases, lost the label its impetus and market role. Stax, after reaching a crossover high point with the huge *Wattstax* concert and film in 1972 (Maycock 2002: 30–5), collapsed soon after in financial disarray. The decline of Motown and Stax contributed to the rise of Philadelphia International, the last great soul label and one based shamelessly on Motown's sophisticated pop sensibility and crossover style.

Countless smaller, often regionally based labels contributed to soul music. Many of the more rare items became the basis of the 'Northern Soul' club scene in the UK, a precursor to later disc and DJ scenes such as rare groove and acid house (Rimmer 2001: 220–1). In particular, mention should be made of Chess in Chicago, and Hi records, responsible for Al Green's hits in the early 1970s. Much of Curtis Mayfield's work, either solo or with the Impressions, was released on small labels such as Vee-Jay, ABC and Curtom. Mayfield's delicate falsetto and gospel-based compositions emphasised optimism and racial harmony, but his early material, such as *Keep On Pushing* and *We're A Winner* also promoted energy and fortitude. Later, his soundtrack for the movie *Superfly* exhibited a keen social awareness of the worsening state of social conditions, particularly in the ghettos.

Although the US was very much the home of soul, Britain did produce successful performers working in the genre, such as Dusty Springfield (Mary O'Brien), Chris Farlowe and Cliff Bennett. However, the 'house band' and studio sound so central to soul was never duplicated in the UK, neither was there a songwriting/production process to match the likes of Holland/Dozier/Holland at Motown, or Isaac Hayes and David Porter at Stax. Soul singers such as Springfield and Kiki Dee (Pauline Matthews) made the move to the US for a period in the late 1960s, with mixed results. Other singers comfortable within the vocal idiom, such as Tom Jones (Thomas John Woodward), Lulu (Marie McDonald McLaughlin Lawrie) and Rod Stewart (Roderick David Stewart), concentrated their attentions on different rock and pop fields. One act that did achieve great success in the mid-1960s was Geno Washington and The Ram Jam Band, a white British band fronted by a black American. As well as having a great reputation as a live act, they also achieved success in the album charts – a great rarity for soul acts before the 1970s.

Soul had a huge impact upon other genres, such as rock (the work of Rod Stewart, for example) and reggae, which will be explored elsewhere in this book. In the hands of early 1980s 'new pop' acts such as Culture Club, Wham, the Eurythmics, Soft Cell and ABC, soul and Motown were given an electronic makeover while still clearly being approached as a direct homage. Equally, soul was prepared to absorb musical elements and production techniques from other pop genres, such as psychedelia and hard rock in late 1960s releases. Conceptual albums, such as Marvin Gaye's *What's Going On*, also reflected the increasing complexity of the format that rock had been exploring since the late 1960s.

However, in overall terms, soul was predominantly a singles form, typically mainstream in terms of its lyrical subject matter and structure, but it did much to prepare the market for more experimental and lyrically challenging forms such as funk and rap. In the era before 'Dance' became a metagenre rather than just an activity, soul music, in all its guises, was one of the dominant forms in the burgeoning discothèques, as well as a staple of the live circuit, particularly in the form of 'revues' or label packages. These toured to huge acclaim in Europe throughout the 1960s.

Historical roots and antecedents

For Ashley Brown, soul comes from three principal sources: jazz, blues and gospel. He describes these styles, not without a degree of accuracy, as the art music, the social music and the religious music of black America. 'Jazz and blues provided form and the beat; gospel gave soul its voice' (Brown 1982: 321). No mention of soul's precursors would be complete without reference to the metagenre of rhythm and blues (R&B). R&B developed alongside the mass emigration of rural blacks to the industrial north (Chicago, Detroit) and to California in the 1930s and 1940s. R&B was an up-tempo, 'urbanised' form of blues, utilising amplification and electrified instruments (the solid-bodied electric guitar was popularised by the Fender company in 1950, followed by a similar bass model in 1951, although the acoustic stand-up bass was the staple until the late 1950s: Burrows 1998). R&B was a commercial success throughout the postwar era. The 'jump blues' recordings of a group such as Louis Jordan and the Tympani Five, built upon twelve-bar blues progressions, 'boogie-woogie' style piano and vernacular, wisecracking vocals, provides us with a clear model for both rock 'n' roll and R&B.

Although it does not fit into the black 'authenticity' paradigm so prevalent among white social commentators, we might also add the importance of 'mainstream' forms of popular music, whether urban – such as doo-wop, Hollywood and Broadway show tunes (or 'Tin Pan Alley'), or rural forms such as country and folk. Many soul writers and players, particularly those from the southern states, have testified to the seminal influence of both gospel and country upon their musical education.

By the late 1950s, jazz had already mutated into a large number of subgenres. A number of its most critically acclaimed offshoots, such as bebop and 'cool jazz', were too esoteric and intellectual to appeal to a mainstream audience. Indeed, this move away from the form's roots in blues and ragtime led to the retro 'trad boom', which was hugely popular among sections of the British music scene around 1960. Soul can be seen in a similar light to trad jazz, as a rejection of jazz's more avant-garde complex tendencies in favour of a more direct approach drawing upon the simplicity of blues and gospel structures. This was combined with something of the electrified drive of R&B to provide the soul or 'funk' – adjectives coming into use to refer to the 'swing' or 'groove' in a song or arrangement. This simplicity of approach led to the song being the most important aspect in soul, rather than the technique. Soul music was strong on ensemble playing, but virtuoso soloing was largely absent.

Most soul music was vocal-led, often featuring a lead vocalist backed by a harmony section. In some cases this vocal tradition owed as much to the broadly *a capella* secular style known as doo-wop (for instance, early Miracles songs such as *Got A Job*, and *Shop Around*, or The Supremes' *A Breathtaking Guy*), as it did to the call and response of the Baptist or Pentecostal congregation. Many soul group members were not instrumentalists or songwriters. Their role was to interpret a lyric and record over a pre-recorded backing track performed by the session musicians of a house band. It should, of course, be noted that prior to the emergence of The Beatles and the beat music boom of 1964, the self-contained writing and performing group was almost unheard of throughout popular music, so soul was only reflecting the strict divisions of labour operating in the 1950s and early 1960s.

Soul vocals were varied, but often made great play of 'call and response', or antiphonal singing associated with but not confined to gospel styles. In the case of much southern soul, harmonies or vocal responses were handled by a brass section 'answering' the main vocal melody. Certainly, in terms of implied soulful emotion and affect, gospel was, again, a major contributor, going as far as to give the genre its name and doing much to create the mythologies of the form. Much use was made of melismatic singing, where a single syllable will be stretched over several notes in a sliding style. While many have read this technique as typically 'black', great use of melisma is also used in traditional and updated forms of European folk music (listen to the vocal style of Joseph Taylor, on one of the earliest 'field recordings' of 1908, for example). Equally, the prominence of the tambourine in soul music does not simply connect with black gospel church practices. The tambourine was also central to white nonconformist religious organisations such as the Salvation Army.

Social and political context

The role of the nonconformist church in both American (particularly southern American) society and upon soul cannot be underestimated. Openly celebratory, unrepressed, 'ecstatic' forms of worship and singing were the vocal firmament for many soul singers (Werner 1999: 28–31). Restraint and formal accuracy were not prized, and the traditional western establishment's 'well-tempered' reliance upon precise pitching and intervals were at least partially dispensed with. This declamatory experience can be observed, to varying degrees, in many soul singers' deliveries. However, the point at which notions of emotion and authenticity become reified as mere technique or a set of generic conventions is deeply ideological in affective and interpretative terms. As we will explore throughout this book, concepts such as 'emotion' and 'honesty' in popular music are 'negotiated' between performers, mediators and audiences – not inscribed within the musical texts themselves.

Despite its overall conservatism, soul also came to symbolise certain radical dimensions in what became known as the civil rights movement, particularly for members of the African-American community. The postwar period saw some advances for African-Americans within mainstream society. Segregation in schools, restaurants and public amenities diminished, although it did not end. In 1954, the US Supreme Court ruled that segregation in educational facilities was 'inherently unequal' (Morse 1982: 781). Martin Luther King first came to international prominence in 1963 when his advocacy of non-violent direct action against segregation in Alabama bore fruit (Morse 1982: 782). In 1966, activist Stokely Carmichael coined the phrase 'black power', and the Black Panther party was founded in California – a more radical organisation reflecting a worsening of race relations throughout the US towards the end of that decade (Morse 1982: 783). Major race-based riots became a common feature in several US cities in the late 1960s, beginning with the disturbances in the Los Angeles area of Watts in 1965, which led to 4,000 arrests and thirty-four deaths (Maycock 2002: 32).

All elements of American society benefited from a general rise in prosperity throughout the 1950s and 1960s. On a basic level, the reality of mixed-race acts, such as Otis Redding/Booker T and the M.G.'s and the Californian soul-funk act Sly and the Family Stone, sent out its own powerful message of ethnic cooperation and equality. In addition, the major soul labels all proved that ethnic minorities could successfully pursue entrepreneurial goals. In addition to Motown's (initially) largely black management team, Stax's vice president, Al Bell, was black, the Chess label was run by a family of Polish descent and Atlantic had been run by Turkish immigrants Ahmed and Neshui Ertegun since the late 1940s.

Prominent soul writers and performers, such as Curtis Mayfield, achieved great success with sweet but impassioned pleas for tolerance and empowerment. The lyrics of a song such as Otis Redding's *Respect* can be read through a gender-based frame as an almost macho exclamation of sexual politics. Equally, it can be read as a cry for black civil rights. In the hands of its best-known cover version, by Aretha Franklin, a feminist reading is also made available. Many songs became rallying cries for a community via a genre that had moved on from the often self-pitying defeatism of the blues and the stoic acceptance of the secular status quo in gospel songs, to one that was proud, forward looking and willing to make changes before the judgement day. As the golden age of Motown and the optimism of the 1960s drew to a close, the Temptations' renditions of the songs and productions of Whitfield and Strong provided a different sort of radical content. *Cloud Nine* and *Ball Of Confusion* reflected upon the debilitating effects of hard drugs moving into the black community, the huge casualties suffered in Vietnam, the deaths of prominent black leaders such as Malcolm X and Martin Luther King, and the general disillusionment suffered in the wake of the aforementioned race riots. .

In Britain, systematic immigration from the Commonwealth began in the late 1940s and accelerated through the 1950s. However, people of African descent had relatively little impact upon the British soul scene, either as musicians or audiences. This was to change as the second generation of black Britons, born in the UK, came of age in the 1970s. In the mid-1960s acts such as Liverpool's The Chants were doubly disadvantaged through both their colour and being 'out of line' with the dominant genres of Merseybeat and R&B. Soul music's chief impact in Britain in the 1960s came about as a result of both its mainstream chart success, but also through its significance to one of the key white subcultures of the period – mod.

The mod subculture (initially 'modernist'), at least in its early 'underground' stage around 1959–63, was overtly elitist and intentionally oppositional to mainstream youth culture (MacInnes 1959). One of the ways this was expressed was through the mod allegiance to then little-known musical forms and performers, in particular in the fields of R&B and modern jazz. As part of the movement's infiltration into the mainstream, mods began to seek out imported US soul, particular favourites being Otis Redding, Motown acts, Booker T and the M.G.'s and later Geno Washington. The early mod scene was as much based upon clubs and records as it was upon attending live performances. Particularly important was the Scene club, where Guy Stevens played obscurities from the US and his own Sue label (Gorman 2001: 56). Mythology has the mods championing hard-driving British R&B from the likes of The Who, Small Faces, The Kinks and The Action and wearing American army parkas. While the link between such acts and the subculture should not be denied, neither should it be over-emphasised. Much of the music of these bands was considered too raucous, unsophisticated and, above all, 'uncool' for the sharpest mod. As we will observe throughout this book, there is a long lineage of marginal, often white subcultures looking abroad, or to black musical forms, for their musical allegiances (see Jones 1988).

The musical texts

Motown and southern soul

As previously indicated, soul music emphasised song over technique, and ensemble playing over virtuoso soloing. In terms of structure, this often meant a standard twelve-bar blues progression (in musicological terms chords I–IV–V, or tonic–subdominant–dominant). This very traditional structure was the bedrock for much southern soul – most up-tempo Otis Redding tracks were twelve-bar blues – but less so for Motown, where the blues structure was less prominent (although still present, for example on Barrett Strong's *Money* or Marvin Gaye's *Can I Get A Witness*). The Motown house musicians and session players came from a jazz or pop background as, to an extent, did Berry Gordy himself. Typically, Motown productions have a pop structure more closely connected to the AABA pattern of 'Tin Pan Alley' or vocal jazz/swing.

In terms of instrumentation, soul typically drew upon a small, amplified combo (bass, rhythm guitar, drums and percussion), often augmented by a brass section. In addition, keyboards such as the electric piano and organ, and subsequently a string section, came to be employed. By 1967, some Motown releases featured such esoteric items as the Theremin, harpsichord and piccolo, alongside the more generically typical saxophone and trumpet.

Much has been made of the 'Motown Sound'. While it is true that many of its most successful releases are instantly recognisable to any devotee of popular music, the degree of uniformity has been over-emphasised. Some Motown artists such as Junior Walker and the All Stars and The Contours had hits with driving R&B and gospel-based material, relatively raucous and 'unpolished'. Others such as Mary Wells and The Supremes occupied a sweeter, almost mainstream pop terrain. Equally, an artist such as Marvin Gaye would tackle a hugely disparate range of material, from jazz-tinged crooning ballads reminiscent of Tony Bennett (Anthony Benedetto) and Nat King Cole (Nathaniel Adams Coles), to blues-based dancefloor grooves.

Another debatable mythology is the widely held assumption that the 'house sound' and Motown backing tracks emanated from one small studio in Detroit. It has been widely assumed that such tracks were the work of a small group of black musicians who became known as the 'Funk Brothers'. Although players such as James Jamerson, Earl Van Dyke, Benny Benjamin and Ronald White were central to Motown in the 1960s, a sizeable percentage of backing tracks were actually recorded in California by session musicians, several of whom were white. In particular, it has now been documented that many basslines accredited to Jamerson were actually composed and played by Carol Kaye, a white mother of two (Abbott 2001: 93–100).

Nevertheless, as a body of work, the Motown releases – particularly in the 'classic' period from around 1964 to 1970 – do possess certain common elements. Most incorporated a small orchestra or at least a string section. Many were deliberately mixed for the transistor radio speaker, with treble frequencies from tambourines, xylophones and hi-hats well to the forefront. While many up-tempo Motown releases (often paced at or above 120 beats per minute) share many common rhythmic characteristics with other soul and pop styles, they also differ in the relative underuse of blues chord progressions. In addition, basslines rarely employ the 'walking bass' style (moving from, and returning to, chordal root notes via crochet intervals), being less tied to root notes and instead adopting a jazzier role, full of flourishes and an almost improvisa-tional feel at times. The drumbeat would often invert the standard kick–snare relationship, with the snare metronomically following each crochet beat in the bar rather than the second and fourth beat, while the kick would punctuate the groove more sporadically. The rhythm guitar would further emphasise alternate snare beats by utilising a 'chop' style similar to the classic reggae 'skank' stroke, although invariably on the on-beat. Examples of all these characteristics can be heard on tracks such as The Four Tops' *I Can't Help Myself*.

A typical example of southern soul, such as Wilson Pickett's *In The Midnight Hour*, was more deliberately paced, at around 112 beats per minute, and in terms of instrumentation and mix much sparser than the Motown model. It is hard not to construct a symbolic opposition between Motown and Stax recordings based upon location or the connotations of urban versus rural characteristics. Equally, southern soul performers such as Otis Redding were born and bred in the southern states, with his rural Georgia accent being identifiable on many occasions (pronouncing ask as 'aks', for example). The Pickett recording was built upon a standard rhythm section and a small brass section, which both underpinned the vocals and offered an ensemble solo during the bridge section. Motown would often conversely employ a solo brass instrument, such as the baritone saxophone, in the break or bridge. The rhythm guitar offered the same 'chop' stroke as found on many Motown tracks, but the bass was much more rooted to a crochet and quaver foundation role. Bass and drums functioned in a pedestrian role, although not in the pejorative sense. The production was also 'flat', with little of the claustrophobia and urgency engendered by the trebly, cluttered mix used by Motown. In particular, the Stax drum sound, much like that found on Al Green's later recordings, situates the listener further from the instrument, and in an acoustically 'dead' space compared to the 'close-miked', echoed Motown drum sound that places us in the midst of a resonant and reflective ambience. On many recordings, the groove of southern soul lies in its restraint and 'playing the gaps', leading to the tension and anticipation also found in much relatively slow and sparse funk. Even in comparing tracks of similar drive and tempo, such as The Supremes' *My World Is Empty Without You* to Redding's *Love Man*, the Supremes' track connotes an urban sense of edge and tension, the Redding track a rural swing with elements of country twang still in the mix.

Small-label soul

As an indication of both the variety of soul styles, and the importance of small, regional soul labels – particularly as a source of songs for British acts of the early 1960s – a few examples of relatively obscure (original) recordings need to be analysed.

Tracey Dey's *Jealous Eyes* barely falls into the genre of soul at all, being an up-tempo waltz built upon a bed of strings and lush 'barber-shop style' backing vocals. The lead vocals have the enunciation more closely associated with the 'torch ballad' style – one not specifically associated with black singers, although at certain points the singer is emoting and almost sobbing out the lyrics in a manner closer to the 'classic' soul delivery. The track is most interesting as an example of how a small label would not necessarily always want to provide a 'roots' or raw antidote to the offerings of the major labels. The production values and crossover appeal are similar to those found in the industry mainstream of the time.

Another example of female soul, much closer to the musical terrain now thought of as typical of the genre, is Betty Everett's *You're No Good*. This features a prominent bass and piano-led rhythm section, interspersed with brass stabs and featuring a short electric guitar lead break. The vocal style, particularly in the lead-out sections, makes greater use of melisma in the 'soulful' upper register. The song is noticeably sparser and more groove-based than *Jealous Eyes*.

Despite its successful incorporation into British Merseybeat in the hands of the hit cover performed by The Swinging Blue Jeans in 1964, *You're No Good* falls marginally into the soul genre stylistically, although still possessing strong connections to the sounds and conventions of mainstream pop. This dimension is also present in Evie Sands' *I Can't Let Go*, which was successfully covered by The Hollies in the UK. This track has something of the swagger and sonic depth of Phil Spector's (Harvey Phillip Spector) girl group recordings, with the call-and-response vocals split between a pop-flavoured backing group countered by the antiphonal soul emoting of Sands moving the track almost into the realms of gospel on occasions. On Linda Jones' *Fugitive From Love*, the terrain is unmistakably that of gospel, with few of the constraints or polite polish of mainstream pop, and some of the more powerful vocal sounds overwhelming the microphone's dynamic capabilities. As with so many elements in popular music, whether this 'error' is an intended stylistic device or the result of technological or economic restrictions is unknown – but the resulting sounds trigger the same generic signals, whatever the reason.

Visual aesthetic

The performers

In common with almost all popular music styles prior to the psychedelic period of 1966–8, dress codes within soul tended to be smart, or at the very least 'smart-casual', for performers. It must be remembered that custom-built venues for amplified music developed concurrently with the 'rock boom' during the late 1960s. For the most part, soul acts played label package tours either in clubs (often set up for cabaret-type entertainment), or, at best, theatres or concert halls. Barry Dickins, a promoter for Stax/Volt tours in 1966 and 1967 described the venues as 'ballrooms . . . It wasn't in the days when you played the Albert Hall and places like that' (quoted in Brown 2001: 119). This factor encouraged a certain formality in dress and appearance, and reflected upon the audience's largely working-class values and expectations relating to 'dressing up'.

Backing groups would usually be attired in sober lounge suits or evening dress, with the lead vocalist(s), if male, sometimes dressed more flamboyantly, but still the suit or jacket and tie was *de rigueur*. Female performers would invariably be attired in the 'party frock' or evening gown; hair straightening or wigs for black performers would attempt to tone down the 'black' elements in the performers' appearance. Motown, in particular, promoted a palatable cabaret appearance and stage demeanour for most of its acts, a famous publicity shot from the mid-1960s showing the touring package resplendent in their so-called 'ice-cream toned' suits and dresses, colour-coded for each act (Palmer 1995: 86). This aspect of Motown was imbued through the 'finishing school' mentality, whereby acts were taught how to dress, move and talk in a 'sophisticated manner'. As Werner commented: 'If the opportunity to dine at the White House arose, Motown's acts would know which fork to use' (Werner 1999: 19). For The Supremes and The Four Tops, cabaret spots at the Copacabana or the Talk of the Town were a natural progression in the Gordy plan to appeal to all sections of the entertainment mainstream.

Even those not party to the Motown grooming process, whose image was more about sweat than poise, such as The Contours, Otis Redding and Geno Washington, still clearly 'dressed up' in the mid-1960s. Soul's visual moves towards nonconformity, flamboyance and radical stage garb occurred later in the decade, and very much in the wake of rock's move to embrace and adopt the visual mores of the counter-culture and underground.

By 1970, acts such as The Temptations had eschewed the uniformity and optimistic smiles of their earlier promo-shots and stage costumes in favour of an altogether moodier and individualistic brand of what we might call 'hustler chic'. This was underpinned by a few psychedelic flourishes, with them sporting wide-brimmed fedoras and bandannas – suede and denim replacing satin and velvet. A group shot of Booker T and the M.G.'s from around the early 1970s shows the members reflecting the bearded and low-key 'back to the country roots' look championed by the likes of The Band and The Byrds. 'Blaxploitation' movies such as *Superfly*, *Shaft* and *Trouble Man* and other films such as *Bonnie and Clyde* had a huge impact upon both ethnic and mainstream dress codes in the subsequent period.

For soul elements uncompromised by the demands of the record company or the mainstream market, just as white musicians in the rock genre let their hair hang down, so black musicians grew 'Afros'. Female performers became less tied to notions of feminine dress and decorum, adopting more casual or 'unisex' modes of dress. The performers at *Wattstax* in 1972 reflected many of these visual shifts. Isaac Hayes took the stage in peach-coloured leggings, chain mail and a multi-coloured cape, with the legend 'Black Moses' flashing on a projection screen behind him.

It is fair to say that many of the wilder excesses of costume lay outside of mainstream soul, but certainly the visual appearance of its performers did radically change in the late 1960s. In addition, British mod or soul-influenced acts such as The Action and the Small Faces were white and associated with a specific youth subculture, which allowed them the licence to break away from the 'showbiz' trappings that influenced much of soul's visual aesthetic in the early 1960s. However, strong echoes of the aspirational 'dressing-up' ethic found among the US soul fraternity are found among UK mods. The Small Faces' Kenney Jones symbolised this dimension when he commented:

> We'd grown up in the post-war era when everything in the East End was black and white . . . When I was 12 I went out and bought a bright jumper and pink jeans and, bang, I was a Mod. Hush Puppy shoes, short trousers to show your socks, backcombed hair, Mod Macs . . . wonderful. (Gilbert 2003: 50)

Audiences

As previously indicated, prior to its crossover into the mainstream in around 1964, soul music was one of the musical genres closely associated with the subculture of mod in the UK. Although, on balance, proletarian and obsessed with notions of 'cool' and 'style', mod did signal a departure from many established values of youth dress and behaviour. Mod males broke with the norms of the 1950s rock 'n' roll/Teddy boy scene by favouring the neat 'French crop' hairstyle or backcombed semi-bouffant over the greased 'DA' and quiff of the teddy boy. Mod was also narcissistic and less about dressing to attract the opposite sex than other subcultures. Similarly, biker garb, or the fabric excesses of the Teddy boy drape suit were replaced by the Ivy League or Italian-style suit. Despite its overall style ethos, mod was also particularly concerned with rapid change – within the space of a couple of weeks, corduroy would be in, then out, cycle shirts and Fred Perry shirts would replace the button-down, or ski pants for females would be replaced by straight skirts and white stockings (Fowler 1982: 801–3).

The air of assumed exoticism and sophistication exuded by much soul music (or interpreted as such by British mods) fitted perfectly into this hedonistic and fashion-obsessed scene. As is ever the case, many elements of underground mod were adopted and adapted by the mainstream pop audience in the mid-1960s, abetted by the explosion of interest in designers such as Mary Quant, Michael Fish, Justin de Villeneuve, Courrèges, John Michael and shop chains such as Lord John and Take Six (Gorman 2001: 50–63, Gilbert 2003a: 50). The constructed 'Swinging London'/Carnaby Street scene of the mid-1960s, including the growth of youth television programmes such as *Ready, Steady, Go* (one episode of which was an important early showcase for Motown, compèred by Dusty Springfield), provided a social context for the marriage of music genres to youth subcultures that is such a characteristic of post-1945 Britain. Twiggy (Leslie Horbie), the proto-supermodel who grew out of mod subculture, claimed that the programme and its presenter Cathy McGowan were 'essentially a mod thing – mod dance, mod clothes' (quoted in Gorman 2001a: 57).

Certainly, the overall paradigm shift from the rock 'n' roll-influenced modes of dress and gender-based codes of behaviour that had held sway for several years prior to the soul and beat boom of 1963–5 was huge and significant. Just as commercial soul became mainstream dance-pop by 1966, modernist elitist subculture mutated into a mainstream form of mod dress and music and the notion of youth 'style' made a similar impact, before both were inevitably challenged by the rise of new musical forms, social conditions, and modes of dress and behaviour around 1967. These will be investigated in the chapter dealing with psychedelia.

Subsequent generic developments

Soul mutated into many subgenres, such as psychedelic soul or Latin soul. Many of the mod sounds and fashions mutated into 'hard mod' or proto-skinhead styles, with mod reggae having an impact. Many obscurities from small soul labels formed the basis for the northern soul dancefloor-based subculture of the 1970s, which has been successively

Dexy's Midnight Runners spearheaded the search
for a new soul vision for the 1980s.

revived since that period. Most significant for popular music as a whole
were the two developments of funk and disco. Funk can be seen as a
radical departure from soul, particularly in terms of its structure, use of
instrumentation and vocal message. For this reason, as well as its huge
impact upon subsequent forms such as rap and various dance subgenres,
funk will be dealt with in detail in a subsequent chapter. At this point, it
should be stated that while much funk is built upon elements of soul, and
while much soul is, indeed, 'funky', we will be making a crucial distinction between the adjective 'funky' and the noun 'funk'. Of course, there
were considerable crossovers, but also some crucial distinctions between
soul and funk.

As well as the fact that the two genres were both mainly African-
American in origin, both soul and funk shared a similar if not identical
relationship to notions of 'groove'. In formal terms groove refers to the
degree of implicit or, more often, overt syncopation within the music,
whereby elements anticipate or drag behind the underlying pulse. This
means that if we divide a four-beat bar into sixteen measures, rhythmic
stresses will be happening at three or five or seven, rather than just on the

semi-quavers of two, four, six or eight within the bar. In affective terms, funkiness encourages informal, rhythmic dancing wherein we metaphorically 'fall in' to the tension points created by anticipation or dislocations in the common metrical pulse. Almost all music, regardless of factors such as genre, race or ethnic origin, has a degree of syncopation; the distinctions lie in the emphasis and the structural and sonic prominence afforded this element. It could be argued that within soul, the prominence of groove was higher than in forms such as rock 'n' roll or beat music (although such conclusions are highly subjective). Furthermore, this prominence was then further emphasised within funk until groove became, in some cases, the most important constituent, sometimes overwhelming elements such as melody or lyrical content.

Unlike funk, disco, although hugely popular and influential in the period 1976–80, does not merit its own chapter in this book, being in overall terms a refinement of soul (in terms of affect and message) rather than a radical departure. This refinement can be mapped through many of the releases on the commercially successful Philadelphia International label ('Philly'), associated with the Sigma studio, and the writing and production team of Kenny Gamble and Leon Huff. Although Philly shared many characteristics with the Motown sound, its releases in the early and mid-1970s were more systematically aimed at the demands of the urban discothèque, with the drums in particular eschewing the improvisational tom-tom fills and jazz feel of Motown for a more stripped down 'four-to-the-floor' metronomic style, making great use of the open/closed hi-hat rhythm central to the disco genre. Equally, the disco sound was very much studio-based, often giving little impression of ensemble playing or a live ambience.

Holland/Dozier/Holland, after leaving Motown, had great if short-lived success with their Invictus label, releasing huge hits for Freda Payne and Chairman of the Board. As with numerous other small labels, Invictus foundered partly on not being able to compete with the business infrastructure and distribution networks of the major or major-affiliated labels. However, the products of these small labels did, as previously mentioned, continue to achieve dancefloor and cult success in specialist markets such as the northern soul scene – remnants of which survive to the present day.

Mention should be made of prominent white musicians such as Daryl Hall and John Oates, Boz Scaggs (William Royce Scaggs) and David Bowie (David Robert Jones). Bowie moved into, or returned to (some of his earliest steps in popular music came from playing sax in a soul/R&B outfit in 1963; see Du Noyer 2002: 81) the genre of soul, or 'plastic soul', with some success in 1974–5 (Buckley 1999: 235–57). The Sigma studio recordings of the *Young Americans* album and Bowie's subsequent work with prominent American soul-influenced musicians did much to 'rescue' soul's status among those sections of the pop audience who found its 'showbiz' trappings too off-putting. Equally, Rod Stewart's music moved – metaphorically and geographically – to the US in the early 1970s. On albums such as the aptly named *Atlantic Crossing*, Stewart moved (or again, returned) from the country rock of his earlier career to the smooth soul style of one of his musical heroes, Sam Cooke. In the early 1980s Kevin Rowland and Dexy's Midnight Runners skilfully updated many elements of the soul sound palette and stage performance with albums such as *Searching For The Young Soul Rebels* and tours such as the Projected Passion Revue. However, it was funk, rather than soul, that provided the bedrock for the many rhythmic explorations of white musicians, particularly in the post-punk era.

Recommended reading

Abbott, K. (2001) *Calling Out Around The World: A Motown Reader*. London: Helter-Skelter.

Barthes, R. (1977) 'The Death of the Author', in *Image, Music, Text*. London: Fontana.

Brown, G. (2001) *Otis Redding: Try a Little Tenderness*. Edinburgh: Mojo.

George, N. (1986) *Where Did Our Love Go?* London: Omnibus.

George, N. (1988) *The Death of Rhythm & Blues*. London: Omnibus.

Gorman, P. (2001) *The Look: Adventures in Rock and Pop Fashion*. London: Sanctuary.

Guralnick, P. (1986) *Sweet Soul Music*. London: HarperCollins.

Hirshey, G. (1985) *Nowhere To Run*. London: Pan.

Jones, S. (1988) *Black Culture, White Youth*. London: Macmillan.

Palmer, R. (1995) *Rock and Roll: An Unruly History*. New York: Harmony.

Ward, B. (1998) *Just My Soul Responding: Rhythm and Blues, Black Consciousness and Race Relations*. London: UCL Press.

Werner, C. (1998) *A Change Is Gonna Come: Music, Race and the Soul of America*. New York: Plume.

Recommended listening

(*Note*: Much soul is now best obtained via reissues and compilations, rather than as original singles or albums.)

Antecedents

Ray Charles (2002) *The Essential Collection*. Cleopatra.

Sam Cooke/Soul Stirrers (1992) *Sam Cooke With The Soul Stirrers*. Fantasy/
Specialty.

Mahalia Jackson (1998) *Gospels, Spirituals and Hymns Vol. 1*. Sony Jazz.

Generic texts

Four Tops (1992) *Motown's Greatest Hits*. Motown.

The Impressions (1997) *Definitive Impressions*. Essential.

Curtis Mayfield (1972) *Superfly*. Charly.

Wilson Pickett (1965) *In The Midnight Hour* [single]. Atlantic.

Otis Redding (1987) *The Dock Of The Bay: The Definitive Collection*. WEA.

Diana Ross and The Supremes (1986) *Anthology*. Motown.

Dusty Springfield (1969) *Dusty In Memphis*. Mercury.

Various Artists (1989) *Motown Chartbusters Volume Three*. Motown.

Various Artists (1999) *Invictus Chartbusters*. Sequel.

Various Artists (1999) *This Is Northern Soul*. Crimson.

Various Artists (2001) *Tamla Motown Big Hits And Hard To Find Classics,
Volumes 1–3*. Motown.

Geno Washington and the Ram Jam Band (1998) *Geno, Geno, Geno*. Sequel.

Subsequent generic developments

David Bowie (1975) *Young Americans*. EMI.

Dexy's Midnight Runners (1980) *Searching For The Young Soul Rebels*. Parlophone.

Rod Stewart (1975) *Atlantic Crossing*. Warner Bros.

Terrence Trent D'Arby (1987) *Introducing The Hardline According To . . .*
Columbia.

CHAPTER 2

Funk: the breakbeat starts here

An overview of the genre

As we have previously argued, in many respects funk was essentially a development of soul rather than a distinctive genre in its own right. However, the sheer radicalism of the sound of funk in terms of its explicit challenge to popular music structure, instrumentation, lyrics and affect means that the form merits its own chapter. In addition, its legacy on musical genres of the past thirty years is almost immeasurable – the funk-based breakbeat is one of the principal rhythmic building blocks in contemporary pop, with wide utilisation in most major genres of popular music. For this reason, and owing to the strong similarities between soul and funk in areas such as social and historical background, this chapter will be rather imbalanced, concentrating upon the musical texts and subsequent developments at the partial expense of the other headings.

From its roots in gospel, soul and jazz (where the term, in its musical sense, originates: see Palmer 1995: 238–9), funk began to carve a distinctive niche in the late 1960s. This occurred in the hands of diverse musicians such as James Brown and his band(s), Sly and the Family Stone, and the Meters, and in specific locations such as Memphis and New Orleans.

Funk differed from soul in several ways:

- Funk was more concerned with the concept of a highly syncopated, relentless 'groove' rather than traditional song structures built upon a smooth 'pulse'.
- Funk employed an insistent riff more extensively than soul.
- Funk changed the role and emphasis of instruments within the sound mix, bringing hitherto partially subsumed elements to the fore and 'relegating' lead instruments to subsidiary, rhythmic duties.
- Funk often used vocals and lyrics as verbal 'punctuations' rather than melodic deliverers of coherent messages, and it constructed polyrhythmic tracks full of syncopated gaps, with intermeshed, often staccato 'stabs' of sound functioning as part of a whole, rather than being significant as individual elements.

All of these individual dimensions can be found throughout popular music. The use of groove or of syncopation can be applied in any genre of music to bring a certain degree of 'funkiness'. However, although funk is always funky, funky music is not always funk (listen, by way of example, to the diverse likes of Little Feat, Japan, Free or Captain Beefheart's *Clear Spot* album, or more broadly dance music genres such as house and techno, for music that is funky, but not 'the funk'). In addition, some acts that worked within the genre have subsequently come to be placed within a different critical terrain. The Commodores, now best remembered for ballads such as *Three Times A Lady* and *Easy*, forged their success with early funk tracks such as *Brick House* and *Too Hot Ta Trot*. The subsequent solo career of Lionel Ritchie was not without its funky moments (*All Night Long*), but his balladeer image – lacking funk credibility – has seemingly erased his more up-tempo offerings from collective and generic memory.

As a result of its musical characteristics and wider cultural connotations, funk proved ideal as the accompaniment to screen narratives in the form of soundtracks, or incidental music. It remains, to this day, one of the most effective signifiers of urban life.

Although typically described in terms of its rhythmic urgency and propulsive drive, much funk is essentially laid back, and even mellow, both in terms of imbued feel and in terms of the actual beats per minute. Much classic funk operates at between eighty and a hundred beats per minute, as opposed to the 120 beats per minute (or higher) of much disco, house, and contemporary dance music. But the result of the inherent rhythmic tensions and contradictions within funk is an implied momentum and restlessness, even in tracks as seemingly 'easygoing' as Bill Withers' *Use Me* (around seventy-six beats per minute – listen to the huge gap left after the bass riff drops out, mainly filled by a skeletal drum rhythm) or the Meters' *Look-Ka Py-Py* (around eighty-eight beats per minute).

Funk became a transcending signifier, with musicians, audiences and critics assigning holistic, even cosmic properties to the term and its sounds: 'Funk is *funkiness*, a natural release of the essence within . . . Funk is at the extremes of everything . . . The Funk is a rush that comes all over your body . . . Funk is what you say when nothing else will do' (Vincent 1996: 3). At the centre of much funk discourse was the concept of 'the one', explained in terms of both a specific structural tendency within the music, and as a communal concept wherein all the musicians, listeners, audiences and, indeed, mythical nations were united 'under a groove'. Both of these concepts will be explored in greater depth during this chapter.

In a similar fashion to the binary opposition between pop and rock that developed in the late 1960s, funk was seen to be, and promoted as, the authentic sound of soul and R&B – elements of which had certainly been assimilated into the pop mainstream in the hands of labels such as Tamla Motown. Funk was the antidote to the showbiz trappings and polite textures of much 'sweet soul'. An early example of the distinctive genre of funk would be James Brown's *Papa's Got A Brand New Bag*, from 1965. Although still built upon standard blues progressions, this track burst out of its blues roots in startling ways, engendering the music with a different feel built upon explicit challenges to instrumentation, vocals, lyrics and structure. With *Cold Sweat* in 1967, Brown's music was helping forge an ever more distinctive path, particularly in the prominence afforded the instrumental break or bridge. A small section of the break, scratched, sampled and looped into the breakbeat by DJs and mixers, became instrumental in the development of rap in the 1970s and 1980s.

Another route for funk lay in the appropriation of psychedelic rock playing and production techniques. The seminal mixed-race, mixed-gender act Sly and the Family Stone achieved huge crossover success with such a formula. Had it not been for huge drug problems in the early 1970s, this band was poised to achieve both huge and long-lasting success and critical status. In many similar respects, the importance of Jimi Hendrix (Johnny Allen Hendrix) for 'the funk' should not be overlooked. During the instrumental break of *All Along The Watchtower*, Hendrix fashions a solo fusing the sounds and techniques of rock, psychedelia and funk. Indeed, with the Band of Gypsys, much of his later work such as *Dolly Dagger* and *Izabella* is closer to funk than any other musical genre.

As funk was played generally by African-Americans, it was seen as uncompromised by the 'white' record industry, and came to embody the struggle for civil rights and the radicalism of the black power movement. Many saw funk's radical dimensions as endemic and symptomatic of the worsening race relations and social conditions in the US following the death of Martin Luther King in 1968 (Palmer 1995: 95). Certainly, Sly and the Family Stone's later work, such as the brooding *There's A Riot Goin' On* from 1971, bears out this scenario. However, funk was too diverse a form to be 'contained' by one set of social conditions. In the 1970s, acts associated with bandleader George Clinton (principally Parliament and Funkadelic) fashioned a more escapist and irreverent, if still political, take on aspects of race and equality (listen, for instance, to Parliament's *Chocolate City*). For other funk outfits, such as Earth, Wind and Fire, cosmology and spectacle were welded to the funk groove. The Ohio Players and Kool and the Gang had no 'master plan', and their take on funk leads us almost seamlessly on to the absorption of certain elements of funk into disco and jazz funk in the mid-to-late 1970s. These latter developments were funky, but not purely 'the funk' in most cases.

In a similar fashion to soul, funk was perceived as a largely American phenomenon, and acts outside the US found it hard to gain an audience or any degree of critical credibility. Scottish outfit the Average White Band did gain some success, but as exceptions to the rule. Disco and jazz funk, with little of the attendant baggage of authenticity or 'ethnic essence', offered a more lucrative career path for the likes of non-Americans such as The Real Thing, Boney M, Imagination and Shakatak.

Historical roots and antecedents

As with soul, the historical roots of funk lay in the long-established 'staples' of the largely African-American music scene: jazz, blues and gospel. However, some important distinctions need to be made in terms of how funk draws upon different elements from these musical antecedents.

Many would see funk as taking the more challenging elements of these genres as their blueprints in order to fashion a sound based upon the demands of a more esoteric or avant-garde or purist (read 'non-crossover' or 'non-commercial') audience. For Ricky Vincent, experimental jazz forms such as bebop and hard bop played a role, both musically and spiritually, with many musicians such as Thelonius Monk, Archie Shepp, Miles Davis (Miles Dewey Davis III) and Art Blakey (Abdullah Ibn Buhaina) exploring polyrhythmic styles and percussion-led outfits drawing upon a 'black roots' or African heritage (Vincent 1996: 42–3). The relationship between African music and Western forms can never be mapped out in any objective sense and is riven with controversy and contentious value judgements. A good example of this would be Vincent claiming that the innovative rhythm guitar role associated with funk was 'later' learned by James Brown to be 'African in origin' without providing any substantiation to this finding (Vincent 1996: 35). More important than the notion that funk was essentially African was the perception that this was the case, regardless of 'hard evidence'. This willing into existence had a huge impact upon the music, ideology and iconography of funk. The subsequent impact of funk upon African styles such as soucous and high life and performers such as Fela Kuti and Manu Dibango would be seen by some as an example of a musical circle being completed. Certainly, much Afrobeat or so-called world music that has made the biggest impact in the West over the past few decades has incorporated a funky element, with James Brown's influence in Africa almost rivalling that of Bob Marley (Robert Nesta Marley).

More directly, clear links can be made between soul and funk, whether emanating from the production line of Detroit or southern centres such as Memphis, Atlanta and New Orleans. One tonal distinction between soul and funk that does largely ring true is that whereas soul was often smooth, funk was invariably staccato, both rhythmically and vocally. This provided artists such as Wilson Pickett, Booker T and the M.G.s, Shorty Long (Emidio Vagnoni), Rufus Thomas, the Meters and Edwin Starr (Charles Hatcher), to name but a few, with the opportunity to deliver a 'funky take' on soul music while still remaining, historically and etymologically, within the soul genre. Too constrained by Gordy's Motown template, The Isley Brothers left the label (and the traditional soul 'vocal group' style) to gain artistic and economic autonomy, resulting in a string of successful soul/funk albums on their T-Neck label. Another hugely successful performer who stayed with Motown but obtained creative autonomy was Stevie Wonder (Steveland Hardaway Judkins Morris). Although never specifically a funk artist, some of Wonder's most popular tracks (such as *Superstition* and *Ain't Gonna Stand For It*) do conform to the style indicators of the genre. In addition, the funky jazz influence on tracks such as *Sir Duke*, *I Wish* and *Do I Do* returns us to one of funk's prime influences.

The point at which soul becomes funk is moot, and is a matter of historical era and definition as much as style. James Brown was known as 'Soul Brother Number One' long into the period when his music was no longer being defined as soul. Indeed, he claimed in 1986 to have never even been an R&B act, although usually classed as one. 'My music came from gospel and jazz, which is called funk and soul. You see funk and soul is really jazz' (Vincent 1996: 73). Nevertheless, funk was a recognisable tendency within soul, years before it got its own generic term, particularly as jazz, as a term, shifted radically during the 1960s and 1970s. For the purposes of simplicity, a cut-off line between funk-in-soul and funk existing in its own right could be drawn at around 1968, thanks to the ground-breaking work of performers to be explored later in this chapter.

Funk can also be associated with timbral and technological developments more usually associated with the experimental or psychedelic rock field. Fuzz-bass, phasing, stereo cross-fading and the incorporation of a broader sound palette – all elements associated with the mid-1960s' 'rock explosion' – began to be employed by some elements of the funk genre by the late 1960s. George Clinton moved in the same musical circles as

Detroit hard rock acts such as the Amboy Dukes, the Stooges and MC5 and learned much about high amplification and stadium presentation as a consequence (see Corbett 1994: 150). In Clinton's own words, 'we had Marshalls all over the place . . . so we became the loudest black band in the world, Temptations on Acid' (Corbett 1994: 148). Such geographic cross-generic influences aided other Detroit acts such as The Temptations to move away from their sweet-soul and gospel roots into a terrain closer to funk, as witnessed by tracks such as *Papa Was A Rolling Stone*, *Law Of The Land* and *Psychedelic Shack*. As well as tonal, structural and rhythmic shifts, such tracks dealt with social issues through a lyrical explicitness far removed from most standard Motown soul tracks. The Temptations were also effectively the musical mouthpiece of production *auteurs* such as, in their case, Norman Whitfield. This matched the shifts in creative status that had occurred in rock, and was duplicated by the growing impact throughout funk of other *auteurs* such as James Brown, Allen Toussaint, George Clinton and Sly Stone (Sylvester Stewart). Brown, in particular, as writer, producer and label and radio-station owner (among many other business interests) was symbolic of the shifts in status engendered by both the times and the genre, elements of which were clearly evidenced by the mood and content of the music itself.

In retrospect, Latin-American music and stylistic tendencies can be seen to have had an often overlooked influence upon funk. In the 1950s, there was a near global upsurge of interest in dance-led forms of Latin music such as the mambo, bossa nova and samba. Shuker claims that salsa (meaning 'sauce' or 'spice'), a term for describing Latin styles, 'has been used in relation to music since the 1920s in a similar fashion to funky' (Shuker 1998: 265). Such styles featured the extensive use of percussion elements (bongos, congas, woodblocks, claves) and extremely propulsive and syncopated brass sections and keyboards, and was popularised by 'Mambo Kings' such as Tito Puente. In addition, many forms adopted an even-measured underlying pulse (as opposed to the common triplets or 6 : 8 time of rock 'n' roll), then countered by a highly mobile bass style not tied to root notes or intervals. Some of these traits filtered into mainstream pop, particularly the work of composers Lieber and Stoller as performed by the likes of the Drifters (*Under The Boardwalk*, *Save The Last Dance For Me*). Something of the crisp syncopation of Latin music shines through these sophisticated pop productions and can be found in later, more hybridised funk narratives (Stevie Wonder's *Don't You Worry 'Bout A Thing*, War's *Low Rider*).

Social and political context

In terms of associating social and political contexts to musical genres, widely held perceptions or moods rather than the specifics of events or government policy shifts are often more historically persuasive when determining a *Zeitgeist*, or spirit of a time. Despite all the inconsistencies that such perceptions efface or deny, it is indisputable that the widely held retrospective perceptions of the 1960s as a time of increased liberalism, optimism and better race relations do ring true, simply because they were held to be true at the time.

Within this timeframe, funk's period of greatest artistic and commercial success (stretching from the end of the 1960s to the end of the 1970s), can be seen to parallel both a general mood of pessimism and disillusionment with the 'end of the dream'. Funk's era also encompasses more quantifiable occurrences. These include the protracted defeat of the American forces in the Vietnam War (and the huge fallout for the black community, statistically over-represented in the armed forces), economic and energy crises, the polarisation of urban America into 'vanilla' suburbs and 'chocolate' inner cities, and the influx of harder and more socially destructive drugs into the North American ghetto. The decline of Sly Stone from a gifted composer, bandleader and multi-instrumentalist to the sad character addled by years of poly-drug abuse is symbolic of these changes (see Selvin 2001: 80–90). As a counter to these negative dimensions, many commentators would also point to the increasing visibility and economic power held by many within the 'black music industry' – leading to the incorporation (or 'absorption') of largely black musical forms such as funk into the mainstream market, with both positive and negative implications.

The film subgenre known as 'blaxploitation' exemplifies both the positive and negative dimensions engendered within black culture during the period of funk's greatest impact. Films such as *Shaft* (1971) (and its sequels), *Trouble Man* (1972) and *Superfly* (1972) all achieved mainstream success. This was due, to no small degree, to the accompanying soundtracks (produced by Isaac Hayes, Marvin Gaye and Curtis Mayfield, respectively). Mayfield's music for *Superfly* spawned two hit singles and a number one hit album in the US, with sales of over two million (Edmonds 2002: 62). However, this success was achieved at the cost of reproducing a stereotypical view of the black-urban experience built around archetypes of pimps and whores, gangster chic, coolness and macho sexuality, partly preparing the terrain for the later 'gangsta rap' genre (see Chapter 9). Thus mainstream culture paid lip service to notions of 'incorporation/

absorption', while still marginalising and reifying black culture's perceived essences. Furthermore, the blaxploitation genre – as the name suggests – was very much a short-lived fad, with many ill-conceived examples besmirching the few films of quality that resulted. The associated music, although not free from cliché and standardised elements, has fared much better in terms of longevity and influence.

For many working within the genre, the concept of 'escape' proved a viable, alternative terrain of symbolic power. This escape could be manifested in a variety of ways – lyrically, musically, iconically, even philosophically. John Corbett argues that figures such as George Clinton

> constructed worlds of their own, futuristic environs that subtly signify on the marginalization of black culture. These new discursive galaxies utilize a set of tropes and metaphors of space and alienation, linking their common diasporic African history to a notion of extra-terrestriality . . . imagining a productive zone largely exterior to dominant ideology. (Corbett 1994: 7–8)

Despite several crossover successes for his outfits between the early and late 1970s, the logistical and economic costs of touring and staging the elaborate spectacles stymied Clinton's long-term plans, resulting in bankruptcy and loss of musical impetus. As is so often the case, the harsh realities of an economic power base exerted a constrictive grip upon the possibilities offered by the symbolic power of a creative superstructure.

The musical texts

James Brown and his band(s)

Terms such as 'ground-breaking' and 'revolutionary' are overused in historical analysis, and are particularly prevalent in pop journalism and fan-based biographical accounts. Nevertheless, it is hard to deny the appropriateness of such superlatives when overviewing the contribution of James Brown and associated musicians to the fabric of popular music, particularly between around 1965 and the early 1970s.

Brown did much to popularise a seismic reappraisal of the role and status of instruments. His music also detached concepts such as swing and groove from their blues and soul foundations and placed them in a more contemporary, yet more primal, setting. This setting often eschewed chord progressions, pop arrangements and conventional subject matter in favour of an unrelenting mesh of elements, many of which only achieve impact in direct contrast to those other components against which they seem to struggle. In this terrain, instruments' percussive and staccato abilities are emphasised. On *Papa's Got A Brand New Bag*, a track still rooted in blues progressions, the expected drum roll signalling the end of the verse/refrain section is played by rhythm guitar – a small, yet unexpected change prefacing the more radical reworkings of the late 1960s. Brown's music turned its back on sustain, full chords and 'washes' of sound. The brass section would play 'stabs' rather than riffs, the rhythm guitar would 'chop' beats while de-emphasising all melodic tonality. The bass, freed from chord root notes or 'following the changes', would typically establish its position with a strong entry on 'the one' at the beginning of the bar, before embarking on a free, highly syncopated journey around the fretboard before its return at the start of the next 'one', where it would again gel with the kick drum – similarly freed for the rest of the pattern to push and drag against the underlying pulse. In a lot of funk, the pulse is implied through absence, rather than emphasised, as in most other forms of popular music.

Although invariably credited as sole composer and producer, Brown's tutelage of his bands, evidenced by both recordings, out-takes, and the testimonies of collaborators, matched the radicalism of the resulting tracks. During the 1960s, Brown would sing, grunt and even dance his ideas for grooves to bandleaders such as Nat Jones and later Alfred 'Pee Wee' Ellis, who would then translate these ideas into a more formal mode for the rest of the band.

> He grunted the rhythm, a bassline to me. I wrote the rhythm down . . . there were no notes. I had to translate it . . . You got a musical palette from hearing him, from seeing his bodily movement and facial expression, seeing him dance . . . So you get a picture of that, and you write it. (Ellis, quoted in Weinger and Leeds 1996)

The resulting music does aptly realise such unfettered composition techniques. In that most oxymoronic of phrases, it is 'loose but tight'. When hearing Brown become a 'human beat box' to exactly demonstrate how he wants the groove to be on an out-take 'false start' of *Cold Sweat* the paradox is made evident – these unfettered and free grooves are 'composed', and this most polyrhythmically complex music seems to be the translation of one man's radical will. As David Brackett suggests, Brown's take on funk, as well as upsetting the accepted musical fabric of pop, also upsets any 'easy assumptions' (Brackett 2000: 154) relating to the constructed oppositions of planning or improvisation, looseness or precision. However, in overall terms, the fact that Brown's autocratic nature resulted in him shedding and replacing musicians with regularity, but still maintaining the music's essence and singularity of purpose, pays testament to assumptions of creative planning, vision and will.

In 1970, a new band, the JBs, was brought in to replace a group of sacked musicians. Foremost in this band was the virtuoso bassist William 'Bootsy' Collins. Brown's ability to mould new players without suppressing their creativity was another great attribute. Brown's statement exemplifies this tendency and the underlying impetus of funk:

> I think Bootsy learned a lot from me. When I met him he was playing a lot of bass – the ifs, the ands, and the buts. I got him to see the importance of the *one* in funk – the downbeat at the beginning of every bar. I got him to key in on the dynamic parts of the one instead of playing all around it. Then he could do all his other stuff in the right places – *after* the one. (Brown, quoted in Vincent 1996: 81–2)

Sly and the Family Stone

In contrast to the singular take on funk fashioned by James Brown and band(s), the funk of Sly and the Family Stone was very much a crossover sound, with rock timbres of sustain, fuzz and distortion contributing to a much 'thicker', often riff-based palette. In addition, the early part of their career (1967–70) embodied many aspects of the hippie and psychedelic subcultures in terms of iconography, race, and gender aspects, and the air of optimistic self-fulfilment embodied in tracks such as *Everybody Is A Star*, *Stand*, *Everyday People* and *Thank You (Falettinme Be Mice Elf Again)*. These elements all contributed to their huge commercial success, in contrast to Brown, whose success in the R&B charts was rarely equalled in the pop market. However, despite the less purist nature of their music, Sly and the Family Stone stand as a classic example of a broadly based funk act whose impact upon subsequent acts was huge.

A large part of this impact rested on the sound and style of bassist Larry Graham. Graham did much to popularise the slap bass style, which was central to much subsequent funk, disco, jazz funk and mainstream pop in the 1980s. In slapping or hammering the bass strings, Graham and others brought the instrument's percussive timbres to the fore, resulting in a 'dirtier' sound. Graham also employed a fuzz unit on tracks such as *I Want To Take You Higher* and *Dance To The Music* that gave these tracks some of their psychedelic feel.

During the latter part of their career, when drugs had done much to fracture the unity of the band, Sly Stone began replacing the drumming of Greg Errico with a rudimentary drum machine on some tracks. In 1971, this was an almost unprecedented move for a 'commercial' dance act. On the *There's A Riot Goin' On* album this mechanical 'anti-funk' component, juxtaposed with archetypal funk elements, does much to contribute to the air of tension and fractured paranoia that so many have drawn from the work (see Selvin 2001: 80–90). This juxtaposition of 'hot' and 'cold' timbres proved to be the aesthetic blueprint for much experimental music in the post-punk field.

The Meters

Although a self-contained recording and touring act, the Meters also functioned as a 'house band' for a large variety of acts based in New Orleans (Lee Dorsey, Aaron Neville/Neville Brothers, Ann Sexton) and were closely associated with the *auteur* Allen Toussaint. The enduring appeal of the Meters' takes on funk rests on the sparseness of their sound, or in 'playing the gaps'. In common with reggae, funk is more reliant upon this aspect than any other genre of popular music. Slow-paced and largely instrumental tracks such as *Tippi Toes*, *Chicken Strut* and *Look-Ka Py-Py* are masterpieces of implied, understated groove, built upon insistent bass riffs, often doubled on skeletal rhythm guitar, intermeshed with organ stabs and trills. Vocal elements are often little more than interjections or percussive examples of 'scatting'. As with so much funk, when taken in isolation, none of the individual elements are in any way strikingly original or virtuoso, but as a complete track, the dialogue between instruments, stretching and pulling the common time pulse into a state of rhythmic disarray, exemplifies funk's ability to upset and disturb in the most pleasurable and seductive fashion.

As with so much classic funk, the kind of rhythmic jolts central to such tracks engenders a sexually charged element to the genre, putting listeners/dancers in touch with their bodies in a manner perhaps unequalled in popular music as a whole. This sexual dimension also accounts for the myriad examples of funk lyrics that do little more that exhort the listener to move, groove or get on down. The use of these, or any other phrases exploiting the dance/sex ambiguities, are widespread throughout pop, and indeed pre-date any form of commercially recorded popular music, but funk typically took this dimension to new levels of explicitness and intensity.

P-Funk

The music of Parliament, Funkadelic and linked acts such as Bootsy's Rubber Band was prolific and varied. Typically, Parliament offered a more conventional take on funk whereas Funkadelic, as the name suggests, incorporated fusion elements of psychedelic rock into the mix: 'Parliament is more groove-oriented and song-driven, where Funkadelic is more loose, jam-oriented, with lots of guitars' (Clinton, quoted in Vickers 1995: 4).

In reality, any objective distinctions between the outfits are blurred, although Parliament made extensive use of a brass section (as on *Bop Gun*), while Funkadelic preferred rock textures from distorted lead guitars (as on the polemical *Who Says A Funk Band Can't Play Rock?*). The collective known as P-Funk was a chaotic mix of styles, icons, structures and alter egos. Although clearly indebted to earlier funk models, P-Funk made far more use of the metronomic four-to-the-floor drum styles, thus linking their funk to disco and jazz funk. However, unlike disco, P-Funk always sounded 'played', with little of the production-line precision of disco and post-disco dance forms.

Nevertheless, to modern ears reared on the timbral excesses and accelerated beats per minute of post-house forms of dance music, P-Funk sounds relatively mellow, even laid-back. Clearly, the overall live package – with elaborate props and costumes and a small army of musicians and dancers on stage – cannot be adequately symbolised by the musical texts in isolation. As with James Brown's backing tracks, P-Funk was one of the most favoured musical sources for subsequent rap producers. Clinton later went as far as to provide sampler CDs full of usable musical snippets, together with 'four point instructions for obtaining permission' (Corbett 1994: 152).

Visual aesthetic

A clear homology existed between many of funk's more radical musical departures and the sartorial wildness of many funk performers. James Brown, although never taking costume to the cosmic limits, signalled the funk ethos through hairstyle changes during his period of greatest success. In 1968, when visiting US troops in Vietnam, Brown was still modelling the slicked and straightened hairstyle redolent of crossover/showbiz values (see Maycock 2003: 66–74). This also reflects upon the peculiar mix of radicalism and conservatism that is found throughout Brown's career and work. Ward states that

in March 1968 . . . Brown dismissed the wearing of natural, unprocessed hair as an irrelevant symbol of racial pride . . . and, of course, in a sense his songs had proudly worn a metaphorical musical Afro for years before he finally succumbed to public pressure and allowed his artificially relaxed coiffure to coil into a natural. (Ward 1998: 390)

George Clinton exemplified the visual excesses of 1970s' funk.

This 'natural', or Afro, became a key signifier for 'unfettered' funk and African-American identity in the early to mid-1970s. It thus mirrored historically the period of greatest excess in post-hippie long hair. The Afro was still widely adopted during the disco era, but has not been deemed suitable as the visual accompaniment to subsequent 'reality' forms of dance or funky music such as rap or jungle.

P-Funk was never visually restrained by any of Brown's sartorial values. Clinton, himself a former hairdresser, promoted a completely laissez-faire, almost cartoon-like philosophy to hair and costume, encompassing long blond wigs, fluorescent dyes and all manner of braids. Members of P-Funk were as likely to take the stage in a nappy or a loincloth or dress as a superhero, a prisoner in stripes, or an extraterrestrial.

This exaggerated 'other-wordly' visual dimension was emphasised by P-Funk's album cover art. Funkadelic's early album covers (the eponymous 1970 album, followed by *Free Your Mind And Your Ass Will Follow* and *Maggot Brain*, both from 1971) are built upon relatively straightforward photographic representation. However, from 1972, the design was taken over by Pedro Bell, whose graphic 'scartoon' or 'sketchadelic' style of drawing, incorporating a myriad range of archetypes ranging from spacemen and gothic demons to African maidens, aptly matched the traits of escape and lunacy symbolised by both the music and the philosophies of the band(s) in this period. Clinton also employed a group of graphic artists to work on costume and stage design. For P-Funk, 'the one' was less of a musical touchstone than a symbol of a totally 'planned', yet chaotically alternative, way of life. This existence enveloped different personae, and even a parallel mode of verbal expression (pseudonyms abounded in P-Funk, as we find in so many other largely black genres such as blues, reggae, and rap). As within other examples of African-American creativity, it is hard not to view this move into a 'magical' surreal terrain as a necessary retreat from a reality that denied much actual socio-economic power or status.

Subsequent generic developments

As previously indicated, many elements of funk helped form the basis for dance subgenres such as disco and jazz funk. Such styles proved hugely popular with a mainstream audience, fuelled in part by the success of the film and soundtrack compilation *Saturday Night Fever*. The importance of the Latino take on funk should not be overlooked. Early disco dancefloors were heavily populated by both African-Americans and Hispanic-Americans, with acts such as The Gibson Brothers drawing upon both their Cuban roots and funk elements. This hybrid sound continued to prove successful with acts such as Gloria Estefan/Miami Sound Machine in the 1980s.

Some of pop's biggest global superstars, such as Michael Jackson and Prince, drew extensively upon funk idioms throughout the period of their greatest commercial successes. In particular, Prince (Prince Rogers Nelson) stands as a classic exemplar of a postmodern pop artist who blatantly incorporates prior musical styles and images in a collagist fashion. However, despite his musical eclecticism, it is funk that has provided the most constant foundation to his work, with some of his most influential tracks, such as *Sign O' The Times* and *Kiss*, being classic examples of the genre. Tracks such as *Housequake* are almost uncannily close to their creative influences, in this case James Brown, but Prince was equally happy updating the psychedelic funk of Hendrix (the guitar work on *When Doves Cry*, for example). In addition, Prince did much to copy the example of Sly and the Family Stone's visual aesthetic, as well as promoting the same blend of races and genders within his bands, most notably with The Revolution in the middle of the 1980s.

Another crossover take on funk was fashioned by reggae artists, who worked upon the huge similarities in pacing, dynamics and 'playing the spaces' to good effect. The work of Third World and Grace Jones (Grace Mendoza) is a good example of this hybrid. On tracks such as Bill Withers' *Use Me* and *Walking In The Rain*, Jones, backed by reggae's 'superstar' rhythm section Sly and Robbie (Lowell Dunbar and Robbie Shakespeare), and Level 42's Wally Badarou, emphasises the parallels between reggae, disco and funk.

As previously indicated, the funk accompaniment to any screen narrative with pretensions towards the representation of 'urban realism' was *de rigueur* for much of the 1970s and 1980s. In television dramas such as *Starsky and Hutch* and later *Miami Vice*, stereotypical funk elements did much to engender 'edge' and physical urgency, and this phenomenon was still proving successful with films such as *Beverley Hills Cop* (1984). The *Theme From Axel F*, its accompanying hit single, replete with 1980s' synthesisers and electronic drums, was as much a sonic signifier of its era as was the wah-wah guitar pattern of Isaac Hayes' *Theme From Shaft* of an earlier point in funk's development.

The funk offshoot of disco was much vilified by both the rock and funk fraternities, but as is ever the case, the subgenre contained much music of worth, with some of it indisputably funky. Where disco differed fundamentally from funk was in its almost total reliance upon the soon-to-be-standardised 'four-to-the-floor' drum pattern, which had the effect of providing a rhythmically comforting metronomic pulse. However, as already noted, a fair proportion of funk (some Parliament/Funkadelic tracks, for example) also adopted the disco beat. Disco's construction of a hegemonic beat did result in a certain degree of blandness in overall terms, but acts such as Chic, later Kool and the Gang, the Jacksons, Shalamar and Sister Sledge built successfully upon such rigid bases. In particular, the music and production team of Bernard Edwards and Nile Rodgers would have comfortably slotted into many a 'hard funk' outfit; Edwards' basslines on Chic's *Good Times* and *Chic Cheer* and the rhythm guitar of Rogers on Diana Ross' *I'm Coming Out* and *Upside Down* are classic funk components. Rodgers' influence as producer also helped add the funk/dancefloor component to acts such as Madonna (*Like A Virgin* album) and David Bowie. Bowie moved from the Philly soul pastiche of *Young Americans* to a harder funk terrain with *Station To Station*, aided by the guitar interplay between Earl Slick and rhythm guitarist Carlos Alomar. After an experimental series of albums with Brian Eno (Brian Peter George St John de Baptiste de la Salle Eno), Bowie turned to Rodgers as producer and the resulting album, *Let's Dance*, was one of the biggest successes of Bowie's career, and was built upon funk grooves.

Jazz funk was very much the 'acceptable' face of dance music in the late

1970s. Jazz funk took its lead from both the jazz rock of Miles Davis' electric period and the small ensembles of Weather Report and The Jazz Crusaders, but also drew upon soul and funk in fashioning a sound aimed less exclusively at the dancefloor than disco. However, as with disco, it could not escape criticisms relating to its politeness, and the sounds of Shakatak and Level 42 did eminently suit the wine-bar culture of the 1980s' yuppie even if the bass work of Level 42's Mark King did take the slap-bass style to new heights of speed and virtuosity. Herbie Hancock (Herbert Jeffrey Hancock), another émigré from jazz and disco, incorporated electro elements into the classic jazz funk of hits such as *Rockit*. A funk dimension was an often integral part in the 'synthpop' music of the early 1980s. Acts such as Heaven 17, Japan, Duran Duran and Spandau Ballet all utilised slap-bass and funk-rhythm guitar styles extensively (this aspect is explored in further depth in the synthpop chapter). In particular, the rhythm section of Japan, featuring the sinuous fretless basslines of Mick Karn (Anthony Michaelides), moved their take on funk into an exotic and unexpected terrain.

Funk's influence upon two other forms of music was less expected, and all the more innovative as a result. Post-punk acts such as Gang of Four, Pigbag, A Certain Ratio and The Fall all drew upon the more fractured and confrontational aspects of funk to fashion a new hybrid. On albums such as Gang of Four's *Entertainment*, the rhythmic disturbances of funk meshed with agitprop lyrics and avant-garde atonality to great effect. Punk rock had made a physical response to music 'socially acceptable' again to the white mainstream rock audience and the punk/funk hybrid garnered credibility as a result.

Another archetypal 'white' genre of music, progressive rock, made tentative steps towards funkiness in its attempt to broaden its appeal and market demographic. In particular, Genesis and Phil Collins became global superstars in the 1980s by stripping their sound of its density and convoluted time signatures and instead exploiting a funk sense of space and dynamics (listen to Collins' *Sussudio* or Genesis' *Invisible Touch* by way of example).

Early forms of rap had consisted of a DJ voiceover and a disco or funk backing or rhythm track, or bass riff. In the early 1980s, aided by new technologies such as programmable drum machines and samplers, developments by the likes of Afrika Bambaataa (Kevin Donovan) and Grandmaster Flash (Joseph Sadler) gave rap a more innovative, and funky basis (listen, for instance, to *Looking For The Perfect Beat* or *Planet Rock* from rap's short-lived 'electro' period). Later in the decade, the sampled funk breakbeat became the basis for huge numbers of rap tracks for the likes of Public Enemy, Ice-T (Tracy Marrow) and LL Cool J (James Todd

Smith). Indeed, the sampled drum pattern from the end section of James Brown's *Funky Drummer* (played by Clyde Stubblefield) can probably lay claim to being the single most sampled piece in popular music, with literally dozens of appropriations by musicians as diverse as Fine Young Cannibals, Jive Bunny, Sinéad O'Connor, Public Enemy and George Michael (Georgios Panayiotou).

The burgeoning and global success of dance music perpetuated the funk legacy. In the 1990s, the same funk breakbeats, slowed down below eighty beats per minute or sped up beyond 160 beats per minute, became the basis for new dance subgenres emanating from the UK, such as trip-hop, jungle and drum 'n' bass, and later speed garage and UK garage. Crossover indie-guitar acts such as Primal Scream and the Happy Mondays made great use of the funk 'shuffle' rhythm, whose influence spread throughout mainstream guitar pop.

In the contemporary music scene, some would argue that the battle that has raged since the mid-1970s between the 4:4 crotchet beat developed from disco, and the breakbeat drawn from soul and funk, has recently tipped in favour of the latter. Post-house dance music, and the whole superclub and superstar-DJ scene based largely upon four-to-the-floor beats, went into decline in the late 1990s in the UK, with prominent clubs such as Home in London and Nation in Liverpool going out of business. In contrast, breakbeat-influenced dance styles, such as the big beat hybrid popularised by performer-DJs such as Fatboy Slim (Quentin 'Norman' Cook) and the Chemical Brothers, were less intrinsically associated with the perceived 'cheesiness' of commercial dance culture, allowing for their critical success amidst the ongoing mutation of funk that shows no sign of ceasing.

Guitar-based forms of rock, such as grunge and nu-metal, did much to unite disparate styles and audiences in the 1990s. American acts such as Red Hot Chili Peppers and Pearl Jam worked within the crossover axes of metal and hard funk to considerable commercial success. Later in the decade, acts such as Linkin Park and Limp Bizkit re-emphasised this crossover, adding a patina of rap vocal style and image to the package. Eminem, the most successful rap superstar, most typically employed a sparse funk breakbeat as the musical accompaniment to his verbal gymnastics, but the same tracks, remixed and augmented with distorted rock guitars, slotted seamlessly into the programming on specialised rock video channels such as *Kerrang!*

The music may most recently be referred to as 'urban' or R&B within record charts or retail categories, but the funk component still dominates these musical genres. Dedicated music TV channels now broadcast funk material in a video-jukebox format. This often consists of the now standardised 'bling-bling' visual style of amounts of bare flesh draped with copious amounts of jewellery and designer labels. Some would see the obvious manifestations of eroticism as making the more symbolic and implied eroticism of funk tracks a little too blatant, but the demands of the media have always encouraged promotion based on youth and (mainly) female sexuality. Within this scenario, funk-based grooves are seen to provide a perfect accompaniment.

R&B, that most overused and non-specific of terms (and now used as shorthand for so-called 'music of black origin'), still relies upon funk idioms, whether in the gospel-tinged vocal work of Destiny's Child, Macy Gray (Natalie McIntyre), Christina Aguilera and Justin Timberlake, or the UK take on groove in the hands of Ms Dynamite and Craig David. Within the 'mainstream', the mutation of artists such as Madonna (Madonna Louise Ciccone) from the up-tempo house-influenced styles of the 1980s and 1990s, to a more sparse funk-based sound on more recent albums such as *Music*, is symptomatic of the enduring influence of funk. Even middle-of-the-road balladeers such as Celine Dion attempted to maximise their demographic appeal and credibility with funk-influenced radio remixes of ballads such as *A New Day Has Come*. This indicates something of the breadth of adoption for the funk idiom.

Recommended reading

Brackett, D. (2000) *Interpreting Popular Music*. Berkeley: University of California Press.

Corbett, J. (1994) *Extended Play: Sounding Off from John Cage to Dr Funkenstein*. London: Duke University Press.

Garofalo, R. (1997) *Rockin' Out: Popular Music in the USA*. Boston: Allyn & Bacon.

Harvey, D. (1989) *The Condition of Postmodernity*. Oxford: Blackwell.

Lipsitz, G. (1996) *Dangerous Crossroads: Popular Music, Postmodernity and the Poetics of Place*. London: Verso.

Palmer, R. (1995) *Rock and Roll: An Unruly History*. New York: Harmony.

Shuker, R. (1998) *Key Concepts in Popular Music*. London: Routledge.

Vickers, T. (1995) *Mothership Connection*. Album sleevenotes accompanying *The Best of Parliament: Give Up The Funk*. Casablanca.

Vincent, R. (1996) *Funk: The Music, the People and the Rhythm of the One*. New York: St Martin's Griffin.

Ward, B. (1998) *Just My Soul Responding: Rhythm and Blues, Black Consciousness and Race Relations*. London: UCL Press.

Weinger, H. and A. Leeds (1996) *It's A New Day*. Album sleevenotes accompanying *Foundations of Funk: A Brand New Bag 1964–1969*. Polydor.

Recommended music

Antecedents
Art Blakey (1958) *1958 Olympia Concert*. Mercury.
James Brown (1996) *Foundations Of Funk: A Brand New Bag 1964–1969*.
  Polydor.
Miles Davis (1949) *Birth Of The Cool*. Capitol.
Jimi Hendrix (1970) *Band Of Gypsys*. Polydor.
Sly and the Family Stone (1968) *Dance To The Music*. Epic.
The Temptations (1970) *Psychedelic Shack*. Motown.

Generic texts
Average White Band (1975) *Pick Up The Pieces*. Atlantic.
James Brown (1991) *Sex Machine* [live recording from 1970]. Polydor.
Funkadelic (1978) *One Nation Under A Groove*. Warners.
Marvin Gaye (1972) *Trouble Man*. Motown.
Isley Brothers (1973) *3 Plus 3*. T-Neck.
The Meters (1970) *Struttin'*. Josie.
Parliament (1975) *Chocolate City*. Universal.
Sly and the Family Stone (1971) *There's A Riot Goin' On*. Epic.
Bill Withers (1998) *The Best Of Bill Withers· Lovely Day*. Columbia.

Subsequent generic developments
Gang of Four (1995) *Entertainment*. EMI.
Japan (1980) *Tin Drum*. Virgin.
Grace Jones (1981) *Nightclubbing*. Island.
Living Colour (1990) *Time's Up*. Epic.
Prince (1987) *Sign O' The Times*. Paisley Park.
Red Hot Chili Peppers (1992) *What Hits?* Manhattan.
Roni Size and Reprazent (1997) *New Forms*. Talkin' Loud.

CHAPTER 3

Psychedelia: in my mind's eye

An overview of the genre

In contrast to several of the other genres covered in this book, psyche-delia[1] was, in the main, contained within a relatively short historical period. In broad terms, psychedelia and the psychedelic era (the two are almost indivisible) stretched between 1966 and 1969. This is not to say that psychedelic elements, whether technological, structural, timbral or social, do not endure to the present day, but rather that the overall 'package', intrinsically linked to the specifics of the late-1960s' period, was unique, and in overall terms unrepeatable.

This era, and particularly the so-called 'summer of love' in 1967, has been mythologised more than any other era in pop's historiography. For Simon Frith, it was 'the year it all came together' (Frith 1982: 4–20), a relatively modest claim compared to other, more hyperbolic statements that grant canonic, even transcendental, status to certain psychedelic acts or albums. What is indisputable is that a large number of important musical and extra-musical conjunctural factors did exercise a great impact upon large social groupings within Western society, and upon the musical artefacts produced around that time.

Psychedelic music was built upon elements contained in a wide range of pop and non-pop genres: beat, R&B, 1960s' garage,[2] jazz, folk, classical, certain north African and Eastern musical idioms and avant-garde experimentalism. Its willing embrace of new technologies and production processes acted to radically change the sound palette, the subject matter and the artistic ambition of mainstream pop. Psychedelic music was influential in establishing the notion that recordings and performances were separate entities, which fed directly into the construction of the binary opposition of rock/pop in the late 1960s.

Unusually for pop innovation, many early examples of psychedelic experimentation emerged from the commercial mainstream. In early

1966, bands such as The Beatles and The Byrds, with the power of major labels and state-of-the-art studios at their disposal, produced tracks that were recognised, even at the time, as ground-breaking. The Byrds' *Eight Miles High* (actually recorded in December 1965) and The Beatles' *Revolver* album (specifically tracks such as *Tomorrow Never Knows*, recorded April/May 1966) signalled a seismic shift in terms of artistic ambition, creative influences and studio craftsmanship. The Byrds willingly acknowledged (and actually referenced) the influence of traditional folk, J. S. Bach, and the jazz exploration of the likes of John Coltrane in their eclectic music. By 1966, The Beatles had progressed from being musical exemplars of Motown, rock 'n' roll and country music, to being acolytes of found sounds, *musique concrète* and raga improvisations.

Such was the welcoming musical and social climate for what remain startlingly innovative explorations in sound and mood that the actual pre-history of psychedelic music was minimal in terms of duration. By the end of 1966, acts such as Donovan, The Yardbirds, Jefferson Airplane, Love and The Beach Boys had all produced canonic psychedelic work, to be followed and augmented by countless acts by the summer of 1967, during what was seen as the full flowering of the psychedelic era.

Aforementioned social shifts and political events were immensely important to the psychedelic *Zeitgeist* and had more of a pre-history. The beat movement, and its influence upon the burgeoning counterculture of the

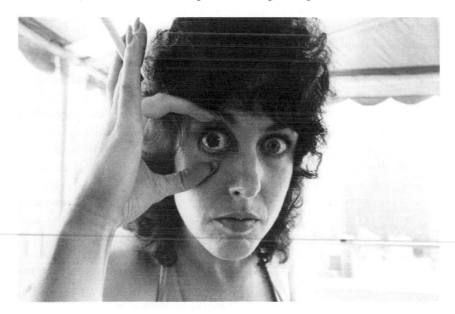

Grace Slick of Jefferson Airplane. In my mind's eye.

1960s, was influential, particularly upon lyrical concerns and styles and the 'dressed-down' aspect of psychedelia. College education and the Art School tradition had made a huge impact, exposing large numbers of young people to 'alternative' or 'bohemian' lifestyles and artworks. The availability of certain drugs, particularly cannabis, amphetamines and LSD, had increased in the early-to-mid-1960s, and had an impact upon many aspects of the musical and subcultural scenes of the time. However, for many, psychedelia was not explicitly linked to drug consumption. This resulted in an often pastoral or whimsical dimension to some music now thought of as 'mind expanding' that was perhaps a reflection upon what the psychedelic experience was thought to be, or should be, as much as how it was actually experienced.

The principal sites of psychedelic music, in terms of production and dissemination, were California and London, although exceptions did of course apply. The Thirteenth Floor Elevators, one of the earliest acts to describe their music as psychedelic, actually hailed from Austin, Texas. To an extent, psychedelia's two main locations were promoted by the media (including the developing 'underground' press) as the centres of psychedelic music, design and fashion, and the reportage became the reality to a large extent. However, many disparate and unfashionable locations developed their own scenes. By 1968, psychedelia, in the widest sense, was being disseminated from territories as far-flung as Australasia and South America (the Tropicalia genre), as well as throughout the Western world, with psychedelic artefacts originating from Holland, Denmark, Spain and Germany.

Psychedelic music and studio and instrumental innovations were largely indivisible. Sound studios, particularly in the US, had adopted stereo and multitrack recording during the 1950s and early 1960s. Processes such as overdubbing and mixing that took place after recording allowed a more artistic production process to come into being that was less tied to notions of organic space and real time. Particular sound indicators, such as phasing, backward tapes, and intentional distortion, were being employed in many of the more sophisticated studios by 1967. Many of these techniques had their historical roots within the earlier avant-garde productions of the likes of the BBC's Radiophonic Workshop, John Cage, Pierre Schaeffer and Karlheinz Stockhausen, and their antecedents such as Edgard Varèse and the Italian Futurists of the early twentieth century. The fuzzbox effects unit became an almost obligatory addition for guitarists working within the genre (Hicks 1999: 12–22). New timbral textures offered by instruments such as the Mellotron and the sitar, often accompanied by the use of 'pedal notes' or 'drones' traditionally associated with folk modes or Asian forms such as the raga, became popular. Indeed, 'the East' and its constructed values of spirituality had a huge influence upon large sections of Western youth who turned their backs, albeit fleetingly or superficially, on the values of materialism and capitalism.

We must add other elements to this psychedelic musical climate: the already long-standing success of the popular music industry; the widespread prosperity of Western youth; the success of cities such as 'swinging' London in partially superseding traditional fashion centres such as Paris; and the publicity given to 'hippie' districts such as San Francisco's Haight-Ashbury (and its subsequent magnetic draw). All these factors reinforce the notion that enough constituent parts were in place to encourage the mythical construction of a whole era, with its musical component a fundamental aspect.

Historical roots and antecedents

As we have previously indicated, there was very little 'pre-history' of psychedelia, in the musical and temporal sense. Part of the reason for this lay in the relative unavailability of the many new technologies and effects fundamental to psychedelia prior to 1966. In particular, studio techniques such as phasing, multitracking and artificial or automatic double tracking (ADT), and new effects pedals such as 'fuzz-tone' and 'wah-wah', simply did not exist in the commercial terrain before this date.

In terms of musical antecedents, the ambition and scope of forms of modern jazz, as explored by the likes of John Coltrane and Ornette Coleman, did have some impact in encouraging groups such as The Byrds and The Grateful Dead to move beyond the conventional structures and tonality of Western pop idioms. Equally, the Indian classical raga form, as exemplified by virtuosi such as Ravi Shankar, proved hugely influential upon musicians such as Roger McGuinn (James Joseph McGuinn III) and George Harrison. But, in the main, it is fair to say that much (although by no means all) psychedelic music consisted of standard pop song structures filtered through new effects, production techniques and 'altered states' of creativity – whether drug-induced or not. The filtering process, whether radical or superficial, did alter empirically the sound palette of pop in the years around 1967.

By 1965–6, it is fair to say that pop's early 'maturation process' was a critical and aesthetic reality, with artists such as The Beatles, The Beach Boys and Bob Dylan (Robert Allen Zimmerman) all garnering considerable praise from the 'establishment'. As well as demonstrating an increasingly eclectic and sophisticated sensibility, popular music was employing lyrical styles drawn from literary and poetic models in the pre-psychedelic era, with Dylan very much in the vanguard of the move away from 'Tin Pan Alley' romantic clichés and standardised subject matter. The wordplay and use of allegory and metaphor found in Dylan's songs connoted both 'high art' and an aesthetic state far removed from the everyday. Dylan's lyrics were 'mind-expanding' and thus psychedelic in the broadest sense of the word, far more so than the musical accompaniment.

The Beatles effectively retired from live performance in August 1966, claiming that their new material was too complex to be adequately reproduced on stage and, in any case, that nobody could hear it above the screams. From this point onwards, they, along with the likes of The Beach Boys' Brian Wilson, became studio artists, taking unprecedented amounts of time over pre-production and studio composition. Their status allowed for the development of a new (for pop) collagist approach, aided by the increasingly sophisticated studio environment, and the willingness of producers such as George Martin to explore and experiment.

The Beatles' meetings with Bob Dylan and the musical exchanges with The Byrds resulted in a fruitful rivalry borne out of mutual respect that encouraged a creative climate open to myriad influences (Williams 1993: 40–62). Certainly, drugs played a part in this process, with most of the burgeoning psychedelic scene's leaders taking LSD by 1967, but the explicit links between psychedelia as an altered state of mind and psychedelia as an altered state of musical expression are difficult to quantify. As Richard Middleton and John Muncie suggest, a psychedelic song can be 'created under the influence of drugs . . . representing or signifying aspects of the drugged state . . . or attempting to produce an altered state' (Middleton and Muncie 1981: 78).

Charlie Gillett stated that the term 'garage band' symbolises two different types of band, both of which are important in terms of psychedelia's antecedents. The first type, based on pre-British invasion models, took elements of R&B as their touchstone, whereas the second were galvanised by the success of The Beatles, Rolling Stones et al. into reworking these Anglo-American hybrids into new forms (Gillett 1983: 313–14). What garage bands did share was a sense of youthful amateurism, suffused with only moderate levels of proficiency, yet linked to a desire to transcend the restrictions of chart-based pop. The music produced by the likes of The Seeds, The Sonics, ? and the Mysterians and Count Five has also been granted the epithet 'punk', and was far removed from the polished, studio-based collages of other elements within psychedelia. Perhaps their true impact was only recognised in the (second?) punk era, which is dealt with in a subsequent chapter. Equally significant to the pre-history of psychedelia were contextual, social and political shifts, many of which will be explored in the following section.

Social and political context

The psychedelic scene, in both Britain and the US, has been historicised as being intimately connected to the hippie subculture. In fact, psychedelia was more heterogeneous, allowing for its appropriation by both the binary poles of establishment *haute couture* and elements of the underground counterculture.

In Britain, society was still in the throes of recovering from the aftermath of the Second World War and austerity, even in the early 1960s. However, a long period of low inflation and near full employment, allied to a general increase in earnings, did give rise to the conditions of the 'consumer society', culminating in the era now encapsulated in the phrase 'Swinging London'. This was accompanied by a loosening of moral and behavioural values that encompassed class, youth and gender relations. In some senses, this was encouraged by the liberal programme of legislative reform on the part of the Labour governments of 1964–70 presided over by Harold Wilson. In particular, the Wilson government

- abolished capital punishment for murder in the Murder (Abolition of Death Penalty) Act 1965;
- legalised male homosexuality (the Sexual Offences Act 1967);
- legalised abortion (the Medical Termination of Pregnancy Act 1967);
- reformed the censorship laws regarding theatre (the Theatres Act 1968);
- outlawed discrimination in housing and employment (the Race Relations Act 1968);
- liberalised the divorce laws: prior to 1969, divorces were only granted when a matrimonial offence (adultery, cruelty, or desertion of three years) had been committed; subsequent to the Divorce Reform Act 1969, divorce could be granted if a marriage had irretrievably broken down.

The general tenor of these liberal reforms, combined with the development of oral contraceptives and increased drug use (yet to be clamped down upon in the Misuse of Drugs Act 1971), laid the foundation for a general loosening of the 'uptight' nature of British society. The global impact of British pop, accompanied by a higher profile for British film, design and fashion, also contributed to a climate of optimism, experimentation and also radicalism – both artistic and political/social.

In the social terrain, the importance of the 'underground' club or scene was a vital component in the psychedelic period. In February 1966, the Spontaneous Underground events began at The Marquee club in London. Sheila Whiteley reported that 'On March 27, [Pink] Floyd played a number lasting half an hour against a background of red and blue lights and projected film' (Whiteley 1992: 28). The fact that such events took place many months before the band became a recording act suggests that important elements of the scene actually pre-date the commercial breakthrough of the music. By October, the band had played in front of 2,000 people at the Roundhouse, and on 23 December helped launch the UFO (Unlimited Freak Out) club evenings (Whiteley 1992: 28–9). Such events were closely allied to the burgeoning underground press (*The International Times*) and the nascent hippie scene/lifestyle. At the same time, more conventional establishment clubs such as the Scotch of St James were also offering nights featuring some of the trappings of the psychedelic mixed-media experience. The term *discothèque* also began to be widely employed around this period.

In the US, a similarly mixed-media scene was established by 1966, centring around 'ballrooms' such as the Avalon and the Fillmore in San Francisco, and featuring live, often semi-improvised music from The Charlatans and Grateful Dead (Whiteley 1992: 119). The term 'psychedelic' had been incorporated into lyrics as early as 1964, and a B-side by surf act The Gamblers had been entitled *LSD-25* in 1960. Indeed, in the pre-psychedelic period, the negative effects of new synthetic compounds such as LSD had not been made manifest, with the US government not banning its distribution until late 1965. Just prior to this point, a loose collective of artists known as the 'Merry Pranksters' had been touring the US and distributing the drug at mixed-media 'acid tests' (Hicks 1999: 59–60).

Important distinctions between the twin poles of Californian psychedelia – the cities of San Francisco and Los Angeles – were also significant. Many of the leading lights of the SF scene came from a folk or bohemian background, which may have contributed to the nature of their appearance and sound. Conversely, LA bands tended to be more influenced by R&B and commercial pop forms. This factor, added to the fact that the entertainment industry and recording studios were concentrated in the city, may have had an impact upon the specific nature of the psychedelia that emerged around the Los Angeles area.

Although American participation in the Vietnam War was long-established by 1966, the escalation of the war and the growing disenchantment with its execution actually comes towards the end of the psychedelic era, following the Tet Offensive and 'carpet bombing' of North Vietnamese cities in 1968 (Savage 1994b: 22). However, events such as the heavy-handed policing of youth 'scenes' (documented in Buffalo Springfield's *For What It's Worth* in 1967, which dealt with the Sunset Strip riot) and the brutal crackdown on campus political activism resulting in students at Kent State University being killed by National Guardsmen in May 1970 (documented in Crosby, Stills, Nash and Young's *Ohio*) evidences an era and a subculture that was often overtly politicised in opposition to establishment values and policies.

In Britain, the non-participation in Vietnam and the lack of the draft as focal points for activist protest did contribute to a less overtly political dimension to the psychedelic era (although the television coverage of the anti-Vietnam protests outside the US embassy in Grosvenor Square were as spectacular as any images from America). Despite this being an era characterised by more overt political protests (particularly by students) compared to others in postwar Britain, for many participants, psychedelia was as much about fashion, alternative lifestyles and hedonism as it was about activism, more a case of 'dropping out' than 'taking over'. For Jon Savage, these factors resulted in British psychedelia possessing a

> curiously precious, toytown ambience . . . In America, psychedelia mattered: although in Britain it let loose the imagination, it was a style, part of our mad parade. In America, it connected with a new youth consciousness . . . defined in opposition to the Vietnam War . . . this bottom line gave American psychedelia its charged, messianic flavour. (Savage 1994b: 22)

A comparison between the archetypal American psychedelic location (San Francisco's Haight-Ashbury district) and its British equivalent (London's Carnaby Street) further symbolises aspects of the cultural divide. Haight-Ashbury was a long-established bohemian quarter (Platt 1982: 918–20), consisting in part of 'alternative' shops: bookstores (beat poet Lawrence Ferlinghetti's *City Lights*), shops selling drug paraphernalia, vegetarian restaurants, help centres run by community activists such as The Diggers, and small cafés and venues. On the other hand, Carnaby Street, just off the main tourist routes of Regent Street and Oxford Street, was already established by the psychedelic era as an alternative fashion and retail location (with well-known shops such as 'Lord John', 'Kleptomania' and 'Granny Takes A Trip'), although one still closely connected to the existing 'rag trade'. In overall terms, London's take on psychedelia was far more 'dressed up' than San Francisco's, with clear echoes of mod or 'urban dandy' style being suffused through an increasingly flamboyant and androgynous range of fabrics and costumes. In 1967, the Small Faces' sound and image became infused with psychedelic elements. However, according to Tony Calder, their take on psychedelic style consisted initially of buying up a particular line of clothing to ensure exclusivity, and later 'having their own stuff made in crushed velvet and other exotic fabrics by Soho style guru Michael Fish' (Gilbert 2003: 50).

As is ever the case, the seeds of a scene's decline are always present within its own distinct 'uniqueness'. What was experimental in 1966 was a tired cliché by 1969. Commercial exploitation was seen to have ruined the 'underground ethos' of many hippie scenes, with San Francisco's hippie district already 'ruined' by exploitative interests: 'By mid-1968, Haight-Ashbury had become a ghetto for speed freaks and muggers' (Platt 1982: 920). Increasing numbers of people connected to the psychedelic scene effectively suffered 'burn out' by late 1967. Some, symbolised by the likes of Moby Grape's Skip Spence (Alexander Spence), the Thirteenth Floor Elevators' Roky Erikson and Pink Floyd's leader Syd Barrett (Roger Keith Barrett), never fully recovered. As the numbers suffering drug-induced psychosis increased, the halcyon atmosphere of peace and love ended.

Two events in 1969 effectively signalled the end of the psychedelic era. The Woodstock festival, attended by at least 500,000, passed off largely peacefully. Later in the same year, a free event headlined by the Rolling Stones at Altamont racetrack in California ended in violence, with elements of the Hell's Angels 'security' force beating to death a member of the audience during The Stones' set amid an atmosphere of 'bad acid' and 'bad vibes' (Palmer 1995: 173). Coming at the very end of the decade that had seen such revolutionary changes in music and youth culture, this debacle sounded the death knell for many aspects of the psychedelic era and the hippie dream.

The musical texts

This section will deal with some of the diverse subgeneric tendencies within psychedelic music, in the process analysing some of the key components in what has been termed 'psychedelic coding' (Whiteley 1992). It is important to emphasise that the relationship between popular music tracks and psychedelia was one of differing degree and intensity, both in terms of the techniques employed, the overall rationale and the intended outcome. Certain acts jumped on the multi-coloured bandwagon for blatantly exploitative motives, hoping that the insertion of one or two 'hip' elements would increase their commercial appeal. For other acts, a certain key element – a distorted guitar, a 'cosmic' turn of phrase, a phased sequence – would effectively 'psychedelicise' an otherwise 'straight' piece of pop or R&B. Yet, for some, psychedelia was fundamental to their worldview and every aspect of the composition and recording process, especially in the period under scrutiny.

Space/raga rock: The Byrds (1967) CTA-102

This track was one of the earliest examples of the band's interest in space travel (later examples included *Mr Spaceman* and *Space Odyssey*). This subject was manifested lyrically and within the structure, production and instrumentation employed. The first section, after almost no introduction, consists of two short verses underpinned by the classic Byrds' electric-folk sound. After twenty-six seconds a long vocal-free section commences, built upon a two-note bass pattern, which allows for the virtual drone-like suspension of the song proper. This section features timbres and oscillations redolent of shortwave radio tuning and Morse code bleeps, with a section of chromatic, almost free-form bass soloing being incorporated. From 1 : 17 the standard song structure and chord progression resumes for one brief, final verse, before the song effectively segues into an almost ambient coda, with backward voices representing the 'aliens' being panned into one channel while a compressed 'ghost' copy of the earlier part of the track repeats in the other channel until the track fades at 2 : 28.

What is remarkable in such tracks is the breadth of imagination and technical innovation that is squeezed into a standard pop-song length. The two 'alternative' sections do connote an escape from the confines of Western pop and Western organisation – structurally, literally and metaphorically. There is little here of the wild excesses in timbre or playing style associated with Hendrix, for instance, but bands such as The Byrds effectively shifted the mainstream parameters of the pop song in the psychedelic era without dispensing with the conventions of tonality, melody and harmony.

Transatlantic connections and divergences: Pink Floyd and Grateful Dead

Pink Floyd's debut album, *The Piper At The Gates Of Dawn* (1967), and Grateful Dead's second album *Anthem Of The Sun* (1968), clearly exemplify some of the key differences in the appropriation of psychedelic coding by British and American bands of the day. Both bands draw upon diverse generic models, but in the case of Pink Floyd these tend to be typically European – avant-garde *musique concrète*, English pastoral and modal folk, and 'nursery rhyme' pop, with some incorporation of elements of R&B and free jazz. In the case of the Grateful Dead, the foundations of their sound are more rooted in American forms of folk such as jazz, country, R&B and blues, and 'jugband'. The Grateful Dead's music was also infused with polyrhythmic patterns resulting from their twin-percussionist line-up, which gives their sound an often African or Brazilian feel.

On tracks such as *That's It For The Other One* and the concluding section of *Caution (Do Not Stop On Tracks)*, the Grateful Dead's sound is fashioned from a segued collage of studio tracks and live sequences, blended and cross-faded together. Towards the end of such sequences are timbres and atonal sections that sound remarkably similar to sequences from Pink Floyd tracks such as *Astronomy Domine* and *Bike*. However, for the most part the tracks on *Piper* are clearly divided into short folk-based vocal-led tracks, with longer, more free-form experimental tracks clearly distinct. The Grateful Dead of this period tend, both compositionally and mix wise, to combine separate compositions into a multifaceted suite, but one more traditionally rooted in standard chord progressions and conventional rock soloing. Pink Floyd are far more prepared to leave tonality behind. Equally, the Grateful Dead's vocals are usually quite sweet, softly sung and harmony based. Floyd's vocals, almost all by Syd Barrett, are strikingly English in diction and phrasing, but at the same time are more clearly 'stoned' in terms of pitch slippage, connoted ambience and lyrical subject matter. The Grateful Dead's electric guitar sounds also tend to be sweet, 'untreated' and relatively undistorted, often consisting of flurries or runs of single notes. Barrett's style is far more abrasive, atonal and chordal, eschewing the mellow tone of the Grateful Dead's sound.

In conclusion, psychedelic coding within these two examples is achieved through different techniques, playing styles and vocal devices. Both bands use studio technology in a self-conscious manner, but to different ends. When Pink Floyd move away from tonality and conventional song structures, the break is more pronounced, but not achieved through edits and the unique mix of live and studio tracks exercised by the Grateful Dead. The generic bases of American rock suffuse the Grateful Dead's psychedelic explorations; Pink Floyd's sound comes, literally and timbrally, from another part of the world.

Psychedelia and effects

As previously indicated, psychedelia was a genre particularly drawn to, and dependent upon, a wide variety of studio and instrumental effects. Not only were the music and the production elements umbilically linked on a symbolic level, but also on a more prosaic, historical one. Seminal tracks such as The Electric Prunes' *I Had Too Much To Dream Last Night* utilised three different guitar effects in a manner not previously possible in commercial pop. Below are listed some of the most important effects utilised within psychedelic music, and brief examples of tracks that exemplify their incorporation, in sonic and metaphorical terms.

ADT – AUTOMATIC OR ARTIFICIAL DOUBLE TRACKING

According to Walter Everett, the engineer Ken Townshend 'invented' ADT during a Cilla Black (Priscilla Maria Veronica White) recording session. The process 'allowed an existing track to be duplicated out of phase, but with steady pitch' (Everett 1999: 34). As well as resolving the problem of recording two near-identical vocal tracks without error, ADT allowed for an affective shift in vocal timbre, which connoted a drugged, or dreamy state very appropriate to the preferred readings of many psychedelic tracks. John Lennon, always a rather undisciplined and inexact singer (he often got the words or phrasing wrong), had his vocal timbre transformed by ADT on tracks such as *I'm Only Sleeping*. On this track, his doubled vocals were panned to both channels, giving a disorienting yet strangely geometric dimension to his lead vocal as it travels from one channel to another with almost imperceptible delay. The effect also reinforces the lyrical message of the track. Other effects, such as 'varispeeding' the recordings and some elements of backward recording on guitar lines (Everett 1999: 50) also add to the classically 'woozy' feel.

PHASING

Phasing, literally 'out of phase' recordings, are possibly the most fundamental style indicator of psychedelic music. The process, similar to but more pronounced than ADT in terms of delay, was more than likely an example of an initial error (a poorly tuned radio signal is 'out of phase') being subsequently incorporated into tracks for deliberate effect. The classic phase effect is affectively read as a soaring or whooshing element with connotations of 'taking off' or 'spinning out of control'. As such, phasing particularly suited specific points of change within tracks, such as lead-ins to solos or pattern changes (for example, the phased drum roll in the Small Faces' *Itchycoo Park*, or the chorus refrain in Julie Driscoll, Brian Auger and the Trinity's *This Wheel's On Fire*).

However, certain psychedelic tracks were seemingly 'drenched' with phasing as a novelty (for example, Status Quo's *Pictures Of Matchstick Men* or Caleb Quaye's *Baby, Your Phrasing Is Bad*) and this overuse did much to effect a musical backlash in the immediate post-psychedelic era, as well as generically 'trapping' many musicians and groups within certain market expectations.

BACKWARD TAPES

The utilisation of backward tape mixing was less widespread than other psychedelic effects, partly owing to the degree of sophistication required within the studio and the painstaking and time-consuming nature of its effective deployment within tracks. Paradoxically, although the over-dubbing of reversed elements on conventional forward-running tracks required considerable discipline and expertise, the resulting collage is easily read as messy or 'undisciplined' – an archetypal psychedelic trope. A classic example of this kind of collage can be found in The Jimi Hendrix Experience's *Are You Experienced?* This track features the aforemen-tioned combination of forward and backward rhythm tracks, with the most clear timbral indicator being the 'sh-thop' sound of reversed drums and cymbals. Again, the sonic disorientation matches the 'stoned' vocal delivery and lyrics, which often suggest alternative states of conscious-ness, distorted modes of perception and fantastic occurrences. This track also makes great use of other stylistic indicators such as the drone note, with the reversed guitar solo towards the end of the track connoting the sitar and suggesting the raga form. The name of the band was most apt. This kind of music was a sonic experience, in which 'musician and listener co-operate in the creation of a kind of virtual reality, a sonic playpen in which sounds can be investigated and toyed with in a spirit of childlike delight and wonder' (Palmer 1995: 162).

FUZZTONE

Fuzztone, the melodic and harmonic distortion of an electric guitar, pre-dated psychedelic music but was widely employed throughout the genre. Foot-operated pedals (such as the Fuzz Face, employed by Jimi Hendrix on *Purple Haze* and other tracks) affectively 'dirtied up' the sound, and were part of a more widespread move away from 'pure' or 'untreated' tone and timbres. Other amplifier-based techniques such as tremolo and reverb were also taken to extremes during the psychedelic era, often single-handedly removing a track from its conventional sonic terrain in the process.

Visual aesthetic

This section will, for reasons of space, concentrate on just two aspects of the particularly rich psychedelic visual aesthetic – the appearance of some of the musicians involved with the genre and the poster art associated with the period.

Hair styles

It is fair to say that hair length and style is usually a recognisable signifier within popular music. Many of the principal acts of the pre-psychedelic era adopted the sartorial model of The Beatles circa 1965, which by the *Rubber Soul* album photograph consisted of outgrown 'mop tops' – fairly outrageous by the staid mores of the time, but comparatively neat and clean-cut by later standards. Facial hair, another key indicator, was almost unknown in pop circles at the time. Even the Grateful Dead still looked fresh-faced and relatively neat in 1966. The Byrds' Chris Hillman, 'born with corkscrew curls, had to actually iron his hair to achieve that immaculate, flaxen, pudding-bowl effect' (Fricke 1996: 3). By late 1966, Hillman, in tune with the emerging *Zeitgeist*, had allowed his hair to grow into its natural 'neo-Afro', a style that had become the trademark of Jimi Hendrix, and one later copied by the likes of Cream's Eric Clapton and members of The Pretty Things. Roger McGuinn was sporting a 'goatee' beard, and David Crosby had adopted the 'walrus' moustache that remains his trademark to the present day. Accoutrements such as the 'kipper' tie, varied pieces of headgear and materials such as flamboyantly coloured velvet and suede replaced styles modelled on the modest but chic Pierre Cardin-style suits modelled by The Beatles and many other beat groups in the pre-psychedelic era.

More extreme, by the standards of the time, were the 'beatnik' or proto-hippie styles adopted by Bay area groups such as the Grateful Dead and Jefferson Airplane. By 1967 musicians such as Pigpen (Robert McKernan), Gerry Garcia, Jack Casady and Jorma Kaukonen had adopted the look now seen as the stereotype for the era – headbands, facial hair, unkempt clothes, hair shoulder length or longer. In fact, the full-blown hippie look was the exception in 1967. The difference in the visual appearance of the crowds at San Francisco's 'Human be-in' in January 1967 compared to those at Woodstock in 1969 or the Isle of Wight Festival in 1970 is striking. Certainly, the visual disparities between dressed-up and dressed-down psychedelia were considerable. The garish and flamboyant appearance of the otherwise 'anti-commercial' Cream in 1967 was far removed from the downmarket look of many (if by no means all) American acts of the same period. As we shall see in the chapters dealing with progressive rock and metal, it is the period around the turn of the decade, even into the mid-1970s, which sees the dressed-down hippie look at its most widespread and archetypal, rather than the psychedelic era itself.

Poster art

Another visual dimension that was contiguous with the musical era was that of poster art – now one of the most recognisable (and valuable) signifiers of psychedelia in the broadest sense. Similarities between British and American designs were considerable, although some interesting distinctions remained. Common features included the 'non-representational' or at least 'difficult-to-read' graphics and fonts, which often rendered words or band names illegible, particularly to the 'unhip'. Colours tended to be garish, almost 'dayglo' or fluorescent, outlines were blurred or distorted, and many images drew upon images of nature or childhood, often infused with a surreal or erotic dimension. In Britain, the 'decadent' art of the *belle époque/art nouveau* period was often referenced, with the work of Aubrey Beardsley a popular source. The work of the art collective Hapshash and the Multi-Coloured Coat was very influential in the UK.

In the US, the graphics and fonts of a similarly 'crazy' age – the Wild West/Gold Rush era – were widespread. John Platt claims that the first flowering of psychedelic poster art began with the graphic promotion of the Charlatans' gig at the Red Dog Saloon in 1965, which featured the phrase 'the limit of the marvellous' (Platt 1983: 1388). From this monochrome example, the form developed rapidly to encompass the visual excesses now seen as symbolic of the era. By July 1967, psychedelic posters were being displayed in art galleries in San Francisco, but the artwork, tainted by association with the media hyping of 'flower power', rapidly fell from favour in design circles.

In overall terms, the attempt to replicate or suggest an altered state was obvious. Equally, the poster art effectively detached itself and its associated subcultural values from 'straight society' and conventional modes of visual representation. The homologies between all aspects of psychedelia were very apparent, and did much to help construct the era as close to a unified, alternative worldview.

Subsequent generic developments

In general terms, the more wholly an act, its image and its sound conformed to the archetypes of psychedelia, the more quickly that act became marooned in what, by 1969, was a largely discredited and clichéd set of signifiers. As previously indicated, elements of psychedelic coding were effectively 'reined in' during the late 1960s, or even totally dispensed with by certain acts looking to progress (or survive).

A band such as Status Quo ditched the psychedelic trappings of 'flower power' pop hits such as *Ice In The Sun*, grew out their neatly coiffured hairstyles, replaced the paisley and velvet with denim, and re-emerged as a commercial force some three years later as a hard-rocking boogie band. Similarly, the Grateful Dead moved away from extended sound collages and exploited the nascent elements of folk, country and bluegrass that had always contributed to their sound by effectively adopting 'roots' genres wholesale on early 1970s' albums such as *Workingman's Dead* and *American Beauty*. However, shorn of some of its most overused trappings, many of psychedelia's studio effects, structural models and compositional innovations in particular continued to exercise a sizeable influence on popular music, particularly when not employed to excess or so self-reflexively as hitherto.

Certain elements of psychedelic coding found their way into genres as diverse as soul, funk, proto-metal (the 'space rock' of Hawkwind, for instance), folk (Roy Harper, The Flying Burrito Brothers), jazzy rock (Steely Dan's early work), indie, dance genres such as acid house and trance, ambient and commercial chart pop. In the case of progressive rock, it is hard to imagine it flowering without the impact of psychedelia. For Whiteley, 'psychedelic' and 'progressive' are largely interchangeable terms (Whiteley 1992). However, we would argue that progressive, as a named genre rather than as a value-based adjective, does exhibit significant distinctions from psychedelia.

If we compare The Nice with Emerson, Lake and Palmer, these distinctions are symbolic of the divergence of the two genres. The Nice's sound, although heavily based on the keyboard work of Keith Emerson, also incorporated many elements of psychedelic coding, including the fuzztones and distortions of Davy O'List's lead-guitar style, song titles and lyrical subject matter (for example, *Flower King Of Flies* and *Diamond Hard Blue Apples Of The Moon*) and the vocal style of Lee Jackson. After O'List's departure, the latter work of The Nice showed evidence of a move into a more classical-based terrain, as evidenced by their reworkings of Sibelius and other composers. After the disbanding of The Nice, Emerson recruited Greg Lake and Carl Palmer to form ELP. This band continued to develop the classical/prog fusions that became very widespread at the height of progressive rock's success (1971–6). As we argued above, psychedelia gave the affective appearance of being 'undisciplined', the polar opposite of progressive rock, in terms of affect, structure, lyrics, vocals and playing style. In addition, many of the archetypal sonic indicators of psychedelia were disregarded (for example sitars, or slurred or 'stoned' vocals), and replaced by newly popularised instruments such as the synthesiser and the Mellotron, and more pure or 'choral' vocal styles (for example, Greg Lake or Yes' Jon Anderson).

For elements of psychedelic coding within genres such as funk and soul, we would refer you to Chapters 1 and 2, but psychedelic coding infused the mainstream of chart music and pop as a whole, although the connotations of psychedelia were more appropriate to certain subsequent styles and historical eras than others. For instance, psychedelic coding was, in broad aesthetic and timbral terms, anathema to the punk-influenced new wave pop of the late 1970s (The Jam, The Tom Robinson Band) or ska revival (Madness, The Specials). However, more wide-ranging connections between psychedelia and subgenres as diverse as easy listening, goth, indie, daisy age rap, indie, acid house, big beat and techno are very evident. A sizeable percentage of post-punk British indie music seemed obsessed by the psychedelic legacy, whether we talk about the feedback-drenched releases of the Jesus and Mary Chain and other Creation label acts, the fey soundscapes of The Lotus Eaters, or the seminal crossover work of Primal Scream. Tracks such as *Higher Than The Sun* and *Shine Like Stars* from the latter's *Screamadelica* album offer a compendium of popular music genres, with, as the title suggests, psychedelia being perhaps the most prominent.

The metagenre of ambient (Future Sound of London, The Orb) has also proven to be indebted to the spirit, techniques and intended moods and uses to which psychedelic music was put. It is very tempting to make connections between any musical scene or genre with a psychotropic dimension (perceived or made explicit) and psychedelia itself, and to read all 'druggy' music as psychedelic. However, as Simon Reynolds argues, some of the most affectively (or symbolically) psychedelic music within dance is the product of often avowedly 'straight' musicians, and by extension this finding will also apply to audiences and consumers of the resulting sounds (see Reynolds 1998).

In the contemporary era, the distinctions between instruments and effects or treatments – given great impetus during the psychedelic era – have been largely effaced within certain genres. An appreciable percentage of contemporary music is not played, or composed, in the accepted sense of the world, but is produced or generated in a collagist manner. Many of the resulting timbres have no organic connection to existing or organic sounds, and could thus be judged psychedelic in the most fundamental sense. The ability to produce sub-bass frequencies that are as much physiological and communal as musical in their affect and appreciation also has strong connections to the 'cosmic' state of 'one-ness' so valued by social and philosophical elements within the psychedelic scene.

Notes

1. The phrase psychedelic generally refers to drug-like experiences, with one dictionary defining it as 'of a drug: producing an expansion of consciousness through greater awareness of the senses and emotional feelings and the revealing of unconscious motivations (freq. symbolically)' (*The Concise Oxford Dictionary*, ed. Judy Pearsall, Oxford University Press, 2001).
2. Not to be confused with the 1980s' and 1990s' dance genre of the same name (see Chapter 11).

Recommended reading

Everett, W. (1999) *The Beatles as Musicians: Revolver through the Anthology*. Oxford: Oxford University Press.

Fricke, D. (1996) Album sleevenotes accompanying the CD reissue of The Byrds' *Younger Than Yesterday*.

Gillett, C. (1983) *The Sound of the City: The Rise of Rock and Roll*. New York: Pantheon.

Hicks, M. (1999) *Sixties Rock: Garage, Psychedelic and Other Satisfactions*. Urbana and Chicago: University of Illinois Press.

MacDonald, I. (1998) *Revolution in the Head: The Beatles Recordings and the Sixties*. London: Pimlico.

Middleton, R. and Muncie, J. (1981) 'Pop Culture, Pop Music and Post-war Youth: Counter-cultures', in *U203 Popular Culture*. Milton Keynes: Open University Press.

Murray, C.-S. (1989) *Crosstown Traffic: Jimi Hendrix and Post-war Pop*. London: Routledge.

Nuttall, J. (1970) *Bomb Culture*. London: Paladin.

Palmer, R. (1995) *Dancing in the Street: An Unruly History*. New York: Harmony.

Reynolds, S. (1998) *Energy Flash: A Journey through Rave Music and Dance Culture*. London: Picador.

Shepherd, J. (1991) *Music as Social Text*. Cambridge: Polity.

Shuker, R. (1998) *Key Concepts in Popular Music*. London: Routledge.

Stevens, J. (1989) *Storming Heaven: LSD and the American Dream*. London: Paladin.

Whiteley, S. (1992) *The Space Between the Notes: Rock and the Counter-Culture*. London: Routledge.

Recommended music

Antecedents

The Beach Boys (1966) *Pet Sounds*. Capitol.

The Beatles (1966) *Revolver*. Parlophone.

The Byrds (1966) *Fifth Dimension*. CBS.
John Coltrane (1995) *The Complete Africa/Brass Sessions*. Impulse.
Love (1966) *Love*. Elektra.
Ravi Shankar (2001) *Master Of Sitar*. Nascente.
The Sonics (1993) *Psycho-Sonic*. Big Beat.

Generic texts

The Beatles (1967) *Sgt Pepper's Lonely Hearts Club Band*. Parlophone.
The Byrds (1968) *The Notorious Byrd Brothers*. CBS.
Country Joe and the Fish (1967) *Electric Meditation For The Mind And Body*.
  Vanguard.
Cream (1968) *Disraeli Gears*. Polydor.
The Grateful Dead (1968) *Anthem Of The Sun*. Warners.
Jimi Hendrix Experience (1967) *Are You Experienced?* Polydor.
Jefferson Airplane (1968) *After Bathing At Baxter's*. RCA.
Love (1967) *Forever Changes*. Elektra.
Pink Floyd (1967) *Piper At The Gates Of Dawn*. Columbia.
The Pretty Things (1968) *S.F. Sorrow*. Snapper.

Subsequent generic developments

Future Sound of London (2003) *Amorphous Androgynous: The Isness*. Artful.
The Orb (1994) *UF Orb*. Island.
Primal Scream (1991) *Screamadelica*. Creation.
Spiritualized (1998) *Ladies And Gentlemen, We Are Floating In Space*. Dedi-
  cated.

CHAPTER 4

Progressive rock: breaking the blues' lineage

An overview of the genre

Progressive rock was one of the dominant genres for the so-called 'serious' market in Europe and the US between around 1968 and 1976. Commercial success was achieved despite a critical climate that was often disparaging and, by the end of the period stated, broadly negative. This was part of a systematic and ongoing critical process that Paul Stump aptly termed 'the cultural exile of all such music' (Stump 1998: 4). In many circles, it was felt that the genre embodied the worst excesses of pretension, expenditure and detachedness from values of 'roots' and social reality deemed important within popular music ideology. This critical approbation survives to the present day, despite several worthy academic attempts to reappraise the genre (see Stump 1998, Holm-Hudson 2002 and Macan 1997).

It is significant that progressive rock (as a musical style rather than as a concept) is one of the few forms that has not, in fact, progressed or greatly influenced other forms. Paradoxically, in a contemporary music scene full of so-called 'underground' scenes and forms, progressive rock is one genre that can truly claim to be 'underground' in terms of its lack of commercial promotion and subcultural appeal. As with other 'marginal' genres, the Internet has proven a boon for the survival of a form now largely ignored by the mainstream.

Progressive rock ('prog') was very much a product of the late-1960s' *Zeitgeist*, wherein virtuosity, complexity and the 'album as art form' assumed greater significance within the newly named 'rock' field. Rock, as a term, was coined to differentiate the music and attitudes of both performer and audience from the 'pop' or 'commercial' form. This rock/pop binarism can be viewed as a false bifurcation on a number of levels (how can an act that sells millions of albums be considered 'uncommercial'?). However, it did serve to reflect the growing fragmentation of the audience for popular music into what we might term 'taste hierarchies' often based upon class, gender, geographical or ethnic distinctions.

Drawing upon a wide range of musical antecedents, prog developed in a similar fashion to jazz, with which it shared many similar values and in some cases musical characteristics. In Europe, jazz had long existed as the bridge between the worlds of pop and classical music. In overall terms, it was an album-based form that valued experimentation and creative integrity over commercial acclaim. This was certainly true for prog, often referred to as 'underground' music in its early manifestation. Prog was also aided by the maturation of the audience 'baby boom' demographic, who had grown up with rock 'n' roll and beat/pop music. As referenced in earlier chapters, central to the burgeoning maturation of both musicians and audiences were the huge leaps in sonic and structural architecture engineered by Brian Wilson and The Beach Boys, and The Beatles and producer George Martin. Equally, as we have seen elsewhere in this book, the impact of psychedelia in all its social, spiritual and musical manifestations had a great impact upon the prog form.

Britain, and more specifically southern England, can be considered the geographical and 'social' home of prog. Its bourgeois roots have been rather overemphasised but an appreciable percentage of prog fans and musicians came from middle-class backgrounds and had a public school, university or art college education.

In the era before dedicated music television channels or video promotion, the music press was hugely important in the popular music scene. During the late 1960s, the long-established weekly pop press was augmented by the periodicals of the rock or underground press: in the US *Rolling Stone* and *Creem*, in Britain *Oz* and *International Times*. Weekly titles such as *New Musical Express* and *Melody Maker* shifted their style from 'fan journalism' to a more engaged analysis of music and its context, and championed forms such as prog in this period (Gorman 2001).

Between 1967 and 1970 groups from a variety of musical backgrounds such as Pink Floyd, The Nice and Procol Harum achieved success in single charts, album charts, and as live acts. What might be called the 'second wave' of acts – the bands today most closely associated with the genre – Genesis, Yes and Emerson Lake and Palmer came to the fore around 1970. Genesis found much of their early success in continental Europe, particularly Italy, and it is significant that within the prog field many European acts managed to break the Anglo-American rock and pop hegemony. In the early 1970s, acts such as Golden Earring, Focus, Gong and PFM all achieved some measure of commercial or critical success.

By 1976 the aforementioned critical backlash, aided by a change in the social *Zeitgeist* and the development of antithetical and critically ac-claimed forms such as punk, pub rock and stadium or adult-oriented rock had had a considerable impact on the attention afforded prog. For many British music journalists, vilifying prog in favour of punk became as much a case of 'bandwagon-jumping' as praising the form had been in 1970. Thus in 1982, Nick Logan and Bob Woffinden could claim that punk sought 'to make rock and roll angry once more . . . to restore its relevance to the street' (Logan and Woffinden 1982: 207). However, acts such as Yes and Genesis had their greatest commercial successes long after the prog era effectively ended, although with a somewhat amended sound.

Despite the cruel though sometimes justified criticism heaped upon the genre (see Macan 1997: 167–78), prog did much to encourage a more conceptual and experimental approach to composition, sound palette and performance. In moving away from the conventions of the pop single, guitar-rock and blues-based idioms, prog reconnected European popular forms with their own historical roots and values. It was much more than just an aberration or a footnote in the history of popular music. Strangely, there was much that was concerned with folk roots and ethnic identity in a genre widely criticised as inauthentic, pretentious and fake.

Historical roots and antecedents

Much of prog's complexity resulted from its broad appropriation of previous forms – some 'popular', such as psychedelic pop and R&B, and some less mainstream, such as jazz, avant-garde, folk and classical. From psychedelia, prog took its willingness to experiment within the studio, particularly regarding effects, overdubbing and stereo imaging. The studio-as-instru-ment approach allowed for the production of complex solo works by composers or multi-instrumentalists such as Todd Rundgren, Rick Wake-man and Mike Oldfield. From jazz and the avant-garde, it took both virtuosity and experimentation in atonality and *musique concrète*. From folk, it took timbres, some lyrical concerns and the use of pre-classical modes and note intervals. From the Western classical tradition, it took extended structures, complex and shifting time signatures, and formal concepts such as counterpoint, recapitulation, the tone poem and the fugue. In addition, the genre was heavily influenced, both structurally and spiritually, by what we could loosely term 'the East' in all its 1960s' manifestations. Literary and artistic genres such as gothic and the pastoral also had an influence, particularly upon instrumentation, lyrics and implied identity.

Prog certainly imbued an audience with a sense of identity often little to do with the more typical African-American model adopted, to some degree, by almost all previous musical genres. It was, as a genre, more to do with Lewis Carroll and Kenneth Grahame than it was with Jack Kerouac or Raymond Chandler. This aspect is made particularly apparent in the vocal styles of the genre, which have little connection to American soul or blues idioms. Of course, as with all genres, the degree of homogeneity (and empathy between acts) should not be overemphasised: some prog acts were strongly influenced by jazz (Gentle Giant, King Crimson) or the classical tradition (ELP, Curved Air), or blues and folk (Jethro Tull), and others less so. Some acts made great use of vocal harmony (Yes), while others largely dispensed with vocals altogether (Camel).

In the period between 1965 and 1969, acts such as The Moody Blues totally transformed their sound from British R&B, through psychedelia, to full-blown prog. During the late 1960s, Jethro Tull moved from tracks built upon slide guitar and harmonica to those making great use of flutes, mandolins and older folk instruments. Many similar examples could be given. Certainly, there was a general mood in rock to embrace the conceptual possibilities that were made manifest in genres such as prog.

What almost all prog acts shared were common racial characteristics (white, male, European) and common instrumental and structural ones. As with other genres, hardly any prog act would refer to itself as 'progressive rock'. Genre distinctions are inevitably imposed, to some extent, upon musicians, particularly by the music press, audiences and, more recently, through radio and record store formatting. In fact, the terms progressive or underground were being employed in the hippie subculture by 1969, according to Paul Willis' ground-breaking ethnographic research. However, such terms were being related to acts more commonly associated with psychedelic or blues and jazz rock in this period, such as Frank Zappa, The Doors, Cream and Jefferson Airplane (Willis 1978: 106–8).

As previously stated, the more experimental work of The Beatles, particularly found on *Revolver* and *Sgt Pepper's Lonely Hearts Club Band*, was hugely influential, as were the jazz experiments of the likes of John Coltrane, Miles Davis and Charlie Mingus, particularly upon acts operating in the prog and jazz-rock areas, such as Soft Machine, Henry Cow and If. Jimi Hendrix (and acolytes such as Jeff Beck), as a polymath of various American idioms (filtered through a British pop/psychedelic frame), opened many ears to the potentialities of tonal and structural experimentation with tracks such as *Are You Experienced* and *Third Stone From The Sun*. The European classical tradition was crucial to many musicians, particularly classically trained keyboardists such as Keith Emerson, Tony Banks and Rick Wakeman. Many classical styles, gestures or indeed whole compositions were routinely appropriated or adapted by prog rock acts, although, simply as a result of disparities in areas such as volume and audience response, the relationship between the classical and the prog rock fraternities rarely moved beyond one of somewhat grudging respect. Soft Machine played at the Royal Albert Hall as part of the BBC's Promenade concerts series, but to limited appreciation (Stump 1998: 90–1).

Instrumental and technological innovations were embraced by prog. Fundamental to most prog acts was the keyboard rather than the rhythm guitar as the basis of the musical track. Keyboards often employed included the versatile Hammond organ and the Mellotron, a rudimentary sampler holding tape loops of strings, flutes or voices, which had the effect of giving a track a 'symphonic' underpinning. From a non-rock background came the utilisation of the grand piano, violin, dulcimer, cello, flute or the twelve-string acoustic guitar. Such elements often replaced more traditional pop textures such as the electric piano or brass section, and gave the sound a more folk, orchestral or pastoral feel. From around 1970, the synthesiser became central to most major prog acts, often as the lead instrument of choice, although the huge expense of early synthesisers did preclude their wide-spread adoption within pop until the late 1970s (Stump 1998: 62). In overall terms, prog communicated using a different timbral sound palette to previous forms. Indeed, some acts such as Pink Floyd made great use of 'found elements' and non-musical timbres in their recordings.

Structurally, the intent was often to 'stretch out': temporally, rhyth-mically, lyrically and tonally. Instead of the long-established song form consisting of variations of verse/chorus and middle section (often referred to as the AABA form), many prog acts recorded extended tracks influenced, in some cases, more by jazz improvisations or the baroque suite of linked themes than the commercial pop model (Macan 1997: 168). Avant-garde experimentation from the likes of Cage, Varèse and Stock-hausen often came into creative contact with English pastoral whimsy within the same track (for example, Pink Floyd's *Interstellar Overdrive*). Indeed, when regarding vocal style and lyrical subject matter, prog was as much concerned with drawing upon archaic influences as it was to appear ground-breaking. In this strange combination of futurism and nostalgia, there did seem to be a deliberate attempt by many prog acts to create a new hybrid form that, at least partially, broke with the accepted funda-mentals of African-American-based popular forms. John Sheinbaum refers to this phenomenon as 'the inversion of musical values' (Sheinbaum 2002: 21 43), and it is significant that much of the recent academic work on prog should originate in North America, where it seems to be viewed as an 'exotic other' in much the same manner that 'roots' forms such as blues have been viewed in Britain.

Social and political context

The 1960s counterculture manifested itself in many forms. For some, it was explicitly anti-establishment and based upon opposition to specific political policies (Vietnam, drug legislation, the draft in the US). For others, it was more about lifestyle and social and sexual mores. Within the prog genre, overtly political dimensions were not widely expressed. The radical challenge to establishment values was more focused within musical structures that encouraged an oppositional stance to composition, the music industry and 'commercialism'. Stump goes as far as to claim that for prog, genres such as soul and Motown were characterised as 'the Fordist Antichrist of mass-produced pop pap' (Stump 1998: 136).

Britain's historical decline in terms of economic influence and imperial power was long established by the late 1960s, but the domestic economy, although increasingly riven by industrial strife and the decline of traditional industries, was still relatively benign, particularly for young people. Unemployment was low, and although the numbers remaining in post-sixteen education were far fewer than today, the art school and technical college did exist as a fulcrum and meeting place for musicians in this period. Maintenance grants also allowed large numbers of student musicians to 'learn their trade' without having to seek paid employment (Frith and Horne 1987).

The art-school model, set up in the postwar firmament of rapid change, existed to give a chance to the often 'unacademic, yet gifted' individual. As documented by Simon Frith and Howard Horne (1987), many subsequently famous and influential musicians passed through the portals of these quasi-anarchic and usually extremely liberal institutions. Because of the slightly more bourgeois demographic of the prog movement, many musicians did take degrees, but often in an arts environment. Moreover, in an overall subcultural climate becoming increasingly intellectualised in this period, the prog genre was well placed to exploit the subsequent rising artistic expectations of the audience. This was manifested graphically and visually as much as musically, with the increasing utilisation of elements such as slides, projections and the lightshow dating from the psychedelic and early prog era (Stump 1998: 23).

Another significant shift in this period was in audience behaviour. By around 1970, a rock concert was a seated and often very sedate affair in terms of physical response. Standing up or dancing were not favoured responses. Of course, this attitude may well have been engendered by the complexity and length of prog compositions. Nevertheless, the result of this combination of factors resulted in a hushed awe that formed a social backdrop to the performances, and encouraged prog audiences to perceive themselves to be elevated, both emotionally and aesthetically, by the experience.

Prog, and its associated subculture, was more aesthetic and even 'escapist' in its concerns than other elements of the counterculture and thus reflected its relative parochialism, in terms of philosophy and geographical origin, if not its subsequent widespread commercial success. Certainly, no North American acts ever adopted the 'classic' British prog sound. The American traditions in jazz, country and blues instead encouraged musicians to hybridise these forms with rock around the turn of the 1970s, leading to country rock, early stadium rock and jazz-rock fusion. Durrell Bowman claimed that the only North American act adopting enough of the prog traits to be included under its banner was Rush and, perhaps significantly, they were Canadian (Bowman 2002: 183–218).

In continental Europe the prog genre flourished. The German music scene, in particular, adopted a progressive-rock/avant-garde hybrid sound to help break the Anglo-American pop hegemony and establish their own native tongue as a viable choice in a market hitherto far more tied to English as the *lingua franca* of commercial pop. Acts such as Faust, Amon Düül II and Can developed a distinctive take on prog which was termed in those less PC times 'kraut rock'. German prog tended to be more confrontational and atonal than its British counterpart in making use of found elements and 'drone' techniques, but was nevertheless hugely influential upon subsequent musicians. As musician Robert Wyatt commented, local authorities, political parties, arts councils and state-sponsored radio ensured that the European prog environment 'had a much more anarchic network of alternative musical dissemination . . . that gave radicalism a moral authority' (quoted in Stump 1998: 122–3).

Other important social changes in this period related to performance staging, packaging and radio formats. The old 'variety package tours' associated with pop and soul were replaced by a 'gig circuit', which for major acts consisted of a variety of theatres, concert halls and university venues. From 1967, these were augmented by open-air festivals in both the US and Europe, and the beginnings of stadium rock date from the same era. In 1971, acts such as Genesis and Van der Graaf Generator (the latter only 'second division' in terms of UK commercial sales) were playing continental stadia and festivals in front of tens of thousands while still being restricted to clubs holding a few hundred in the UK (see Cavanagh 2002). In the same year, Genesis were astonished to find their second album, *Trespass*, at number one in the Belgian album charts before they had progressed beyond underground obscurity in the UK. In this period, their 'best gig' in their homeland was a small club called The Friars in rural Aylesbury, Buckinghamshire (Fielder 1984: 58). By the 1970s, seated audiences would indulge the musicians' penchant for extended solos or improvisatory passages. The audience for prog favoured the album form over singles; indeed, many prog acts did not even bother to release singles in this period. By 1974, most major prog acts had released a double or even triple album, often based partly or wholly on a single conceptual theme. The album artwork became hugely important in the rock metagenre as a whole (see Thorgerson and Powell 1999). In some cases album package, staging, costume and performance all became fused into a powerfully unified whole work of art.

> Clearly what was at stake here was no longer simply music, but the entire artistic realm, a striving towards *Gesamkunsterwerk* that the modernist pioneer and archangel of Romanticism, Richard Wagner, would have recognized; music, once again, sat at the centre of a multi-artistic endeavour. (Stump 1997: 26–7)

There was little television coverage for non-single forms of music in this era, particularly in the UK. However, the development of FM radio in the US, accompanied by some faltering moves in the same direction in the UK from 1967 onwards (see Barnard 2000 and Chapman 1992), did provide a valuable media outlet for genres such as progressive rock. By 1973, the 'underground' or alternative subcultural beginnings for prog had shifted into a much more mainstream rock identity, although musicians and audiences would have still seen themselves as existing outside the perceived limitations imposed upon commercial pop by the 'music biz'. However, as many have rightfully commented 'the commitment to musical truth informed an "anti-commercialism" which turned out to have a remarkable selling power' (Frith and Horne 1987: 90). This last factor did much to encourage the major labels to set up 'progressive' subsidiaries, such as EMI's Harvest and Philips' Vertigo. These coexisted alongside labels that then were at least partly independent, such as Island and Charisma, to 'assure the kids that they were all on the same side' (Stump 1998: 73).

Visual aesthetic

As previously stated, with little television exposure for prog, the principal modes of visual exposure for the genre were through the concert experience and album-cover artwork (Macan 1997: 57–68). Audience dress codes could be defined as 'post hippie', with some of the more flamboyant colours and materials replaced by a functionalism that resulted in the army-style greatcoat rubbing shoulders with the Afghan. Prog did attract a largely male following, not exclusively middle class, but certainly not proletarian. Genesis drummer Phil Collins summed up their audience in the prog era thus: 'Our fans were mainly college-goers – spotty blokes, most of them. We never had girl fans at all, until very recently. It was long trenchcoats, with fishing hats and a pile of albums under the arm' (quoted in Fielder 1984: 82). As this observation indicates, 'dressing down' was more approved of than dressing up. Hair length reached its maximum in the early 1970s, and the overall impression of a prog audience compared to one for psychedelic rock was of less ostentation, with the Eastern or 'utopian' trappings diminishing. Indeed, before the new wave of heavy metal in the late 1970s, there was little to choose between the appearance of the two audiences and, in many cases, the musicians in prog and metal.

Prog musicians took their music very seriously. For most stage performers, costume or stagecraft had low status. In addition, this was often music of great complexity, making huge demands upon players (and audiences) and discouraging movement by either element. This resulted in some musicians performing almost anonymously, while seated (Michael Rutherford and Steve Hackett of Genesis in the early 1970s, Robert Fripp of King Crimson throughout his later career). The occasionally flamboyant front man, such as Peter Gabriel of Genesis or Ian Anderson of Jethro Tull, was the exception. As Gabriel himself stated, the costume changes and surreal monologues that punctuated his performance were as much about expedience as stagecraft – they provided much-needed focus, and gave him something to do during protracted instrument changeovers, or during extended instrumental passages (Fielder 1984: 60–2). For Anderson, his pre-industrial or 'Faginesque' stage dress seemed an extension of the kinds of archetypes (minstrel, sea-dog, down-and-out, lecherous squire) that formed the basis for many of his songs (Moore 1993: 91–2). Lead vocalists that did not play were also unusual. Even Gabriel, an able flautist, felt obliged to accompany the group on additional kick drum during up-tempo instrumental passages in their early career. Other leaders of groups, such as Keith Emerson, did attempt to project to their audience via costume or gesture, but being partially trapped behind (by 1973) banks of keyboards limited this aspect of performance. Guitar showmen such as Hendrix, or The Who's Pete Townshend would not have suited the demands and mythologies of prog.

For Macan, both the prog concert experience and associated cover art were most indebted to styles and developments associated with the psychedelic era (Macan 1997). Pink Floyd's staging developed from the rudimentary in 1967 to the spectacular by 1973, and was only rivalled in scale by ELP. Greg Lake performed standing on an expensive Persian rug at the height of their success, which tells us much about the pretensions of the genre.

Prog stagings deliberately diminished the stage presence of the musicians to the minimal or so they could even be considered incidental. Backdrops and visuals reinforced the cover art of the most recent album and some acts formed long creative partnerships with specific designers and artists (Pink Floyd with Hipgnosis, Yes with Roger Dean).

Between the psychedelic and the mid-prog eras, a general move away from psychedelic abstraction and Eastern mysticism took place, with a shift towards a more surreal yet representational set of styles, often based upon fantasy, mythology, science fiction or 'little England'. The 'careerist' nature of prog was also emphasised by the ongoing continuities in style from one album design to the next. This sometimes went as far as self-consciously referencing past works and then developing the band logo – later to become a copyrighted commodity during the stadium rock era.

By 1972, most prog acts had adopted the gatefold sleeve format. This allowed for the incorporation of large designs spread over two sides of an album, as well as accompanying notes, lyrics and promotional shots. On occasions, even more material was enclosed in the form of booklets or on dust sleeves. The importance of this visual dimension for 'culture' and prog in particular cannot be underestimated, and a great deal of creative freedom was granted to album designers in the prog era (Thorgerson and Powell 1999: 9–16). Peter Blake, the designer of the *Sgt Pepper's* cover, noted wryly that his artwork nestled between Chartres Cathedral and Tolstoy's *War and Peace* at number 15 in *The Sunday Times* 'Top Fifty Millennium Masterworks of the Twentieth Century' (Thorgerson and Powell 1999: 8).

The relationship between concert, album artwork and music was very much homologous, as far as audiences, industry and musicians were concerned. The return of 'functional realism' with punk and new wave in 1976–7 did much to expose some of the visual excesses of prog. The rise of the CD package in the mid-1980s, concurrent with the development of music television, also did much to shift the visual emphasis away from the album-package-as-artwork and there seems little likelihood of its return.

The musical texts

Because of the nature, scope and complexity of musical texts within prog, more attention has been paid to these aspects of the genre than is usually the case within popular music analysis. In fact, in some cases, the formal, musicological nature of the analysis is as exclusive as that found in fields such as jazz or even classical music. Within academic circles, debate has raged with regard to the most appropriate musicological methodology to employ (see Brackett 2000). For the purposes of this book a more inclusive, culturalist approach is employed, regardless of the musical characteristics of the genre.

European prog

CAN (1971) *OH YEAH*

As previously indicated, European prog was far more influenced by avant-garde and anti-commercial experimentalism than British prog. This often resulted in the use of atonality, free-form improvisation and non-standard song structures. All these elements can be found in this track. Band members Holger Czukay and Irmin Schmidt had studied under Stockhausen, while other members had rock or improvised jazz backgrounds (Patterson 1996: 22). Uncommonly for prog, *Oh Yeah* is built around a repetitive groove, with no multiple-key or tempo changes. Over an ascending bass pattern, washes of keyboard, backwards cymbals, and stopped guitar chords interspersed with blues licks drop in and out of the mix. The vocals intermittently appear to offer an exotic Japanese or German texture built upon the repetition of one simple melody line. The drums are perhaps the most interesting feature, setting up a simple, hypnotic pattern in 'common time' without any of the complex rolls or time signature changes associated with either the genre or the era. This song demonstrates the facets of prog in conceptual terms – as a challenge to pop traditions – rather than in its timbral or structural execution.

Folk prog

JETHRO TULL (1971) *MOTHER GOOSE*

Having started out as part of the British blues boom movement in 1967–8, Jethro Tull's style shifted towards a quintessentially British folk-prog sound by 1971's *Aqualung* album. The album was also their first 'conceptual' work, with each side featuring a suite of songs linked to a common theme, one side dealing with the life of a vagrant, and the other a treatise on the nature of faith and organised religion. *Aqualung* was a staging post towards the full-blown (although self-conscious and parodic) concept of *Thick As A Brick*, which featured two side-long compositions.

Despite the quintessentially British nature of their music, the band became a major act in North America in the 1970s, in fact more popular than in their homeland. This provides us with an inversion of the more usual scenario whereby certain American acts (whether working in blues or punk) have to travel abroad to find success. Other prog acts have continued to flourish in the States, long after their British audience has diminished. By the 1980s, the band had ceased to be a major commercial force in fickle Britain, whereas in Germany their biggest album success came as late as 1986.

Although full of the cyclical riffs and guitar-driven elements associated with rock, *Aqualung* made great use of folk textures and instrumental fills, particularly through Anderson's own acoustic guitar, recorder and flute. By later albums such as *Songs From The Wood*, such timbres would dominate their sound to the extent that that there is barely any explicit relationship to African-American styles or their British derivatives. For the first 2 : 24 of its duration *Mother Goose* is close to a solo performance, with Anderson's vocals – very English in their clipped diction and lack of melisma – accompanied by acoustic guitars, double-tracked flutes and recorders, and minimal percussion. At this point electric bass and guitar do enter the mix, but in a much understated manner. The track's sparseness and the connotations of a pastoral sense of landscape and tradition can only be understood fully in the overall context of the album. Aqualung intersperses aggressive tracks such as *Locomotive Breath* with folksy 'interludes' to produce a loosely unified 'concept album' that, in the context of its genre, helped forged a new terrain for popular music little to do with blues style, vocal idioms or subject matter.

Psychedelic prog

HAWKWIND (1971) *MASTER OF THE UNIVERSE*

This track is the sonic and structural meeting place of three genres: psychedelia, prog and metal. Hawkwind emerged in the post-psychedelic era, and forged a reputation on the live and free festival circuit. The band was always heavily influenced by science fiction and worked closely with author Michael Moorcock at one point. Many of their tracks deal with notions of androids, space travel and escape from dystopian worlds. Therefore they are lyrically and conceptually 'expansive' and psychedelic/prog. In many tracks, they also make use of drone-like grooves.

On *Master Of The Universe*, the simple drone is overlaid with psychedelic effects such as a long phased sequence and a 'wah-wah' saxophone solo. It also features two rhythm guitar tracks, one funky and choppy, and a second, which joins the track later than the first, highly distorted and 'dirty'. This textural component immediately removes the track from its psychedelic and prog terrain, edging it into a heavily hybridised territory closer to metal. In addition, the track is in a simple 4 : 4 time, imbuing it, in parts, with something of the classic metal 'headbanging' quality. However, the extensive use of rudimentary synthesisers and what the band termed 'tone generators' provided a far more varied range of timbres than found on a classic metal track, the connotations again being too 'spacey'. Hawkwind's tracks also made use of 'light and shade' and some acoustic interludes. In addition, some of their longer tracks were 'concept' length and featured a number of linked sections, although without the time-signature trickery of classic prog. This hybrid terrain allowed the band to straddle several audiences, granting them both commercial success and longevity.

Classical prog

GENESIS (1974) *ANYWAY*

In 1974, Genesis released the double album *The Lamb Lies Down On Broadway*, which was performed in its entirety for a subsequent world tour. The concept, based around the character of Rael and his attempts to return to 'the real world' after being sucked into a cloud that transports him into a nightmarish succession of scenarios, was redolent of Lewis Carroll, John Keats or J. R. R. Tolkein. This ambitious framework allowed Gabriel to adapt his vocal style to a more raspy Americanised delivery in keeping with his constructed alter-ego and the setting of the fable in New York City. In a similar fashion, the album saw the band move away from their earlier practice of constructing long tracks from linked themes and movements to one where separate tracks of a more standard song length and structure were segued together, often via ambient instrumental interludes.

Anyway exemplifies this new song-based approach, but still exhibits a complexity and a debt to the European classical tradition that are central to the prog genre as a whole. The track lasts for 3 : 08 and begins with a short grand piano intro of nine seconds, which then leads into a verse, followed by a second verse at forty-nine seconds. All this occurs in standard 4 : 4 time. So far, so conventional. Then at 1 : 14 an abrupt and seismic change occurs, with the solo piano signalling a change in tempo, key and time signature simultaneously in moving to furious triplet patterns in 12 : 8 time. The piano is then joined by the remaining rhythm section emphasising certain chords under the arpeggiated piano lines before an atonal synthesised tone signals a shift into a double tracked guitar solo underpinned by a return to common time and a regular beat. At 2 : 18 the track recapitulates its intro section and then a third verse follows. The track ends by segueing seamlessly into the following track via the chordal wash of a synthesiser. Barring the lack of a chorus, the opening and closing sections of this track are relatively standardised in structural pop terms.

What removes the track from a position within the balladic mainstream of pop is the remarkable middle section. Firstly, at just over a minute long, it is too protracted for the standard pop solo, bridge or break section, particularly in a song of this short length. Secondly, its dramatic intrusion into a hitherto constructed mood and tempo that has been 'comfortable' disturbs the usual flow of a standard pop song. This factor, together with the style of the keyboard playing – more redolent of Liszt, Chopin or Rachmaninov than pop keyboard styles – moves the track into what we could term classical prog.

In microcosm, *Anyway* demonstrates many of the strengths of the genre, in particular the relationship (and, to an extent, unresolved dichotomy) between pop modes of playing and mood and the differing demands and connotations evoked by a classical sensibility. Despite the standardised A section ultimately 'triumphing' over the disturbing B section, the overall impression, in terms of pop sensibility, is one of dislocation and disunity.

Subsequent generic developments

As previously indicated, the development of prog as a musical style was effectively halted, particularly in the trend-conscious UK, by the rapid emergence of punk in 1976–7. The period since this point of reappraisal has seen prog return to its 'underground' roots, particularly in terms of critical coverage and approval, although surviving prog acts such as Yes continue to fill large auditoria, particularly in the US and mainland Europe. The classic prog sound, already by 1976 becoming heavily standardised, has been drawn upon with some success by later acts such as Pendragon, The Enid, Twelfth Night and particularly Marillion. The latter were a major commercial act in the early to late 1980s with a sound and image unashamedly drawing upon the example of mid-period Genesis. Their vocalist Fish (Derek Dick) had a voice uncannily close to Peter Gabriel's, and their music combined elements of the prog penchant for the protracted suite (*Grendel*), time signature trickery (*Garden Party*), the linked songs in a concept album (*Clutching At Straws*) and the standard pop song with prog flourishes (*Kayleigh*), to sometimes impressive ends.

Many original prog acts continued to produce music in a mode close to its original manifestation and suffered falling sales as a result (Emerson, Lake and Palmer). Both Genesis and Yes adopted a more stadium-rock style to their work, which consisted of leaving behind some of their more flamboyant metrical and structural flourishes in favour of a more basic rocky or even funky feel. This resulted in even greater commercial success than in their supposed classic period. By the late 1980s, Genesis were one of the biggest rock acts in the world, aided by the somewhat unexpected success of their drummer and vocalist, Phil Collins, who assumed Peter

Gabriel's role, almost by default, in 1976. Collins' own solo work had little to do with prog, being typically a more standard 'rock-lite', soul and funk mix that reached a huge crossover audience. In contrast, Gabriel produced some ground-breaking work in the 1980s that veered from prog to world music styles via collaborations, and made great use of 'progressive' rudimentary sampling techniques. This typifies the dichotomy between prog as a genre and as an adjective. Many diverse acts would consider themselves progressive, but never prog. However, Radiohead have often been discussed using such terms.

A more logical progression for many prog musicians was into fields such as ambient, 'new age' or minimalist and avant-garde music, styles that were built upon the construction of cyclical repetition, reflective moods or timbral experimentation rather than song structures and lyrical meaning. The influence of composers working only on the periphery of popular music, such as Steve Reich, Philip Glass and Terry Riley, was as important as any other prior model. Following on from their example, King Crimson's Robert Fripp (Rodney Frock) and former Roxy Music member Brian Eno produced influential works in this area, as did the German group Tangerine Dream. The music produced, being 'atmospheric' and largely instrumental, proved an effective accompaniment to visual images and thus ideal soundtrack or incidental music.

The legacy of prog as a concept has continued and manifested itself in many unlikely places over the past two decades. In the wake of the acid house movement of the late 1980s, subgenres such as ambient house, progressive house, trance, techno and drum 'n' bass began exploring structures and timbres within a framework of extended or linked-movement tracks. Although elements within such genres could be highly rhythmic, drawing upon dancefloor grooves, there were also concerted moves to provide complex, reflective, almost symphonic pieces more suited to the concept of 'chilling out'. Prominent acts in this area included System 7, The Orb, Pentatonik, Orbital and T-Power. Despite certain links to prog in conceptual terms, most of the acts mentioned stayed resolutely within the comforting parameters of common time, building upon the four-to-the-floor or breakbeat dance grooves that have dominated the metagenre of dance since the funk and disco era of the 1970s.

Recommended reading

Barnard, S. (2000) *On the Radio*. Milton Keynes: Open University Press.

Brackett, D. (2000) *Interpreting Popular Music*. Berkeley: University of California Press.

Chapman, R. (1992) *Selling the Sixties: The Pirates and Pop Music Radio*. London: Routledge.

Fielder, H. (1984) *The Book of Genesis*. London: Sidgwick & Jackson.

Gorman, P. (2001) *In Their Own Right: Adventures in the Music Press*. London: Sanctuary.

Holm-Hudson, K. (ed.) (2002) *Progressive Rock Reconsidered*. London: Routledge.

Macan, E. (1997) *Rocking the Classics: English Progressive Rock and the Counterculture*. Oxford: Oxford University Press.

Moore, A. (1993) *Rock: The Primary Text*. Buckingham: Open University Press.

Stump, P. (1998) *The Music's All That Matters*. London: Quartet.

Thorgerson, S. and Powell, A. (1999) *One Hundred Best Album Covers*. London: Dorling-Kindersley.

Toop, D. (1995) *Ocean of Sound: Aether Talk, Ambient Sound and Imaginary Worlds*. London: Serpent's Tail.

Willis, P. (1978) *Profane Culture*. London: Routledge & Kegan Paul.

Recommended listening

Antecedents

The Beatles (1967) *Sgt Pepper's Lonely Hearts Club Band*. Parlophone.

The Moody Blues (1967) *Days Of Future Passed*. Deram.

Pink Floyd (1967) *The Piper At The Gates of Dawn*. EMI.

Generic texts

Can (1971) *Tago Mago*. Spoon.

Emerson, Lake and Palmer (2001) *Fanfare For The Common Man: The Anthology*. Sanctuary.

Focus (1972) *Focus III*. Polydor.

Genesis (1974) *The Lamb Lies Down On Broadway*. Charisma.

Mike Oldfield (1973) *Tubular Bells*. Virgin.

Pink Floyd (1971) *Meddle*. EMI.

Todd Rundgren (1975) *Initiation*. Bearsville.

Jethro Tull (1971) *Aqualung*. Chrysalis.

Van der Graaf Generator (1975) *Godbluff*. Charisma.

Various Artists (1996) *Supernatural Fairy Tales: The Progressive Rock Era*. Rhino.

Yes (1972) *Close To the Edge*. Atlantic

Subsequent generic developments

The Orb (1991) *The Orb's Adventures Beyond The Ultraworld*. Island.

T-Power (1995) *Police State: Prospects For Democracy And Synthesis* [EP]. SOUR.

Various (1996) *Progressive House Classics*. Firm.

CHAPTER 5

Punk rock: artifice or authenticity?

An overview of the genre

The term 'punk' can be used adjectively in order to qualify a range of activities. Recent academic analyses of punk phenomena point towards the possibility of there being punk politics, punk journalism (such as the work of Lester Bangs), punk clothing and fashion (including both the *haute couture* work of Vivienne Westwood and Zandra Rhodes and the no less spectacular clothing of punk bands and everyday punks), punk poetry (as performed by the Mancunian wordsmith John Cooper Clarke), punk cartoons (such as the commercially successful comic *Love & Rockets*), punk art (the work of 'young British artist' Gavin Turk or the Sex Pistols' art director Jamie Reid), punk fanzines (such as *Sniffin' Glue*), punk fiction (Gideon Sams or Stewart Home), punk cinema (Derek Jarman's *Jubilee*) and even punk etiquette (which often involved spitting).[1] What these cultural forms have in common is debateable, with the majority of the leading commentators disagreeing as to what connects these disparate cultural forms. For Roger Sabin, punk involved 'an emphasis on negation (rather than nihilism); a consciousness of class-based politics (with a stress on "working class credibility"); and a belief in spontaneity and "doing in yourself"' (Sabin 1999b: 3). For Jon Savage, British punk was a form of 'dole queue rock' that was directly related to the economic and social upheavals that the country was going through at the time (Savage 1994a). For Greil Marcus, punk was a combination of situationist and anarchist politics (Marcus 1989). For Stewart Home, there is no 'core' to punk rock at all – it is a fluid category with its boundaries subject to 'ongoing renegotiation' (Home 1995: 7–9).

While discussions of the non-musical elements of the British and American punk explosions of the 1970s are of interest, this chapter will concentrate primarily on punk rock as a music genre. In generic terms, there are essentially two contrasting styles, and these contrasting two styles are seen on both sides of the Atlantic.[2] The first of these styles is a plebeian or social-realist style. Plebeian punk rock places a lyrical emphasis on providing an exposition of working-class dissatisfaction with 'normal' society, and frequently focuses upon concerns that are particular to young people. Musically, the plebeian style is likely to be more aggressive in feel and played in a seemingly untutored style. Contrasting with the plebeian mode is an 'art-rock' style that specifically references modes of communication found in theories of art. This music is more intricate and layered than the plebeian style, and lyrically more complex. A situationist or art-school influence often surrounds this style of punk rock. In many ways, these two categories conform to a classic Cartesian split, with plebeian or social-realist punk rock having corporeal (bodily) characteristics (for example 'muscular'), with art-rock being seen as more 'cerebral', 'intelligent' and experimental.

PLEBEIAN OR SOCIAL-REALIST PUNK ROCK
- Chelsea
- The Clash
- Cortinas
- Eater
- The Jam
- The Lurkers
- The Ramones
- Sham 69
- Slaughter and the Dogs
- Tom Robinson Band
- The Vibrators
- UK Subs

ART-SCHOOL INFLUENCED PUNK ROCK/'ART ROCK'
- Blondie
- Buzzcocks
- Generation X
- Magazine
- Patti Smith
- Penetration
- Richard Hell and the Voidoids
- Siouxsie and the Banshees
- Television
- Wire

Chronologically, American punk rock pre-dated British punk rock, and American bands playing a form of early punk rock in the 1960s and 1970s (often termed 'garage') were a strong influence on subsequent British and

American punk rockers. The garage music of the 1960s rejected the concurrent move towards complex rock styles in favour of a simplistic and 'stripped down' approach that relied on a minimum of musical instruments and musical ability. In the United States in the late 1960s and early 1970s this musical approach was twinned with lyrical concerns that included alienation, disenchantment with society and youthful rebellion, and came to be termed punk at around the turn of the decade.[3]

In 1976 and 1977 there was a qualitative shift in punk rock, which occurred when both the American and British punk-rock scenes achieved commercial success and mainstream media coverage. While the 'stripped down' musical aesthetic remained, lyrical concerns become more explicitly political and, on occasion, nihilistic. While American garage bands were referred to as punks, the label punk rock was not widely used to describe British bands in the 1960s or early 1970s, although come 1976 a range of UK-based bands (such as the Sex Pistols, The Damned and The Clash) were being referred to as punks or punk rockers. Within British punk rock the art-school influence is strongest at this point, with 1978 and 1979 seeing a shift towards a more socially realist plebeian mode.

A further difference between American and British punk rock is the relationship between the punk scene and the mass media. In America, early punk-rock bands such as The Ramones, Suicide and Television played concerts and released records away from the media limelight, and consequently American punk rock, and the scene surrounding it, developed at a relatively leisured pace. This is in contrast to events in Britain, where the punk-rock bands formed in 1975 and 1976 soon received national notoriety. While the Sex Pistols played their first gig on 6 November 1975, they received their first national review in February 1976, with *New Musical Express* writer Neil Spencer suggesting that the band played '60's styled white punk rock' (see Heylin 1998: 6). Throughout 1976 music magazines such as *Sounds* and the *New Musical Express* reported on the explosion of a punk subculture, while punk rock's national notoriety was sealed following the Sex Pistols' explosive interview on Thames TV's *Today* programme (broadcast on 2 December 1976). During this interview, the band followed the drunken provocations of the interviewer Bill Grundy with a stream of expletives. The popularity of British punk rock, and its social visibility and political importance, increased dramatically from this point onwards.

Following the explosion of media interest in punk rock in 1977 and 1978, many bands began to adopt a more sophisticated and nuanced approach to music making, and as a consequence many punk acts began to play a form of music dubbed 'new wave'. In 1979, there was a significant decline in the popularity of punk rock. Media coverage also declined and the 'punk scene' shrunk considerably at this point, although the generic form of punk has continued to exist until the present day. (Indeed, the commercial potential of punk rock was only ever fully exploited following the decline of punk.)

Historical roots and antecedents

An examination of punk rock's antecedents is complicated by the use of the punk-rock soubriquet to describe American 'garage' music from the late 1960s onwards. Further confusion is added by the fact that punk-rock music pre-dated punk's subcultural formation by many years. As Dave Laing suggests 'unlike nearly every other youth subculture (the Teddy boys, mods, skinheads, etc.), punk began as music and punks themselves began as music fans and performers. In every other case, the youth subculture adopted an already existing type of music' (Laing 1985: ix). In short, punk-rock bands from 1976 onwards were staffed by punks (subcultural formation), whereas those bands that played punk rock before 1976 were not.

For the purposes of this chapter, punk rock from the mid-1970s will be examined in the section entitled 'musical texts', while the influence of bands that pre-date this period are dealt with in this section.

1950s' rock 'n' roll

With its sexual immorality and rebellious spirit, rock 'n' roll as developed in the mid-1950s was a punk antecedent. Indeed, there can have been few things more shocking to sections of European and North American society than seeing Elvis Presley wiggling his hips on television. Equally, Bill Haley's *Rock Around The Clock* single was, at the time, perceived to be a clarion call for rebellious youth to take over the streets, and take over the night, through dancing to supposedly dangerous black rhythms. This reading of the song was particularly heightened by the furore surrounding the release of the films *Rock Around The Clock*, banned by at least twelve local councils, and *Blackboard Jungle*, which featured *Rock Around The Clock* on its soundtrack (see Laing 1985: 37). There are connections between this early period of rock 'n' roll and 1970s' punk rock, not least the Sex Pistols' love for early rock 'n' roll records by the likes of Eddie Cochran.[4]

American pop

Certain forms of American pop from the 1950s and 1960s pre-dated the formal simplicity of the punk-rock genre. These include the following:

- *Doo-wop.* Acts such as Archie Bell and the Drells and Dion and the Belmonts employed a simplistic form of music production that was characterised by its musical immediacy and came to influence many American punk-rock bands.
- *American surf-oriented instrumental bands.* These included The Beach Boys, Jan and Dean, Dick Dale, The Astronauts, The Riveras and Ronnie and the Daytonas. The influence of these bands can be heard clearly in the partially submerged melodies of bands such as The Ramones. While many consider punk rock as being not particularly tuneful, this is mistaken; it is merely the case that in punk rock melody is not as foregrounded, or as complex, as in other popular music genres.
- *American fuzz and bubble gum.* Bill Osgerby points to the influence of The 1910 Fruitgum Company, Ohio Express, The Archies and The Monkees on punk rock, stating that 'it was from here that punk's pop sensibility drew many of its motifs and reference points as it elaborated a theatrical parody of the mythologies of teenage suburbia' (Osgerby 1999: 160). While Osgerby concerns himself with the antecedents of the American punk-rock scene, the same is true for British punk. For example, the Sex Pistols played The Monkees' *(I'm Not Your) Steppin' Stone* at gigs, and the teenage suburban influence can be seen in the art-school influenced 'Bromley contingent', who were a group of young punk-rock fans and musicians (such as Siouxsie and the Banshees) from a south London suburb. In addition, worth noting in this respect is the 'second-wave' British punk act the Members and their single *The Sound Of The Suburbs*.

1960s' British rock and pop

Punk rock also draws influence from the simplicity of 'stripped down' British pop music from the 1960s that emphasised enthusiasm over technical ability, and simplicity over complexity. Acts such as The Rolling Stones, The Kinks, The Who, Small Faces and The Yardbirds were all an influence on 1970s' punk rock. Some of this music is almost as violent as punk rock in its intensity (this is aided by the primitive recording technologies used in its production), while the simplicity and 'authenticity' of this music also appealed to 1970s' punks.

Garage

In the mid-1960s, a generation of mid-East and mid-West American bands began to record a form of punk rock that was fast, loud and short, and which required a minimum of musical ability to be able to play. This 'proto punk rock' is more frequently termed garage, a phrase that refers to the kinds of places where this music is rehearsed and played.[5] Few of these bands had any commercial success, but they did make a blueprint for the kind of stripped-down amateurish rock 'n' roll that 1970s' punk rock revived. In 1960s' garage music, 'spirit' and 'feeling' are prized far more than musical ability or complexity (although lyrical concerns were not as explicitly political or as nihilistic as punk rock from the 1970s).

Examples of this style are found on the series of compilations entitled *Nuggets*, compiled by the American journalist Lenny Kaye, with the most famous example being The Kingsmen's raucous single *Louie Louie*, which became a live staple for many punk-rock bands of the 1970s.

The American 'post-Pepper underground'

Clinton Heylin cites America's 'post-*Pepper* underground' as being a significant precursor to American punk (Heylin 1993: xi). For Heylin this consisted of the Velvet Underground, the MC5, the Stooges, the Modern Lovers and the New York Dolls (who many consider to be the first punks). According to the music journalist Lester Bangs, what linked these groups was an attempt to redefine rock as 'a raw wail from the bottom of the guts', which consisted of 'rock honed down to its rawest elements' (quoted in Heylin 1993: 33). In particular, these groups experimented with fuzz, distortion and feedback, with some of these bands using these elements melodically. As we will see, this became a central feature of 1970s' punk rock.

British punk's immediate antecedents in 'pub rock'

British punk rock was, in many ways, a reaction to the progressive rock of the early 1970s. In particular, punks objected to the overt displays of musicianship inherent within progressive rock, where prog-rock bands employed an array of musical technologies to produce a complex and intellectualised musical form. The standard modes of distribution of progressive rock were long, musically complex tracks played at stadium concerts and released on double or sometimes triple albums. When in concert, a progressive rock band was considered 'authentic' if they could re-create their music in a live setting.

Pub rock, as developed and popularised in the early to mid-1970s, was a precursor to punk's objection to progressive rock, with bands playing stripped-down rock 'n' roll and country rock in a network of pubs and clubs. This was seen by many as an attempt to return rock to its 'primitive' roots. In comparison to the stadium gigs of progressive-rock acts, this led to an enhanced feeling of intimacy and 'connectedness' between band and audience. Like many early punk acts, pub rock performances were interspersed with cover versions of 'standards' from the rock 'n' roll canon. Pub-rock venues also had a central importance to the later punk scene, with the Sex Pistols, The Stranglers and The Damned playing at the Nashville, a leading pub-rock venue. Equally, the small economies of scale of independent pub-rock record labels (such as Chiswick and Stiff) showed punk entrepreneurs that small production runs of individual records were financially viable (whereas major labels had a 'breakeven point' of approximately 20,000 sales, Stiff and Chiswick could break even when selling just 2,000 records: see Laing 1985: 10). Pub-rock artists included Dr Feelgood (who had a number one album released on a large semi-independent label), Eddie and the Hot Rods, Kilburn and the High Roads and Nick Lowe. Other pub rockers, such as Joe Strummer (John Mellor) from the 101ers, went on to form punk bands (in Strummer's case The Clash).[6] For a further examination of pub rock, see Will Birch's tome *No Sleep Till Canvey Island: The Great Pub Rock Revolution* (Birch 2000).

Social and political context

It was surely no coincidence that punk rock arrived on the streets of Britain in 1976 and 1977, for this period represents the fault line between the two dominant conjunctures[7] of postwar Britain: the postwar social-democratic consensus and Thatcherism. While American punk rock had been in existence before the explosion of British punk rock in 1976 and 1977, it remained an obscure musical cult limited to New York and certain other cities. In comparison, British punk rock became both commercially successful and socially notorious in the space of a few months. This is because British punk rock seemed to be a musical genre that was purpose-built for the articulation of young people's dissatisfaction with the few remaining fruits of the postwar social-democratic consensus. Many American punk-rock bands went on to achieve widespread commercial success; however; none seemed to shake the foundations of society in the same profound way as certain British punk-rock bands. None seemed to have the social resonance of the likes of the Sex Pistols. While Chapter 7 examines the effect Thatcherism had on British music in the 1980s, and while Chapter 10 deals with the relationship between Thatcherism and New Labour Blairism, this section will examine the essential nature and eventual collapse of the postwar social-democratic consensus.

The postwar social-democratic consensus[8]
The post-Second World War Labour governments of 1945–51 and the Conservative governments of 1951–64 were in broad agreement concerning the way governments should manage the economy. Influenced by the economist John Maynard Keynes, the postwar governments presided over a mixed economy, with state ownership of key industries such as telecommunications, coal, steel, electricity and gas production. A system

of 'National Insurance', welfare benefits, free secondary education and a
National Health Service were also key factors in postwar society, and
there was a consensus that a social-democratic mix of public and private
ownership was preferable to the liberalism of American economics or the
'command economies' of the Eastern Bloc (see Hennessy 1991).

The sum total of these economic and political reforms was a 'high wage,
mass-production, domestic-consumer-orientated modern economy' (Hall
et al. 1978: 229) that produced full employment, rising standards of living
and a mass consumer market. For young people without dependants or
other major financial responsibilities, the rise in actual income was
translated as a roughly equal rise in disposable income. A considerable
proportion of this disposable income was spent on music-related products, and from the mid-1950s onwards, this resulted in an expansion of
the British record industry. Throughout the 'golden age' of rock 'n' roll,
rising incomes, leading to an increase in spending, facilitated an expansion
in the music industry. From the 1950s until the 1970s, a gradual decline in
heavy industry was matched by an increase in the production of consumer
durables and an increase in the size of British service industries. An
expanded popular music industry fitted neatly into this model. As well as
fuelling the economic base of rock 'n' roll, the sense of a new youthful
economic freedom fuelled the narratives found within rock 'n' roll
records.

However, come the 1960s and 1970s, the economy was slowing down
and unemployment was increasing. In 1964, the Labour Party won its
first General Election since 1951, but the two Labour governments of
Prime Minister Harold Wilson (1964–6 and 1966–70) were beset with
difficulties. These included successive balance of payment crises that led
to a devaluation of sterling, unpopular cuts in public investment, tax
increases, strikes in British dockyards and other industrial unrest caused
by a legally binding pay freeze (Coxall and Robins 1998). The overall
impression was of an emerging national economic crisis as Britain began
to cope, both emotionally and economically, with the decline of empire
and the decline of Britain as a world superpower. The end result was that
voters eventually returned a Conservative government in 1970, while
within a few years the negative effects of the emerging economic crisis was
reflected within the lyrics of key punk tracks as well as within punk's
general emphasis on 'negation'.

If respected commentators such as Alan Sked and Chris Cook char-
acterise Wilson's administration as one of 'overall failure' (Sked and Cook
1979: 280), judgements concerning Prime Minister Edward Heath's
government of 1970–4 are invariably worse. Heath's government initiated

widespread cuts in public expenditure and instituted monetary restrictions that led quickly to economic stagnation. Unemployment rose to just short of one million, and a balance of payments crisis led to a sterling crisis, which then led to high inflation.

Heath's eventual undoing was an attempt to invest in industry without investing in wages, with Heath instituting a freeze on wages, prices and rents. This led to a series of coal strikes that resulted in a national state of emergency and a so-called 'three-day week'. This crippled industry, and an international rise in oil prices combined with an all-out coal miners' strike led Heath to call an election in 1974 that he subsequently lost (Coxall and Robins 1998). All these events served to heighten the sense of national crisis that had begun during the previous Wilson administration, while providing a kind of emotional fuel for punk's leading songwriters.

The postwar democratic settlement, the age of rising wages and full employment, had been replaced by economic stagnation and a bitter feeling that Britain was trading on its former glories. This feeling was made more acute by the crisis in Northern Ireland, where internment without trial was introduced in a failed attempt to halt the Provisional IRA's campaign for a thirty-two-county Irish Republic, and the devolved Ulster Unionist government was abandoned in favour of direct rule by Westminster (see Mulholland 2002). A heightened sense of awareness of Irish politics can be seen within such seminal punk tracks as Stiff Little Fingers' *Alternative Ulster*, while other bands from the north of Ireland, such as The Undertones from the city of Derry, chose a more escapist mode of representation.

The so-called 'Irish question' was not answered by the Labour governments of 1974–9, nor were the telling questions regarding what was to replace the postwar social-democratic consensus. Under the Prime Ministership of both Harold Wilson and his successor, James Callaghan, Britain's economic plight did not improve significantly. In 1976, when the ferments of punk rock were brewing in London and elsewhere, unemployment rose to 1.2 million, interest rates rose to a record high and the government announced a further spending cut of £3 billion. By mid-1977 unemployment was over 1,500,000, higher than in any other Western industrial nation (Morgan 1990: 397–414, Childs 1984: 266, and Sked and Cook 1979: 332–65). The 'baby boomers' of the 1950s had grown into the disenfranchised and disenchanted teenagers and 'twenty somethings' of the punk era, and the spectre of unemployment is a lyrical feature of many punk-rock records.

The 1970s not only saw industrial unrest but also racial tension. Britain had seen a rise in immigration in the 1950s as Caribbean migrants travelled to Britain to fill vacancies in an economy that was buoyant. However, by the mid-1960s some began to call for an end to Commonwealth immigration. In 1968, the Conservative demagogue Enoch Powell contributed to racial unrest when he made his infamous 'rivers of blood' speech, stating that immigration into Britain amounted to 'a nation busily engaged in heaping up its own funeral pyre' (quoted in Berkeley 1977: 80). While Powell was sacked from the Shadow Cabinet, the political repercussions of Powell's speech continued to reverberate through the 1970s, with some political commentators suggesting that it alone had inflicted damage on the postwar consensus (Schoen 1977: 34). A significant rise in support for the extreme right National Front during the 1970s also caused further racial tension. Battles between the newly emergent far right and street-fighting left wingers connected to organisations such as the Anti-Nazi League became regular features at punk-rock gigs, and the use of the swastika within punk became ever more complex as some punks flirted with Fascism and Nazism. Punk's reaction against the rise of the far right took the form of Rock Against Racism, and a growing sense of unity between certain punk acts such as The Clash and X-Ray Spex and reggae bands such as Steel Pulse and Misty in Roots (see Widgery 1986).

In summary, the rise of punk in 1976 and 1977 took place against a backdrop of great political, social and economic turbulence. The Prime Minister of the time James Callaghan subsequently suggested that 'amid the debris of political controversy we yearn for the symbols of national unity' (quoted in Whitehead 1985: 307). While this was true for the majority of the population in 1977, a significant minority looked towards the politics of the punk-rock scene for affirmation that they were not alone in feeling distinctly uncomfortable with the direction in which Britain was sailing.

The musical texts

Structure

Most punk-rock tracks are songs, and there are very few instrumental examples within the genre. Most punk-rock songs conform to a simple verse/chorus/verse/chorus format. It is also worth noting that few punk songs have what Dave Laing refers to as 'atmospheric solos' (Laing 1985: 61). This reflects the relative lack of importance of melody in punk rock, and the consequent heightened sense of both noise and rhythm.

Instrumentation

As opposed to the numerous keyboards and other miscellaneous electronic instruments used in progressive rock, punk rock insisted on a pared-down line-up of guitar, bass and drums (with a few notable exceptions including The Stranglers and X-Ray Spex).

Lyrics

Punk-rock lyrics frequently tackled taboo subjects. Whereas the lyrics of chart singles of top fifty groups in 1977 were dominated by romantic themes or were self-referential in their allusions to music and dancing, punk lyrics more often than not tackled explicitly political issues. These political issues were precisely the same issues being debated within society at large, and were generally related to issues concerning the postwar social-democratic consensus and the state of Britain in 1976–7.

Most famous of these political punk-rock tracks are the Sex Pistols' songs *God Save The Queen* and *Anarchy In The UK*. Other notable political topics included unemployment (for example Chelsea's *Right To Work*), racial politics (for example The Clash's *White Riot*) and the criminal justice system (for example The Clash's *Bankrobber*, Sham 69's *Borstal Breakout* and UK Subs' *C.I.D.*).

Whereas many of the punk-rock bands working within a plebeian mode wrote lyrics dealing explicitly with specific political issues, art-rock punks more frequently wrote in terms that were more general, outlining a non-specific disenchantment with British society. Songs within this category include Buzzcocks' *Boredom* and The Damned's *Smash It Up*. Equally, many art-rock-influenced tracks dealt with sexual politics, including Buzzcocks' *Orgasm Addict*, X-Ray Spex's *Oh Bondage! Up Yours!* and the Tom Robinson Band's *Glad To Be Gay*. Other punk acts of a more nihilistic bent discussed and celebrated drug use in their lyrics; for examples see *Chinese Rocks* by Johnny Thunders and the Heartbreakers and *Another Girl, Another Planet* by The Only Ones.

Vocals

In many respects, punk rock ushered in a completely new mode of vocal delivery. Indeed, whether punk-rock 'songs' were ever 'sung' is debateable. In the punk-rock tracks of 1976–8, we see a variety of different approaches including speaking, shouting, chanting, muttering and recitation. This non-musical approach opposed the usual melodic singing style for good reason. In order to break out from the romantic ideologies of the traditional pop song, punk vocalists used non-singing modes to emphasise both their separation from previous music genres and the importance of their political message. Laing pinpoints this quite accurately in his statement that the implicit logic would seem to involve the conviction that by excluding the musicality of singing, the possible contamination of the lyric message by the aesthetic pleasures offered by melody, harmony, pitch and so on, is avoided. Also avoided is the prettiness of the mainstream song, in its forms as well as its contents. (Laing 1985: 54)

As important as this different style of 'singing' is the accent of the 'singer'. With punk rock we see the partial banishment of the notorious 'mid-Atlantic' accent popular in the rock music of the early 1970s, in favour of a working-class accent that is, on occasions, also regional (with, for example, Pete Shelley from Buzzcocks singing in a Mancunian accent).

Guitar

Punk-rock tracks invariably feature one or more guitars, which are invariably 'treated' with distortion or feedback. In the mid-1970s, this was a reaction to the 'clean' sounds of mainstream pop. Guitars are generally played in a somewhat simplistic manner with few chords. Those chords that are used often 'bleed' into each other, giving the suggestion of a 'buzz saw' or drone, where individual notes or chords are barely distinguishable.

Punk-rock guitars are also played in a seemingly untutored style. Overt displays of musicianship or virtuosity, such as the guitar solo, are also largely absent from British punk rock, although certain American punks, such as Tom Verlaine (Thomas Miller) and Richard Lloyd of Television, play the guitar in a more complex and sophisticated style.

Percussion

Punk-rock drum rhythms tend to be regular and repetitive. Laing gives the clear example of the Sex Pistols' track *Holidays In The Sun*, which begins with the sound of marching feet, which are then replaced by drums. This march emphasis is a 'rhythmic monad', where four equally emphasised drumbeats are placed 'on the bar'.

Bass

Like punk-rock drumming, punk-rock basslines are simplistic and frequently monadic. Such bass playing is even more untutored than punk-rock guitar playing, and therefore appealed to those punk 'musicians' such as Sid Vicious who had extremely limited musical abilities (see Heylin 1998).

Tempo

The unsyncopated nature of drumming and bass playing combines with punk rock's relatively fast tempo to give the impression of both relentless energy and a form of insurgent urgency. This is perfectly in tune with the ideology of punk. Punk rock's fast tempo combines with its monadic march emphasis to suggest that time is literally running out, and that the quicker the punk rocker's message is delivered to his or her audience the better. Again, this can be connected to the somewhat apocalyptic feel of mid-1970s' Britain, where the 'old order' of the postwar settlement was coming to a speedy end.

Furthermore, the fast tempo of punk rock, combined with its lack of syncopation, tended to disinhibit the listener from dancing in any previously acceptable manner. Syncopation encourages a loose-limbed and 'funky' approach to dancing, whereas monadic percussion does not. Again, the emphasis is therefore not on dancing and getting 'into' the music, but on the lyrical message of the vocalist. However, punk rockers did not remain seated during punk performances.

Visual aesthetic

Punk-rock graphics and art

One of the most interesting aspects of the punk-rock genre is the packaging in which the musical texts were distributed. In many respects, there was such a close ideological 'fit' between musical text, punk ideology and the record sleeve that we can suggest that there was a homology between musical text, visual text and the subjectivity espoused by punk groups and punk fans.

This was certainly the case with the work of the Sex Pistols, who employed the graphic designer Jamie Reid to produce the artwork for all of their recorded releases and publicity materials. In Reid's work we see the radical anti-authoritarian message of punk rock being communicated through a set of visual images rather than through the primal roar of the Sex Pistols' stripped-down rock 'n' roll. Popular music artists as diverse as Paul McCartney (*Give Ireland Back To The Irish*) and MC5 (*Kick Out The Jams*) had flirted with lyrical and musical radicalism. Equally, visual artists had used record sleeves as 'canvasses' (for example Peter Blake's famous cover for The Beatles' album *Sgt Pepper's Lonely Hearts Club Band*). However, Reid's work with the Sex Pistols managed to draw the worlds of the visual and recording arts together, providing a clear visual espousal of the central meaning of the Sex Pistols' lyrics and music. Of note were the following designs:

- Virgin Record's release of *God Save The Queen* came in a sleeve that contained a blue and white half-tone reproduction of the Queen, based on an official portrait by Cecil Beaton. In ransom-style lettering the Queen's eyes had been torn out and replaced by 'God save the Queen', and the Queen's mouth torn out and replaced with the band's name. Variations on this theme were also used on posters, T-shirts, promotional badges, mugs and stickers (although a version where the Queen's eyes had been replaced by swastikas was deemed to be too controversial even for the Sex Pistols).
- On promotional material for the single *Pretty Vacant* Reid incorporated an image of two buses originally produced for inclusion in an American situationist magazine entitled *Point Blank*. These old buses were labelled as travelling to 'NOWHERE' and 'BOREDOM'. This concept of a society and culture going nowhere certainly mirrored punks' feelings concerning the state of British society in the mid-1970s.
- Reid's design for the *Holidays In The Sun* single was also reminiscent of situationism. For the single cover Reid 'adapted' a cartoon contained in a brochure concerning tourism to Belgium. However, Reid removed the original words spoken by the drawn characters (for example 'Belgium has everything a young girl could ask for'), and replaced them with the lyrics from the single ('I don't want a holiday in the sun, I wanna go to the new Belsen').
- Elsewhere, Reid conducted a full-scale assault on the values of the band's record label. Reid coined the phrase 'Never Trust A Hippie' (allegedly aimed at Virgin's owner, Richard Branson) as part of a series of fluorescent banners for general distribution. Elsewhere, a poster for the Sex Pistols' film *The Great Rock 'n' Roll Swindle* used a fake American Express card and referred to the band's record company as a pimp. (American Express took objection to the use of their name and brand logo and forced the poster to be withdrawn.)
- A promotional poster for the single *Something Else* contained a 'Sid Vicious Action Man' that consisted of a crude model of the late John Ritchie (a.k.a. Sid Vicious) in a miniature coffin, while the single itself came in a record bag that contained a drawing of a so-called 'Vicious Burger'.

American punk-rock fashion

Savage suggests that as early as 1974 the band Television had adopted a style of dress that would later dominate punk rock in both Britain and America. It is worth quoting Savage at length to show that there is a clear connection between the sartorial and the musical styles contained within punk:

[Richard] Hell had also worked out a visual package to go with the chopped musical style [of Television]: large fifties shades, leather jackets, torn T-shirts and short, ragamuffin hair. This was a severe aesthetic, that carried a series of meanings: the existential freedom of the fifties beat, the blazing, beautiful self-destruction of the *poète maudit*, and the razor-sharpness of the sixties Mod. It spelt danger and refusal, just as the torn T-shirt spoke of sexuality and violence. If such a thing is possible to identify, it was the origin of what would become the Punk style. (Savage 1994a: 89)

The Slits. Punk provided new role models for female musicians.

British punk fashion

At the same time as Hell was developing his early punk sartorial aesthetic, Malcolm McLaren was also visiting New York in a doomed attempt to work with the band the New York Dolls. While the New York Dolls fell apart amid excessive hard-drug use, McLaren returned to his clothes shop in London and began to experiment with various clothing styles including Teddy boy clothes and fetish wear. During 1976 and 1977 McLaren, along with his business partner Vivienne Westwood, began to develop a style that was to become as synonymous with British punk as Hell's style was for the New York scene. In their west London boutique 'Sex', McLaren and Westwood sold loosely knitted mohair sweaters, leather boots, tartan bondage trousers, 'rapist masks', muslin shorts, feather ties and a range of T-shirts stencilled with slogans and 'iconic' images. Included in this range of T-shirts were images of Karl Marx, two gay cowboys baring their penises, anarchist 'logos', swastikas, and phrases such as 'try subversion', 'destroy', 'only anarchists are pretty', 'for soldiers, prostitutes, dykes + punks' and 'too fast to live too young to die'. Most controversial of these items was a T-shirt containing an image of a fetish mask with the word 'Cambridge Rapist' superimposed on it, above a short biography and a photograph of The Beatles' manager Brian Epstein. 'Sex' withdrew this item from sale after the police voiced their suspicion that one of their customers might be the 'Cambridge Rapist' (see Burgess and Parker 1999: 52–77).

Subsequent generic developments

Punk's influence was widespread and long lasting. The DIY ethos of punk, whereby potential musicians were encouraged to make music using limited resources, has had an influence on indie, rap and other dance-based genres such as acid house and techno. The simplicity of punk's guitar-based approach was also highly influential on the American grunge music of the late 1980s and 1990s. However, it is possible to take the view that for a musical movement to be included in the punk-rock category, it should share significant formal characteristics with punk rock rather than merely sharing a 'spirit' or political ethos. For example, the fact that techno music sounds so radically different to punk rock excludes it from the category of 'subsequent generic development'.

New wave

Come 1979, the art-influenced wing of punk rock had all but abandoned the musical simplicity and anger of punk rock in favour of 'new wave' music that began to experiment with both formal structure and musical and lyrical content. British examples include John Lydon's post-Sex Pistols band Public Image Limited, Howard Devoto's (Howard Trotter) post-Buzzcocks band Magazine, Elvis Costello's (Declan MacManus) first album *My Aim Is True*, Joy Division's two studio albums *Unknown Pleasures* and *Closer*, and the early work of The Pretenders. American examples include Blondie's string of chart hits including *Heart Of Glass*, *Sunday Girl* and *Call Me* (which were also UK number ones) and the B52s' hit single *Rock Lobster*.

Oi!

In seeming opposition to the shift from art-school punk rock to new wave, we have the development of Oi! In particular, Oi! led to a refocusing upon both musical simplicity and working-class 'street' authenticity. This involved the lyrical articulation of a narrowly defined set of working-class youthful concerns ('violence, drinking, police oppression': Home 1995: 86) in a specifically plebeian voice. Musically simplistic, Oi! also shunned new wave's use of electronic keyboards in favour of a return to traditional guitar-led rock songs. British bands such as the Cockney Rejects, Peter and the Test Tube Babies, the Exploited, the 4 Skins and the Angelic Upstarts quickly attracted a male-dominated working-class audience, with a significant number of skinheads. While the working-class focus of Oi! led many artists (such as the Angelic Upstarts) to become engaged in left-wing politics, the populism of Oi! also led some bands and their fans to the neo-Nazi politics of the National Front and the British Movement. Oi! subsequently collapsed under the weight of antagonism between these two wings, with some far-right bands such as Skrewdriver and Condemned 84 dropping the Oi! name in favour of labels such as 'white-power rock and roll' or 'nationalist rock'. Musically this form is almost indistinguishable from certain forms of heavy metal (see Home 1995: 81–105).

Goth

Of particular influence throughout the 1980s, 1990s and 2000s is the discourse within punk rock that led to a variety of goth styles. Many suggest that the term derives from a quotation by Mancunian entrepreneur Tony Wilson, who described the music of Joy Division as 'gothic compared with the pop mainstream' when introducing the band on the Granada-made television programme *So It Goes* (www.goth.net). In many respect the punk-rock band Siouxsie and the Banshees sowed the seeds of goth, with a sartorial and musical aesthetic that emphasised darkness over light and deviance over conformity. Come the 1980s, bands such as The Cure (whose lead singer Robert Smith had been in the Banshees), Bauhaus, Sisters of Mercy, Rosetta Stone and The Mission had attracted a broadly goth following. These fans dressed themselves almost entirely in black while using white and red make-up (on both sexes), and whose extra-musical interests included romantic literature, horror fiction and occultist religions including Satanism (see Hodkinson 2002). In the 1990s, goth merged with a variety of other subcultures, and in the twenty-first century we can find industrial goths, whose musical tastes extend to an aggressive techno-rock hybrid, hippie goths, whose interests include Victorian art and literature, occultist goths, whose interests are predominantly religious, and 'moshers', a partially goth hybrid connected to the massive success of nu-metal. One possible reason for the massive success of goth since the 1970s is that it appeals equally to female as well as male subcultural members, and seems well suited to the more emotionally turbulent years of adolescence that seem to be a feature of socialisation in the vast majority of Western cultures.

Anarcho-punk

Of particular influence in the 1980s were a group of punk bands attracted to the political ethos of anarchism. Connected to the rise of 'new-age travellers' (itinerant anarchist-influenced hippies), bands such as Crass, Conflict and The Subhumans played a form of punk that placed an emphasis on political polemics while paying little attention to melody and harmony. While its rise can be seen as connected to the free festival scene of the time, the decline of the anarcho-punk scene is also partly connected to the decline of the 'hippie convoy' amid official harassment, police brutality (as witnessed at the 'Battle of the Beanfield'[9]) and a legislative assault that culminated in the Criminal Justice and Public Order Act 1994.

Riot grrrl

Riot grrrl is a music genre that developed in the 1980s and which contains clearly delineated punk-rock roots. In particular, riot grrrl draws on the feminist individualism of punk-rock bands such as X-Ray Spex and The Slits. The lyrics of riot grrrl acts are focused upon a reaction against societal oppression, while the DIY ethos, musical simplicity and amateurish guitar playing of punk are mirrored clearly in the riot grrrl scene. Central to the ethos of riot grrrl was a distrust of the media, with many bands refusing to talk to mainstream media organisations, preferring to rely upon a proliferation of fanzines to put their message forward (a message that consisted of a form of feminist punk individualism). The notoriety and subsequent popularity of the punk-rock acts of the mid-1970s was fuelled by mainstream exposure. Barring Huggy Bear's brief flirtation with controversy after an appearance on Channel 4's youth programme *The Word* (http://www.wiiija.com/artists/catalogue/huggy_-bear/biog.htm), riot grrrl received little media attention and consequently bands such as Bikini Kill, Lunachicks and L7 fell into obscurity. Come the mid-1990s, riot grrrl's radical edge had been replaced and tamed by the so-called 'girl power' of the Spice Girls. Out went the radical collective feminism, to be replaced by a form of individualised femininity.

American and other punk rocks

While punk rock received a boost in popularity in Eastern Europe during the period after the fall of state communism, American punk rock reached its highest point during the same period with the rise of 'grunge'. Built upon the 'hardcore' of 1980s' bands such as Black Flag and the sardonic punk of The Dead Kennedys, grunge music contained all the necessary punk-rock generic attributes (lyrics that focused upon a non-specific disenchantment with society, melodies buried beneath a multitude of overdriven guitars, an indie ethos), while also appealing to mainstream audiences in both America and Europe. Bands such as Pearl Jam, Nirvana and the Butthole Surfers showed that there was a great deal of life left in a genre that prefaces amateurism over musicianship and disenchantment over positivity.

Original punk bands still performing

While the lyrics sung by punk-rock acts in 1976 and 1977 often focused upon youthful disenchantment, this has not prevented many punk bands from continuing to tour and release records some twenty-five years later. Most notable are the Sex Pistols, who re-formed in the mid-1990s with the original studio line-up of John Lydon, Glen Matlock, Steve Jones and Paul Cook. Other punk acts such as The Damned, UK Subs, Blondie and 999 also continue to tour and release records.

Notes

1. For an examination of many of these categories see the collection of essays edited by Roger Sabin entitled *Punk Rock: So What?* (Sabin 1999).
2. As with all categorisations, the distinctions between these two styles do blur occasionally. It could be suggested that the best bands managed to straddle this divide. For example, the Sex Pistols had a situationist and art-school influence through the role of their manager Malcolm McLaren and art director Jamie Reid, as well as a plebeian influence through the roles played by their guitarist Steve Jones and drummer Paul Cook.
3. Clinton Heylin quotes Alan Vega (Alan Bermowitz), from the American punk-rock band Suicide, talking about a 1970 Suicide booking at an event called 'Punk Best'. However, Vega states disingenuously that this usage was 'before the word punk was ever used' (Heylin 1993: 66). Perhaps this can be taken as meaning 'before the word punk was *widely* used'. Having made this point, readers should not worry unduly about when the phrase punk rock was first used to describe a band's material. As Laing suggests 'it would be extremely difficult, if not impossible, to unearth the first reference to these musics as "punk", but the aim and effect of the process of identifying them as such was to establish the value of a particular strand running through American rock music' (Laing 1985: 11).
4. In many ways, the cover versions the Sex Pistols performed at gigs (some of which were also recorded on their 'posthumous' film and album *The Great Rock 'n' Swindle*) serve as a useful summary of punk-rock's antecedents. On *The Great Rock 'n' Swindle* we find punk-rock versions of Eddie Cochran's *C'mon Everybody* and *Something Else* (with Sid Vicious on vocals), Bill Haley and the Comets' *Rock Around The Clock* (with Tenpole Tudor on vocals), The Small Faces' *Watcha Gonna Do About It*, The Monkees' *(I'm Not Your) Steppin' Stone*, Dave Berry's *(Don't You Give Me) No Lip Child*, Chuck Berry's (Charles Anderson) *Johnny B. Goode*, Jonathan Richman's

Roadrunner and The Who's *Substitute*. At a variety of gigs, the Sex Pistols also performed cover versions of the Small Faces' *Understanding*, The Stooge's *No Fun* (which was also the b-side to their *Pretty Vacant* single) and The Creation's *Through My Eyes* (see Heylin 1998).

5. 1960s' garage rock should not be confused with the subgenre of house music that is also termed 'garage'. For an examination of this use of the term, see Chapter 11.

6. It is worth noting that American punk bands were also influenced by pub rock, with Clem Burke, the drummer in an early incarnation of Blondie, crediting Dr Feelgood as showing American bands that a major record deal was not necessary in order to have a hit album (Heylin 1993: 164–5).

7. In cultural studies, the term 'conjuncture' refers to a period of economic, cultural, social and political life where social relations remain relatively stable. The term was popularised after the first English publication of Antonio Gramsci's *Prison Notebooks* in 1971. See Hall (1988: 161–74) and Gramsci (1971: 177–80).

8. For a useful examination of the relationships between the postwar social-democratic consensus and youth culture see the A4 booklet produced by the Open University that accompanied their seminal course *U203 Popular Culture* (Bennett 1981). For an overview of the postwar social-democratic consensus, see Henness (1993), Bogdanor and Skidelsky (1970), or the relevant chapters in Marwick (1982) and Marwick (1991).

9. 'The Battle of the Beanfield' occurred in 1985 when police officers attacked hippies intent on gathering at Stonehenge for the summer solstice. For further details, see www.tash.gn.apc.org.

Recommended reading

Arnold, G. (1998) *Kiss This: Punk in the Present Tense*. London: Pan.

Burgess, P. and Parker, A. (1999) *Satellite*. London: Abstract Sounds Publishing.

Colgrave, S. and Sullivan, C. (2001) *Punk*. London: Cassell Illustrated.

Heylin, C. (1993) *From the Velvets to the Voidoids: A Pre-Punk History for the Post-Punk World*. London: Penguin.

Home, S. (1995) *Cranked Up Really High: Genre Theory and Punk Rock*. Hove: Codex.

Laing, D. (1985) *One Chord Wonders: Power and Meaning in Punk Rock*. Milton Keynes: Open University Press.

Lydon, J., with K. and K. Zimmerman (1996) *Rotten: No Irish, No Blacks, No Dogs*. London: St. Martin's Press.

Marcus, G. (1989) *Lipstick Traces: A Secret History of the 20th Century*. London: Faber & Faber.

Sabin, R. (ed.) (1999) *Punk Rock: So What?* London: Routledge.

Savage, J. (1994) *England's Dreaming: Anarchy, Sex Pistols, Punk Rock and Beyond*. London: Faber & Faber.

Stephenson, N. and Stephenson, R. (1999) *Vacant: A Diary of the Punk Years 1976–79*. London: Thames & Hudson.

Recommended listening

Antecedents

Various (1998) *Nuggets: Original Artyfacts From The First Psychedelic Era 1965 1968*. Rhino.

Velvet Underground and Nico (1966) *Velvet Underground And Nico*. Polydor.

Generic texts

Buzzcocks (1977) *Spiral Scratch* [EP]. New Hormones.

Clarke, John Cooper (1978) *You Never See A Nipple In The Daily Express* [single]. Virgin Records.

The Clash (1977) *The Clash*. CBS.

The Damned (1977) *Damned Damned Damned*. Stiff.

Generation X (1978) *Generation X*. Chrysalis.

The Ramones (1976) *The Ramones*. Sire.

Sex Pistols (1977) *Never Mind The Bollocks, Here's The Sex Pistols*. Virgin.

Sham 69 (1977) *Tell Us The Truth*. Polydor.

Siouxsie and the Banshees (1978) *The Scream*. Polydor.

Slaughter and the Dogs (1977) *Where Have All The Boot Boys Gone?* [single]. Decca Records.

The Stranglers (1977) *No More Heroes* [single]. UA.

Suicide (1977) *Suicide*. Red Star.

Television (1976) *Marquee Moon*. Elektra.

X-Ray Spex (1977) *Oh Bondage! Up Yours!* [single]. Virgin.

Subsequent generic developments

Crass (1982) *Christ – The Album*. Crass.

Dead Kennedys (1985) *Frankenchrist*. Alternative Tentacles.

Nirvana (1991) *Nevermind*. Geffen.

CHAPTER 6

Reggae: the aesthetic logic of a diasporan culture

An overview of the genre

Unlike some of the more short-lived genres examined in this book, reggae has been in existence since at least the late 1960s, and still thrives today. Originally a purely Jamaican form, reggae can now be found throughout the world, and is particularly popular in Africa and with Jamaican diasporic communities in America and Britain. In many respects, reggae is a truly global form that is characteristic of musical developments in the postcolonial world. In other respects, reggae is a unique and peculiarly localised phenomenon, with all major shifts in its development emanating from a small Caribbean island.

Like much of Jamaican popular culture, reggae is a 'syncretic' form that draws upon African and European forms. Percussion, rhythm and a counter-ideological aesthetic of Afrocentricity are drawn from African musical discourses, while from Europe come vocal styles, lyrical content and melodic and harmonic structures. Add Jamaica's penchant for American jazz and R&B, along with the massive influence of an essentially syncretic religion (Rastafarianism), and we have a fascinating musical form that has shifted and mutated for forty years, yet still retains many core thematic and musical features.

The most important driving force of reggae is the Jamaican dancehall. The vast majority of stylistic changes in the development of reggae (with the exception of the international success of Bob Marley and the roots reggae style) originated with changes at the level of Jamaica's three hundred or so outdoor soundsystems. These soundsystems consist of a selector (analogous to the European or American DJ), a deejay (analogous to the rap or garage MC), one or two record decks, amplifying equipment and banks of speakers. These soundsystems date back to the 1940s when the development of amplification equipment allowed the soundsystem to usurp the jazz band as the dominant mode of distribution of music within

Jamaica. The soundsystem soon became synonymous with Jamaican popular culture, and competition between soundsystems is the 'dynamo' of reggae culture. The search for new sounds and rhythms to entertain soundsystem patrons led to the development of reggae precursors such as ska and rocksteady, as well as subsequent subgenres of reggae such as rockers, deejay version, dub and dancehall. The central role of dancehall patrons, along with the centrality of Rastafarianism within reggae (with its emphasis on the poor Jamaican 'sufferahs'), has led many commentators such as Lloyd Bradley to suggest that reggae is a form of folk music (see Bradley 2000: 65).

In the 1960s, with the popularity of imported American jazz and R&B in decline, soundsystems such as Downbeat (owned by Clement 'Sir Coxsone' Dodd) and Trojan (owned by Arthur 'Duke' Reid) turned their attention to record production, and a generation of Jamaican record labels such as Dodd's Studio One and Reid's Treasure Isle were born. This development set a pattern for Jamaica's record industry, with relatively small record labels (at least in global terms) owned by individual 'producers', who built studios, sponsored recordings, hired bands, singers and studio engineers, and consequently owned the intellectual property rights of the music recorded at their facilities. This form of rights ownership is different to the European model, where songwriters own the intellectual property rights of the songs they write, although they may choose to sell these rights either prior to or after writing specific songs. The relative freedom offered by the Jamaican model has meant that musicians have continually borrowed rhythmic structures and lyrics from each other without necessarily being accused of musical plagiarism.[1] Indeed, the communal use of specific 'riddims' by producers within contemporary dancehall reggae is one of its unique features. Other notable Jamaican record company entrepreneurs include Chris Blackwell, founder of Island Records, and Edward Seaga, a Jamaican anthropologist who would become a controversial Jamaican Prime Minister in the 1980s.

Historical roots and antecedents

Jamaican folk music traditions can be traced back to the origins of Jamaica itself. At least three-quarters of the population of Jamaica are the descendants of slaves from Central and West Africa, brought to the Caribbean by British slave masters (Jamaica became a British colony in 1655) to work on sugar and other plantations from the mid-seventeenth century until the abolition of British slavery in 1838. The development of Caribbean folk culture and folk music is related closely to these developments.

Prior to the development of a market for pre-recorded music in the 1950s, Jamaican folk music included a variety of forms, all of which went on to influence reggae. These include

- Kumina drumming, connected to the West African religion of Pocomania/ Pukkumina (Bradley 2000: 83);
- Burru drumming. In many cases, this was the only drumming allowed on plantations, as it set the rhythm of work (Hebdige 1987: 56). Burrus, originating from a specific West African tribe, became outcasts following the abolition of slavery, but continued to exist in rural areas of Jamaica throughout the nineteenth and twentieth centuries. Burru drumming employs three drums: a bass drum carrying the rhythm, a 'repeater' carrying the melody and a 'fundeh' which produces harmonies (Bradley 2000: 83);
- work songs;
- the fife and drum music of Jonkanoo;
- Maroon drumming and singing (the Maroons were freed slaves or escapees);
- non-conformist Christian church music, especially the music of Revivalist cults but also including more traditional hymns;
- 'churchical' and 'heartical' drumming within Rastafarian Nyahbingis (a specific form of religious gathering and worship);
- itinerant troubadour chanting, such as that performed by Slim and Sam, who spoke lyrics over tunes in a similar way to the dancehall deejay.

All of these forms went on to influence reggae, with Christian sermons influencing the 'call and response' of artists such as Clayton 'Toots' Hibbert and the 'talk-over' style of 1970s' deejays (see Hebdige 1987: 49), as well as influencing the biblical themes found in much roots reggae and Rastafarian dancehall.

Before the development of electrically amplified music in the 1950s, the predominant way of 'distributing' music in Jamaica was in the form of a band or orchestra at a dance, playing mento[2] or jazz. However, by the mid-1950s the soundsystem had largely replaced live musicians. The popular recorded musics of the 1950s' soundsystem included Afro-Cuban forms like rhumba and mambo, and, in particular, American boogie-based R&B and jazz (initially imported onto the island by American sailors during the Second World War and then heard on AM radio stations broadcasting from Miami, Memphis and New Orleans). When in the mid-1950s American R&B merged into rock 'n' roll and became popular with American and British youth, the old 'blacker' style of US R&B diminished in popularity in the US. This left a gap in the Jamaican market, where soundsystem fans still preferred the traditional R&B sound. The most important soundsystem pioneers of the late 1950s, such as Arthur 'Duke' Reid, Clement 'Sir Coxsone' Dodd and Prince

Buster (Cecil Bustamente Campbell), began to produce Jamaican R&B and went on to play a central role in the later development of reggae.

Within Jamaican R&B, the American blueprint was merged with local influences, with a rhythm guitar strumming on the afterbeat in a similar manner to the off-the-beat banjo of mento (see Bradley 2000: 52). Once Prince Buster added handclaps to this sound (drawn from the 'clap hand' songs sung in Jamaican churches), and began to emphasise the afterbeat (that part of the musical rhythm and sound immediately after the beat), a new genre began to develop. With its emphasis on the afterbeat, this new genre was known initially as upside-down R&B, Blue Beat, Rudie Blues or Jamaican Boogie.

It is certainly no coincidence that a shift towards indigenous Jamaican music should have occurred at a time when Jamaica was gearing up for independence from its British colonial 'masters'. The island became self-governing in 1959, and as Bradley suggests 'cultural independence from the USA was every bit as important as political independence from the UK' (Bradley 2000: 51). The nature of this musical independence was also shifted by the introduction of religious themes within the Jamaican music of the early 1960s. A good example would be the role played by Count Ossie (Oscar Williams – a noted Rastafarian drummer influenced by the Burrus) in Prince Buster's soundsystem and recordings. From this moment onwards, the rhythms of Jamaican music took on an Afrocentric spiritual air.

From its roots in 1950s' Jamaican R&B, ska, an early reggae precursor, began to develop through the late 1950s and early 1960s. Drawing influence from Jamaican R&B but played at a faster tempo and emphasising the 'skippy' beats of 'heartical' Rastafarian drumming, ska consists of a fast and frantic dance music often characterised by its distinctive use of horn instruments and by its fast choppy rhythm guitar. By this stage, most instruments, especially the guitar, lingered on the afterbeat, a distinctive feature of subsequent reggae forms. As Norman Stolzoff suggests, 'ska turned the R&B rhythmic pattern inside-out by employing a syncopated after-beat on the second and fourth beats' (Stolzoff 2000: 60).

The lyrics of prominent ska tracks in early 1960s' Jamaica often celebrated Jamaican independence (Jamaica had been granted full independence in August 1962). Examples include Jimmy Cliff's (James Chambers) track *Miss Jamaica*, and the Folkes Brothers' 1961 hit *O Carolina*,[3] recast some forty years later by Shaggy (Orville Richard Burrell) as a widely selling dancehall anthem. While songs eulogising Jamaica were popular, nothing could top the popularity of innuendo and ribaldry (a phenomenon that would reach ludicrous extremes in post-

1980s' dancehall), so the biggest hit of this period was the ska version by Millie Small (Millicent Smith) of Barbie Gaye's R&B track *My Boy Lollipop*, with Small's version selling six million records worldwide (Bradley 2000: 151).

As the 1960s went on, Jamaican artists turned towards the militant black nationalism of Marcus Garvey, the religion of Rastafari, the American civil rights movement, and the rebellious youth culture of 'rude boys' for influence. While ska was reaching its creative and popular peak in Jamaica during 1965 and 1966, the hopes born of independence were fading amidst a general increase in political violence between supporters of the ruling Jamaica Labour Party (JLP) and the opposition People's National Party (PNP). British rule had been replaced by an economic overdependence on the United States, and the deleterious effects of this economic dependence were exacerbated by high levels of migration from the Jamaican countryside to cities such as Kingston. Violent slum-dwelling young men of the 1960s and after became known as 'rude boys', and when Jamaican music was not focused upon love and courtship, it invariably commented on the rude-boy phenomenon, with Obika Gray suggesting that the rude boys

> defied political authority, rejected the dominant cultural sensibility, and affirmed ghetto culture and ideology as legitimate rivals to the Anglophile tendency. This celebration of ghetto morality exalted a combative refusal to be submissive, a spontaneous militant affirmation of blackness, a disposition to adopt menacing postures towards those perceived as 'oppressors' and a readiness to challenge those found guilty of vaunting their class position and 'high' [i.e. pale] skin color. (Gray 1991: 72)

Lyrically, Jamaican music began to reflect the rise in civil disobedience and emphasise the political protests of the time. This was most noticeable during the official State of Emergency declared before the General Election of 1967 (Stolzoff 2000: 84). During this time, the rude boys secured many of the political themes of reggae in the 1970s into place. Notable exponents of rude-boy music included the Wailing Wailers, who would go on to achieve international success as Bob Marley and The Wailers.

While the lyrics of ska became more oppositional to the status quo, the music became less frantic, fitting in more closely with the rhythmic demands of the dancehall audience. The electric bass guitar (which replaced the stand-up bass in the early 1960s) was brought to the fore and used as a lead instrument. Basslines deepened and were stretched out, with the horns moving into the background and subsequently disappearing to be replaced by lead guitars and electric organs (which by this time were beginning to replace the piano). Instead of ska's emphasis on the second and fourth beats of the bar, rocksteady stayed in 4 : 4 time but emphasised a kick drum of the third beat of the bar, while most other instruments were syncopated on the afterbeat. This rhythmic formation became known as the 'one drop' (Bradley 2000: 165). The choppy rhythm guitar was maintained and a slower more soul-influenced vocal was added to the mix, often provided by vocal trios. This latter addition was the result of the influence of Jamaican gospel and America soul (as epitomised by the releases from Motown Records and Stax), and the resulting musical mix became known as rocksteady. A notable example of this development is Alton Ellis' single *Rock Steady*. Both Ellis' track and the subgenre itself were named after a popular dance style of the time.

Rocksteady was a short-lived musical form and by 1968 it was rapidly changing. Rocksteady had foregrounded drums and the bass guitar; however, after the summer of 1968 the bassline began to spread out and became more emphatic, the rhythm slowed further and the drums came to the fore with an emphasis on rim shots and cymbals. Equally, guitar playing loosened with emphasised chords on the upbeat. In particular, the arrival of delay and echo units in Jamaica and their use with guitars led to the creation of a distinctive 'chikka–chikka' guitar rhythm (sometimes called the chicken scratch), which seems to cut against the hypnotic, grumbling bass (Hebdige 1987: 45). By this time, melodies had faded into the background and rhythm became all. In many respects, this was a result of reggae turning away briefly from European influences and looking back to Africa for musicological sustenance.

While the lyrics of ska had often referred to violent rebellion, the lyrics of late-1960s' rocksteady often had a more soulful and reflective feel, and were broadly anti-violence (good examples include Alton Ellis' *Cry Tough*, Derrick Morgan's *Cool Off Rudies* and Slickers' *Johnny Too Bad*). Some lyrics had explicitly religious themes, such as Desmond Dekker's (Desmond Dacre) *Israelites*, and this, combined with a further slowing of the music, led to the creation of reggae, a name at least partly derived from a dance style popularised by Toots and the Maytals on their 1968 track *Do The Reggay* (Hebdige 1987: 45).

Social and political context

The dominant political contexts during the development of reggae were the spread of Rastafarianism within and beyond Jamaican culture, and the changing nature of socio-economic forces and party politics in Jamaica.[4] With regard to the latter aspect, the development of reggae is intrinsically linked to the fates of Michael Manley and Edward Seaga, the two dominant figures in postcolonial Jamaica.

Rastafarianism

Rastafarianism[5] is a religion based on the worship of Ras Tafari Makonnen, also known as Haile Selassie, Emperor of Ethiopia from 1930 to 1974. Selassie, who claimed to be a descendant of King Solomon, was also known by many other titles including Negus Negusta, living God, the Lion of Judah, or simply 'Jah' (the name given to God in the King James Bible translation of Psalm 68). Rastafarianism is a syncretic religion that draws upon West African spirit worship, Judaism, Ethiopianism, Coptic Christianity and Western Christianity as 'imported' during colonialism. Although Selassie died in 1975, he is still worshipped as a living god, in much the same way that Christians worship Christ. Rastafarians believe that Selassie will lead the black man out of exile in the West, allowing them to return to Ethiopia or Israel, terms used to describe the promised land of Africa.

Rastafarianism draws heavily upon Garveyism. Marcus Mosiah Garvey was a Jamaican political activist and black nationalist who founded an organisation called the Universal Negro Improvement Association. By the 1920s, the UNIA had five million members, a newspaper and the Black Star Line, a shipping company set up to transport black people back to Africa. From this moment onwards, repatriation to Africa (be it physical or merely spiritual) became a central aim for all Rastafarians. Following Garvey's statement that black people should 'look to Africa for the crowning of a Black King, he shall be the Redeemer' (quoted in Barrett Sr 1997: 81), many saw the crowning of Emperor Selassie as having deep significance for the future of people of African descent all over the world, and began to see Selassie as not merely an emperor but also as a deity.

While Garvey went on to reject the Rastafarians' spiritual allegiance to Selassie (Stolzoff 2000: 78), Rastafarians retained a commitment to Garvey's politics. In Selassie, the Rastafarian had a living god who they perceived as resisting the ways of the white men who had enslaved the black body and mind. Rastafarians shun 'Babylon', the phrase used to describe the capitalist culture of the white man with its reverence for capital and property. Equally the Rastafarian abstains from alcohol and gambling, while also consuming herbal cannabis, seen as a sacred herb.

Politics and economics in Jamaica
during the Michael Manley years

Twentieth-century urbanisation in Jamaica led to the creation of slums in Kingston, with poverty feeding both the demand for Rastafarian redemption and repatriation as well as street violence. A series of economic crises followed the granting of independence, with a collapse in the banana and sugar trades and a worrying reliance upon American capital investment. As early as the rocksteady period of the mid-1960s, artists such as Desmond Dekker were warning that Jamaican towns were turning into slums, with the chorus of Dekker's *007 (Shanty Town)* containing the plaintive line 'them a loot, them a shoot in shanty town'.

In 1969, with the JLP in government, the leadership of the opposition People's National Party passed from Norman Manley (leader since 1955) to his son Michael. In preparation for the General Election of 1972, Michael Manley began to use reggae music to define the nature of Jamaica's economic and political problems, while also making a point of visiting Haile Selassie, who presented Manley with a staff that Manley dubbed the 'Rod of Correction' (Stolzoff 2000: 95). Recasting the PNP as the party of the underprivileged masses, Manley used slogans drawn from popular reggae songs, such as Delroy Wilson's *Better Must Come*, to gain popular support. With further help from tracks such as Clancy Eccles' *Power For The People* and *Rod Of Correction*, Manley's populist approach won him the 1972 election. Following Manley's victory, the influence of reggae upon Manley's policies was reciprocated by musicians such as Prince Far I, whose album *Under Heavy Manners* was titled after a phrase used by Manley to describe his martial law policy of 1976. However, the support of the likes of Prince Far I was only ever conditional. While some welcomed Manley's attempt to speak the language of Jamaica's poor, others criticised Manley for populism, with, for example, Junior Byles (Kerrie Byles Jr) responding to Manley's use of the *Better Must Come* slogan with *When Will Better Come?* Others were more hostile, with Max Romeo's (Max Smith) *No Joshua No* and *One Step Forward* being thinly veiled attacks on the Manley regime (see Hebdige 1987: 44, and Bradley 2000: 470–1).

As the 1970s continued, Jamaican politics became increasingly dominated by violent turf wars between 'garrison' communities that supported either the PNP or the JLP, with PNP suggestions that the JLP-supporting American CIA had flooded Jamaica with weapons. Reggae moved centre stage within this period with the One Love Peace Concert of Saturday, 22 April 1978. Both Manley and Edward Seaga (leader of the JLP) were invited to attend the concert, which starred Bob Marley and The Wailers along with Peter Tosh, Dennis Brown, Inner Circle and the Mighty Diamonds. During the concert, it came as a shock to everyone when, during a rendition of his song *One Love*, Marley invited Manley and Seaga to join hands on the stage. Through sheer force of personality, Marley had managed to briefly unite two seemingly implacable opponents.

The rise and fall of Edward Seaga

Edward Seaga had risen to prominence in Jamaican society in the early 1960s when, as an anthropologist of Jamaican music, he inaugurated a National Festival to coincide with independence, cementing the rule of Alexander Bustamente's newly elected JLP. As leader of the JLP throughout the 1970s, Seaga, a fervent 'anti-Communist', preached conservative economic liberalism in contrast to Manley's Socialism. Continuing economic decline in Jamaica, at least partly exacerbated by covert CIA-funded operations that increased political violence among the 'garrison' (politically aligned) communities of Jamaica, led to a flood of cocaine and cocaine-related gangsterism (Gunst 1995) and resulted in the collapse of the PNP government in 1982 and the election of Seaga. In a move that mirrored political changes in North America and Europe, the newly elected Seaga accepted the 'structural adjustment' plans of the IMF and World Bank, privatised nationalised industries, floated the Jamaican currency, brought in anti-trade union regulations and reduced barriers to 'the free market' (Payne and Sutton 1993). Following the country's adoption of free-market economics, reggae turned away from Rastafarianism and began to adopt consumerism, unbridled sexuality and gangsterism as dominant themes (see the section on 'dancehall' below). Many commentators such as Stolzoff and Gilroy suggest that the rise of 'slack' deejays is at least partly attributable to the changes wrought by Seaga's economic liberalism (Gilroy 2002, Stolzoff 2000), with Stolzoff suggesting that the decline in the influence of Rastafarianism is attributable to the association of Rastafarianism with Manley's failed democratic-socialist project. Stolzoff argues that once Prime Minister Manley had 'adopted' Rastafarianism, it gradually ceased to have effect as an oppositional force (Stolzoff 2000: 103).

During the 1990s, Jamaica slipped further into social unrest and economic turmoil, with Brian Meeks characterising the situation as one of long-term 'hegemonic dissolution', whereby the post-independence ruling class have finally lost their ideological grip over Jamaican society (Meeks 1996). Out of this social chaos arose a Rastafarian renaissance headed by the turban-wearing Bobo Dreads, a hard-line Rasta cult who preached 'fire on Babylon' and who maintain a puritan lifestyle free of decadent trappings (see Masouri 2002). Shorn of its association with the Manley regime, this new form of Rastafarianism dominates the lyrical context of much contemporary dancehall reggae, with notable exponents including Capleton and Sizzla.

The musical texts

Roots reggae

Come 1970, the deeper and slower rhythms of reggae had replaced rocksteady, and Rastafarianism was dominating lyrical themes. In 1973, Island Records released Bob Marley and The Wailers' first album *Catch A Fire*, and having rejected their 'rude boy' past, The Wailers' style of 'roots reggae' came to dominate the growing international reggae scene. In many respects, *Catch A Fire* was the first reggae album. While the Jamaican and British reggae markets had been dominated by singles and compilation albums (such as the popular *Tighten Up* compilations released by Trojan in the UK), *Catch A Fire* saw a reggae band develop a series of themes across a single album. Importantly, the main recording took place in Jamaica, and mixing and overdubs by British and American rock musicians were completed in London (legend has it that the tempo of the record was also increased in London to make it appeal to rock fans used to a faster beat). The record itself was packaged within a cardboard cut-out of a Zippo lighter and marketed to a Western audience (Bradley 2000: 414).

As the 1970s progressed, Marley took up the mantle of champion of the Jamaican 'sufferahs', with songs such as *Concrete Jungle* emphasising the gulf of inequality between Jamaica's slum-dwelling blacks and middle-class blacks and whites in the affluent suburbs (see Hebdige 1987: 22). Marley's political opposition to the Jamaican ruling class is clearly derived from the strong discourse of opposition to slavery and colonialism from the 'discovery' of Jamaica to the granting of independence in 1962. Even the instrumentation of Marley's reggae can be seen to be related to slave rebellions, and beyond that to West African music. Drumming was central to African, slave and Maroon communities, with specific percussive rhythms being used for a form of communication that might be best described as 'paralinguistic'. Drumming was a particularly important form of communication during the era of slavery, as many plantation owners forbade the speaking of traditional African languages, and, in some cases, forbade slaves from speaking at all. Equally, the use of horn instruments can be traced back to the use of the abeng, a cow horn, by Maroons to signal for slaves to take up arms (Hebdige 1987: 26–9).

The themes of roots reggae are often simply referred to as 'culture', and contain anticolonialism, black consciousness, communality, Afrocentricism and opposition to Western capitalism. Musically, the popularity of African percussion styles lent the music an ability to 'carry' a variety of different vocal styles, some of which were derived from Rastafarian

Nyabhingis, psalm singing and mento. The tempo of roots is particularly slow, with a prominent bass guitar. Other 1970s' exponents of the languorous roots-reggae sound include Bunny Wailer (Neville Livingston) following his departure from The Wailers, Burning Spear, Israel Vibration and in the 1990s Morgan Heritage and Luciano (Jepther McClymon).

Dub

The origins of dub reggae are to be found in the late-1960s' studio experimentation of engineers such as King Tubby (Osbourne Ruddock). Engineers such as Tubby would take the studio tapes for ska and rocksteady songs and remix their respective elements, cutting between vocals and instrumental tracks while also adjusting the relative levels of bass and treble within each track and the piece as a whole. At a loosely defined post-production stage, echo, phasing, flange and reverb were then added to key elements. Pressed onto 'dub plates', these one-off versions became particularly popular on the soundsystem of King Tubby's employer, Coxsone Dodd, and as these dub plates were not available for sale, this enabled Dodd to maintain a set of reggae tracks that were exclusive to his soundsystem. In time, King Tubby's dub version would also appear on the B-side of Coxsone's releases instead of a separate original tune.

Later in the 1970s, Lee 'Scratch' Perry (Rainford Hugh Perry – another Coxsone studio engineer) and King Tubby would take this process further and sculpt seemingly entirely new creations out of the original structure of reggae. In particular, multitracking studio technology allowed these producers to develop dub as 'the musical expression of the sound engineer as musician' (Stolzoff 2000: 92). In many respects, this phenomenon pre-dates the fashion for remixing within American and European dance musics such as house and techno.

Deejay talk-over

Within the Jamaican soundsystem scene, a DJ, known as 'the selector', would often be accompanied by a 'deejay' who would 'toast' over popular records of the day, adding nonsense verse, nursery rhymes or simple excitations. One of the earliest examples of this style is the work of Count Matchukie (Winston Cooper), with Stolzoff describing the style initiated by Matchukie as

a form of extemporaneous speech making similar to what occurs in the tea meeting and other folk forms, involved the creation of interesting verbal sounds, delivered in a rhyming verse that offered some commentary on the proceedings. Successful toasting, or dee-jaying as it would later be called, depended on the ability to embody several different roles (i.e., cheerleader, wisecracker, and jive talker) and voice registers (i.e. talk, singing, and high-pitched squeals). Men such as Matchukie specialized in speaking in several tongues: from the Queen's English to Jamaican patois. Sometimes these toasts were boastful, satirical, or even totally nonsensical. A deejay's tone, timing, and rhythm were as important as what he was saying. (Stolzoff 2000: 56)

Jamaican deejays became so popular that soundsystem owners such as Coxsone Dodd and Duke Reid began to offer deejays studio time to record their toasting over particularly popular records, or to add spoken vocals to exclusive soundsystem dub plates. In 1970, at Duke Reid's Treasure Isle studio, the first deejay star U Roy (Ewart Beckford), aided by King Tubby, employed the formula of taking popular rocksteady tracks such as John Holt's *Wear You To The Ball* or Alton Ellis' *Girl I've Got A Date*, fading out the singing at crucial moments, and adding speech, shouts and mutterings to the track. This 'versioning'[6] (the separation of the vocal track from the instrumental track which would become known as the 'riddim') is a crucial development that would lead to the development of dancehall reggae in the 1980s (see below). Early signs of rampant 'versioning' include Rupie Edwards' 1974 album *Yamaha Skank*, which contains fourteen versions of one single 'riddim'. Again, this pre-dates the popular 'riddim' album series by Greensleeves in the 1990s and 2000s, on which Greensleeves have collected dancehall variations of single 'riddims' such as the sleng teng, diwali, Egyptian and Far East.

During the 1970s, deejays such U Roy, along with successors such as Big Youth (Manley Augustus Buchanan), I Roy (Roy Reid), Dennis Alcapone (Dennis Smith) and King Stitt (Winston Spark) became phenomenally popular, with their 'versions' of certain songs selling more widely than the originals. Each deejay had their own specific style, with U Roy specialising in clicks and mutterings, Big Youth developing a heavy 'dread' style influenced by Rastafarianism and King Stitt making much use of specific catchphrases. Big Youth is also credited with moving deejay music away from the versioning of rocksteady tunes towards the addition of toasting to more roots-sounding dub. In particular, the deejay version was more often than not spoken or chanted in patois rather than 'standard English'. This meant that there was a clear linguistic distinction between deejay talk-over and the more 'international' style of roots reggae popular in the 1970s.

Rockers

By 1974, a much heavier version of the reggae blueprint known as rockers became popular within Jamaica. Within rockers reggae, the bass is foregrounded and becomes more complicated, with bass rhythms becoming the focus of the track. This bass is accompanied by steady regular percussion. Probably the most famous musician working within this style is Augustus Pablo, whose album *King Tubby's Meets Rockers Uptown* combines the dub effects of King Tubby with the rockers style of rhythm section Sly and Robbie.

Lovers rock

While righteous Rastafarianism dominated 1970s' reggae, there remained a strong undercurrent of romantic ballads running through the genre, with singers such as Alton Ellis, John Holt and Ken Boothe playing smooth, soulful reggae, while Marcia Griffiths and Susan Cadogan also released some notable tracks. This style of balladeering was at least partly derived from the love songs (as opposed to the rude-boy protestations) of rocksteady, and became particularly popular outside of Jamaica and outside of reggae's core audience. Within lovers rock we also have a range of records that incorporate sexually explicit lyrics with, for example, Max Romeo charting in the UK in 1969 with *Wet Dream*, a song banned by the BBC (Hebdige 1987: 76).

The British style

The global popularity of Bob Marley and The Wailers in the 1970s led to a general increase in popularity for roots reggae, and within Britain there was a demand for a form of reggae that addressed specifically British concerns. Anglo-Jamaican artists such as Misty in Roots, Aswad and Steel Pulse took the basic roots formula but emphasised the concerns of the Caribbean diaspora, which in Britain meant racism, police harassment and unemployment. Rastafarianism, with its focus of ethnic displacement, was also prominent. Paradoxically, lovers rock, essentially reggae at its least political, was also popular with Anglo-Jamaican audiences in the 1970s and 1980s. Bradley hints at a class distinction between the audiences for roots and lovers reggae. As working-class blacks were more likely to suffer unemployment and poverty than middle-class blacks, they were more likely to approve of the politicised roots form. On the other hand, 'the intrinsic shininess of lovers' rock sat well with the notions of self-improvement or upward mobility that was part of so many second-generation immigrants' psyches' (Bradley 2000: 441). Equally, there was a gender split; Rastafarianism contains traditional and constrictive gender roles, and as such it is less appealing to women than it is to men. Lovers rock studiously ignores Rastafarian themes and is therefore of more appeal to Anglo-Jamaican women.

Come the turn of the 1970s, a full-blown ska revival also occurred in the wake of the collapse of the punk scene. Multiracial English bands such as UB40 (who specialised in an accessible form of chart-friendly reggae), Madness (who gradually moved away from ska towards well-crafted chart pop), The Specials, The Selector and The Beat subsequently had a great deal of chart success throughout the 1980s. Reggae also had an influence on mainstream pop during this period with, in particular, The Police and The Pretenders having chart hits that were based on reggae rhythms. Also worth noting in the context of the British reggae scene is the role of dub poets such as Linton Kwesi Johnson, who put a distinctive form of Anglo-Jamaican patois poetry to a roots reggae beat. Kwesi Johnson is also known for his political activism and his involvement in the journal *Race Today*.

Visual aesthetic

Ethiopianism and the visual influence of Rastafarianism
Many of the symbols found on record covers can be traced to the influence of Rastafarianism in reggae. In particular, the red, green and black of Garvey's UNIA, and the red, green and gold colours of various African flags (the latter seen on Bunny Wailer's *Just Be Nice*, held aloft and contrasted with the Stars and Stripes of the USA), can be found on roots reggae album covers from the 1970s onwards. Within these pan-African colours, red symbolises the blood of the slaves, green symbolises African vegetation, black the 'negritude' of Africans and yellow the gold found throughout Africa. Equally, the six-pointed Star of David, symbolising the Rastafarians as Israelites and descendants of King David, is also found on numerous record covers. Representations and photographs of Marcus Garvey (such as on Burning Spear's *Garvey's Ghost*) and Haile Selassie (such as on Bob Marley and The Wailers' *Soul Captives*) are also widespread, as are drawings and depictions of regal lions (such as on Culture's *Lion Rock*). These lions denote 'the Lion of Judah' (Selassie) and connote natural strength and power.

Other Afrocentric images found on record sleeves include drawings of the continent of Africa (such as on Hugh Mundell's *Africa Must Be Free*), Rastafarians themselves (such as on Big Youth's *Dread Locks Dread*), the visual representation of the problems of Babylon (such as war and conflict – including Peter Tosh's *No Nuclear War*, Mikey Dread's *World War III* and The Mighty Diamonds' *Stand Up To Your Judgement*), ganja (such as on Peter Tosh's *Legalise It*, the Joe Gibbs Family's *Reggae Christmas* and Bob Marley and The Wailers' *Catch a Fire*), and dreadlocks (see below). Other non-Rastafarian images include the map of Jamaica (Prince Buster's *Ska-Lip-Soul*) and Jamaica's countryside (see Morrow 1999).

Dreadlocks

One of the most visually striking aspects of Rastafarian aesthetics, and the visual style of reggae musicians and fans, is their dreadlocks. Dreadlocks are uncut hair that has formed naturally into locks. Metaphorically, the concept of 'dread' refers to rebellion and individualism. The first dreadlocks were developed in the 1920s among Garveyites beginning to take up the Rastafarian religion, and some suggest that the Garveyites were influenced by African tribes (Barrett 1997: 137). The style became increasingly popular among Rastafarians in the 1940s, who were influenced by photographs of Ethiopian warriors with locked hair.

The Rastafarian has a biblical justification for dreadlocks ('They shall not make baldness upon their head, neither shall they shave off the corner of their beard, nor make any cuttings in the flesh', Leviticus 21: 5) and a cultural one, as dreadlocks fit in with an 'Ital' (meaning natural or organic) lifestyle. Dreadlocks also visually confirm subcultural membership and emphasise the exclusivity of the Ras Tafari cult. The act of growing locks in one's hair is also symbolic of the refusal to adhere to the dominant society's notion of self-grooming and part of the Rastafarians' celebration of their negritude. Negro hair grows into locks more easily than Caucasian hair, and in refusing to straighten their hair the Rasta emphasises and celebrates his or her blackness.

Dreadlocks are a powerful visual statement of the Rastafarian's, or the reggae fan's, refusal to conform. Bob Marley is influential in spreading the style with the lyrics and artwork for the album and single entitled *Natty Dread*. In the 1990s, there began a stylisation of dreadlocks whereby this hairstyle became partially disarticulated from its religious or Afrocentric origins.

The English skinhead reggae style

While dreadlocks and Rastafarian colours and insignia dominate the Jamaican reggae scene (and record covers as imported into the West), a footnote to reggae's visual style is the 'rude boy' look as adopted by English reggae fans. During the 1950s, there was a developing tradition of Jamaican musicians visiting Britain and playing on the British jazz and R&B scenes. During the early to mid-1960s, ska and rocksteady became popular among the English mod and emerging skinhead scenes. As such, mods and skinheads turned towards the Jamaican rude boys for sartorial

Bob Marley and The Wailers. Dreads inna Babylon.

influences. By the 1960s, the 160,000 Jamaican migrants to Britain (Stolzoff 2000: 41) were beginning to make their presence felt within British society. The result of combining rude boy and English skinhead clothes was that reggae-listening English skinheads would wear 'pork pie' hats, plastic-framed sunglasses, Ben Sherman shirts, sheepskin jackets, 'Harrington' jackets, donkey jackets, overcoats in the style of the English gentlemen's outfitters Crombie, 'Sta-Prest' trousers, tight Levi 501 jeans and work boots. For the smarter skinhead, mohair, two-tone 'tonic' or Prince of Wales check suits were worn with polished brogue shoes. While the skinhead subculture declined in popularity, the English ska boom of the late 1970s and early 1980s saw a revival of this clothing style, with the addition of Fred Perry tennis shirts and Dr Marten boots. Generally, skinheads or young people wearing these clothes in the 1980s could be safely categorised as ska fans.

The Jamaican dancehall style

Following the rise of dancehall music in Jamaica in the 1980s (see below), Jamaican dancehall culture produced a new sartorial aesthetic for both male and female dancehall attendees, and these styles have been adopted in those areas of the world where dancehall reggae is popular. Stolzoff describes female dancehall fans as wearing

> 'batty riders', which Chester Francis-Jackson defines as 'a skirt or pair of shorts which expose more of the buttocks than it reveals'. 'Puny printers' (pants that show the outlines of a woman's genitalia), wigs of all colours, mesh tops, large jewellery (gold bangles, rings, earrings, nose rings), and elaborate hairdos . . . Men's dancehall fashions changed as well, shifting from the hippie and African-inspired garb of the roots era to flashy suits, abundant jewellery, and hairdos made popular by American rappers. Unlike the women, however, male dancehall fans and performers continued to cover their bodies in long, draping outfits that hid rather than revealed their shape. (Stolzoff 2000: 110; see also Francis-Jackson 1995)

Subsequent generic developments[7]

Following the death of Bob Marley in 1981, the Jamaican reggae scene experienced a lull in both sales and creativity. The musical vacuum created in the wake of Marley's death and the eventual decline of 'international reggae' was filled with the latest innovation from Jamaica's dancehalls, a subgenre of reggae that became known simply as dancehall. The 1980s' dancehall saw the return of the deejay to the epicentre of reggae, but instead of the nonsense rhymes of the 1960s, or the Rastafarianism of the likes of Big Youth in the 1970s, 1980s' dancehall saw the rise of sexually explicit lyrics, with the phrase 'slackness' used to describe this new style. Deejays such as General Echo (Errol Anthony Robinson) and Yellowman (Winston Foster) went further than 1970s' artists such as Max Romeo (who had cleaned up his act and turned 'culture' with the album *War Ina Babylon*), and began to write lyrics that were essentially pornographic and derogatory to women. Lyrically, this slackness not only defied the morals of the Jamaican upper classes, it was also an affront to the Rastafarians. Importantly, whereas much roots reggae was sung in English, dancehall was dominated by the deejay's patois, and as such 1980s' reggae looked back inwards to Jamaica after the global success of Marley et al. in the 1970s.

While dancehall saw a significant shift in lyrical content, changes in the music were no less dramatic. In 1985 came the release of Wayne Smith's tune *Under Mi Sleng Teng*, which featured a digital 'riddim' loop produced on a Casio Rhythm Box that was entirely devoid of a conventional bassline (produced by studio producer King Jammy, a.k.a. Lloyd James, an apprentice of King Tubby). This inaugurated the era of 'ragga', an entirely digital form of dancehall. Over the next few years, King Jammy's percussive loop came to dominate dancehall reggae, with more than two hundred releases featuring different deejays chatting over a basic

Sleng Teng 'riddim'. This process of producing a digital 'riddim' and hiring the services of a deejay to provide a vocal track now forms the basis of dancehall, the most significant 'post-reggae' development in Jamaican music. Modern dancehall now contains a mix of simple two-chord melodies, newly produced and rhythmically complex digital 'riddims' (often influenced by mento, Burru, and Pocomania and Kumina percussion), or freshly sampled and digitally manipulated 'riddims' drawn from the rocksteady and early reggae days (see Bradley 2000: 518–30).

In the late 1980s, matching slackness for its shock value, dancehall returned to rocksteady's obsession with rude boys, only the cocaine-fuelled rudies of the late 1980s surpassed their 1960s' predecessors in their levels of violence. Deejays such as Ninjaman (Desmond Ballantine) and Bounty Killer (Rodney Price) began to produce 'gun lyrics' that glorified symbolic and actual violence.

The 1990s saw the return of a significant female presence within reggae, sidelined following the rocksteady era by the rise of Rastafarianism in the 1970s. In particular, Stolzoff sees the rise of female deejays such as Tanya Stephens and Lady Saw (Marion Hall) as being a partial reflection of the increased economic power of women in post-Manley Jamaica. Seaga's economic liberalism had broken the male-dominated trade unions, and women began to obtain more employment in new professional, technical and administrative jobs (Stolzoff 2000: 111).

In 2004, there has been no shift away from the domination of deejays over singers within the Jamaican reggae scene. However, no thematic style dominates dancehall, with the situation remaining similar to Stolzoff's analysis of the mid-1990s (the following categorisation is loosely based on Stolzoff 2000: 163–73, and encompasses both dancehall and the roots revival of recent years).

- *The cultural Rasta deejay.* Harking back to the Rastafarian deejays of the 1970s, contemporary artists such as Tony Rebel (Patrick Barrett) emphasise Afrocentricism and Black pride.
- *The rude-boy Rasta deejay.* Deejays such as Anthony B (Keith Anthony Blair) and Terry Ganzie combine the 'attitude' of the rude-boy gangsters with a commitment to the violent overthrow of Babylon. Anthony B's *Fire Pon Rome* is a good example of such a track.
- *The reality deejay.* Non-Rastafarian 'ghettocentricity' that attempts to expose political corruption, exploitation and needless violence. Women are notable exponents of this form, with Tanya Stephens producing key tracks such as *The Other Cheek*.
- *The gangster/gunman deejay.* Prominent in the 1980s, this style is still popular among Jamaican youth, with Bounty Killer in particular scoring a succession of hits.
- *Slackness and the loverman deejay.* Defined by Yellowman (Winston Foster) in

the 1980s and mass marketed (and toned down) by Shabba Ranks (Rexton Rawlston Fernando Gordon) in the early 1990s. A defining feature of the late 1990s was the rise of the female slack deejay Lady Saw, whose tracks such as *Life Without Dick* and *Stab Out The Meat* leave little to the imagination. Perhaps the increase of women in the Jamaican recording industry and economy more generally explains the fact that women deejays such as Lady Saw can match the male deejays for vulgarity while also producing tracks such as *What Is Slackness?* that provide a critique of political corruption and the sexual double standards of many Jamaican men.

- *The comedian/gimmick deejay*. Deejays such as Red Rat (Wallace Wilson), who toasts in an almost impossibly high register, and Snagga Puss, who adopts the sound of a cartoon character, are particularly popular at the younger end of the market. Such deejays generally keep their lyrics free of gun talk and slackness. A notable album is *Oh No It's Red Rat!*, which although littered with his trademark phrase 'oh no!' also contains *Nuh Live Nuh Way*, a 'cultural' version of the South African standard *Wimoweh*.

- *Singjays*. Halfway between the singers of the 1970s and the dancehall deejays of the 1990s sit those artists choosing to combine traditional singing with patois toasting. This development, highly influenced by the 'sound boy burial' style of Tenor Saw (Clive Bright) on tracks such as *Ring The Alarm*, is now led by Sizzla (Miguel Collins), a Bobo Dread who works with 'cultural' Rasta themes.

- *Combinations*. This phrase is used to describe tracks that include two deejays, or a singer (or singjay) and a deejay.

- *Post-dancehall roots and the new culture singers*. The mid-1990s saw a general decline in the provision of live reggae, with modern dancehall events more closely mirroring European-style club events featuring a DJ plus MC. However, the mid-1990s' Rastafarian renaissance also saw the return to popularity of traditional singers, such as the late Garnett Silk, who work within the dancehall setting. This tradition is carried on by Everton Blender (Everton Williams) and Luciano.

- *Lovers singers*. Examples include Beres Hammond, Sugar Minott (Lincoln Minott), Wayne Wonder (Von Wayne Charles) and Frankie Paul.

- *Old-school singers*. Singers from the 1960s and 1970s, such as Jimmy Cliff, Desmond Dekker, Alton Ellis, Ken Boothe and Marcia Griffiths, still complete international tours and remain popular in Jamaica and Europe.

- *All-Rounders*. At the top of the Jamaican recording industry are artists such as Buju Banton (Mark Anthony Myrie) who combine roots reggae-style instrumentation (*Mama Africa*), loverman lyrics (*One To One*), 'cultural' Rasta themes (*Up Ye Mighty Race, Mama Africa*) and reality toasts (*Mr Nine*) on a single album (*Friends For Life*). Other all-rounders include Beenie Man (Moses Davis), and Lt. Stitchie (Cleveland Lang) who produce a wide range of toasts on a number of different themes.

Notes

1. The passing of a law on copyright by the Jamaican Parliament in 1993 (Stolzoff 2000: 177) has had no noticeable effect on the production and appropriation of 'riddims' within the reggae industry.

2. Stolzoff describes mento as a

> creolized fusion of European- and African-derived styles. It was performed by ensembles that combined European instruments, such as the fiddle, flute, and guitar, with instruments "wholly or partly of African origin" (Bilby 1995: 153) such as the banjo, rhumba box, drums, rattle and scraper. In this sense, the origins of mento parallel those of popular dance musics throughout the Caribbean, such as merengue, calypso, and konpa, which arose out of similar processes of musical creolization. (Stolzoff 2000: 23)

3. Noticeable on the Folkes Brothers' original is the use of a distinctly Jamaican accent rather than the adoption of an American accent found on earlier recordings (Bradley 2000: 60).

4. Stolzoff goes as far as suggesting that the political rivalry between the PNP and JLP shaped the entire social landscape of Jamaica from 1966 onwards (Stolzoff 2000: 83).

5. For an in-depth exploration of Rastafarianism within its Jamaican context, readers should consult Leonard E. Barrett, Sr's book *The Rastafarians* (Barrett 1997).

6. Dick Hebdige's introduction to *Cut 'n' Mix: Culture, Identity and Caribbean Music* contains the following useful exploration of the term 'version':

> One of the most important words in reggae is 'version'. Sometimes a reggae record is released and literally hundreds of different versions of the same rhythm or melody will follow in its wake. Every time a version is released, the original tune will be slightly modified. A musician will play a different solo on a different instrument, use a different tempo, key or chord sequence. A singer will place the emphasis on different words or will add new ones. A record producer will use a different arrangement. An engineer will stretch the sounds into different shapes, add sound effects, take notes and chords or add new ones, creating empty spaces by shuffling the sequence of sounds into new patterns. (Hebdige 1987: 1)

7. In the context of this chapter, 'subsequent generic developments' refers to developments that followed the 'fixing' of the generic characteristics of reggae in the 1970s. Therefore, the naming of this section should not necessarily be seen as supporting the view that dancehall is not reggae. Unlike other genres examined in this book, reggae is as popular now as it has ever been, and in its dancehall form it is as innovative now as it has ever been in the past.

Recommended reading

Barrett, L. E., Sr (1997) *The Rastafarians*. Boston, MA: Beacon Press.

Barrow, S. and Dalton, P. (1997) *Reggae: The Rough Guide*. London: Rough Guides.

Bradley, L. (2000) *Bass Culture: When Reggae Was King*. London: Penguin.

Hebdige, D. (1987) *Cut 'n' mix: Culture, Identity and Caribbean Music*. London: Comedia.

Jones, S. (1988) *Black Culture, White Youth: The Reggae Tradition from JA to UK*. London: Macmillan.

Morrow, C. (1999) *Stir It Up: Reggae Album Cover Art*. San Francisco: Chronicle Books.

Potash, C. (1997) *Reggae, Rastafarians, Revolution: Jamaican Music from Ska to Dub*. London: Music Sales Limited.

Stolzoff, N. C. (2000) *Wake the Town and Tell the People: Dancehall Culture in Jamaica*. Durham, NC, and London: Duke University Press.

Recommended listening

Antecedents

Various (1989) *The Liquidators: Join The Ska Train*. Trojan.
Various (1998) *Trojan Rocksteady Box Set*. Trojan.

Generic texts

Big Youth (1973) *Screaming Target*. Gussie.
Burning Spear (1975) *Marcus Garvey*. Island.
Ellis, Alton (1993) *Cry Tough*. Heartbeat.
King Skitt (1996) *Reggae Fire Beat*. Jamaican Gold.
Kwesi Johnson, Linton (1998) *Linton Kwesi Johnson – Independant Intavenshan: The Island Anthology*. Island.
Bob Marley and The Wailers (1972) *Catch A Fire*. Island.
Pablo, Augustus (1976) *King Tubby Meets The Rockers Uptown*. Rockers/Telstar.
Perry, Lee (1997) *Arkology*. Island Jamaica.
Romeo, Max (1976) *War Ina Babylon*. Island.
Steel Pulse (1978) *Handsworth Revolution*. Island.
Toots and the Maytals (2001) *54–46 (Was My Number)*. Trojan.
U Roy (1971) *Version Galore*. Trojan.
Various (1999) *Trojan Lovers Box Set*. Trojan.
Various (2003) *Trojan Reggae Sistas Box Set*. Trojan.

Subsequent generic developments

Buju Banton (2003) *Friends for Life*. Epitaph.
Lady Saw (1996) *Give Me A Reason*. Diamond Rush.
Sizzla (1997) *Black Woman And Child*. VP.
Various Artists (1990) *Hardcore Ragga: The Music Works Dancehall Hits*. Greensleeves.

CHAPTER 7

Synthpop: into the digital age

An overview of the genre

In this chapter, we are adopting the term synthpop to deal with an era (around 1979–84) and style of music known by several other names. A more widely employed term in pop historiography has been 'New Romantic', but this is too narrowly focused on clothing and fashion, and was, as is ever the case, disowned by almost all those supposedly part of the musical 'movement'. The term New Romantic is more usefully employed to describe the club scene, subculture and fashion associated with certain elements of early 1980s' music in Britain. Other terms used to describe this genre included 'futurist' and 'peacock punk' (see Rimmer 2003). As well as its evident connections to early twentieth-century art and radical values, futurist carried more elitist connotations. It is certainly ironic that the Italian-in-origin futurist art movement was a reaction to the alleged sentimentalism of the original Romantics (see Lista 2001). Dave Gahan commented that Depeche Mode

> were Futurists because we were involved with people who wanted to be individual. The New Romantic thing meant people all looking the same, however flamboy-antly. Futurists were an extension from punk. That was our following at the time. (Quoted in Malins 2001: 24–5)

The term 'New Pop' was also used to describe many of the bands studied in this chapter. However, while 'futurist' was seen to be a kind of technological punk, 'New Pop' was often defined according to its opposition to more seemingly credible genres such as punk. As former *Smash Hits* journalist Dave Rimmer suggests:

> The New Pop isn't rebellious. It embraces the star system. It conflates art, business and entertainment. It cares more about sales and royalties and the strength of the dollar than anything else and . . . it isn't the least bit guilty about it. (Rimmer 1985: 13)

The term 'new musick' (most associated with the journalist Jon Savage) was also used to describe some of the music examined below. However, whereas our term synthpop crosses the high/low cultural divide, Savage specifically developed the term 'new musick' to describe a post-punk move into experimentation, avant-gardism and a more synthetic and mythically European sound (noted as early as November 1977 – see Savage 1977).

Our term synthpop, while not 'value-free', can be employed to transcend many of the other terms' limitations. In particular, it can cover the wide terrain between groups such as Adam and the Ants, who made little use of synthesiser technology but whose post-punk style was both resolutely pop and populist, and Cabaret Voltaire, who used synthesiser technology in an avant-garde 'industrial' style (and therefore achieved high credibility and low sales). Somewhere between the two is New Order, who despite massive success with their single *Blue Monday*, never fully capitalised on their popularity, at least partly due to the esoteric business practices of their label Factory Records.

The influences of punk rock, glam rock, synthesiser technology, disco and the Germanic ambience of groups such as Can and Kraftwerk, and of David Bowie in his 'Berlin' period (1976–7), were all crucial components in the construction of synthpop. By the height of the punk era, relatively cheap synthesisers and sequencers had infiltrated the pop landscape sufficiently for them to be considered a viable alternative to more traditional instruments. Synthesiser-based music from artists as diverse as Jean-Michel Jarre, Donna Summer (LaDonna Andrea Gaines) and Kraftwerk had made inroads into the British singles charts, and groups such as The Human League and Ultravox were releasing their first work. Tubeway Army's (Gary Webb, a.k.a. Gary Numan) *Are 'Friends' Electric?* was a chart-topping UK single in 1979 and gave synthpop its first 'teen idol' (cf. Savage 1979).

The more theatrical and flamboyant side of punk encouraged a small group of London-based 'style victims' to congregate around mostly gay clubs such as Bangs, Louise's, Chaguarama's and the Global Village in the late 1970s. In 1980, scene entrepreneurs and prime movers such as Steve Strange (Steven Harrington), Rusty Egan and Robert Elms began to fashion their own 'Bowie Nights' or 'Heroes Nights' at Billy's and later the Blitz (Rimmer 1985: 30–1). This was a club-based scene based on recordings. However, by the summer of 1980 performing groups such as Spandau Ballet and Duran Duran were beginning to tour and garner publicity in the British pop and newly-formed style press (magazines such as *The Face* and *i-D* that looked as much at the newly termed 'lifestyle' as they did at its musical accompaniment).

By 1981, a host of acts connected to a synthpop sound had tasted chart success, including Depeche Mode, Visage, Orchestral Manoeuvres in the Dark, Ultravox and the 'market leaders' Spandau Ballet and Duran Duran. These were followed by the likes of Japan, Soft Cell, Culture Club, Eurythmics, and Blancmange. As with any genre, the music was diverse but was characterised by a broad set of shared values that eschewed rock playing styles, rhythms and structures, and implied 'feelings'. The rock aesthetic was replaced by synthetic textures often redolent of alienation, 'European-ness' and a robotic rigidity that was as much to do with the limitations of the new technology as any formulated artistic credo. For Savage, the sound and credo was 'the reaction to the cardboard cut-out that punk had become. Glamour replaces grubbiness' (Savage 1995).

By around 1984, many of the biggest names had moved on from synthpop and its rather rigid musical constraints. Others simply entered the commercial pop mainstream. More sophisticated instruments and techniques removed some of the amateurish 'rough edges' from the songs and sounds, and in the wider world of popular music there was something of a critical backlash against the flamboyance and self-conscious artifice of the style, which Savage named 'the New Authenticity' (Savage 1985). This can be seen in the success of performers such as Bruce Springsteen and Bryan Adams, and events such as 1985's Live Aid. Thanks to music video and dedicated channels such as MTV, the synthpop sound – a largely British phenomenon – did provide a platform for worldwide success for some acts, many of whom, paradoxically, ended up as stadium-rock successes.

For a style much vilified, synthpop gave the atrophying post-punk scene a much needed jolt. As well as popularising new instruments and production techniques, it encouraged 'non-musicians' to create in much the same manner that punk had. Gary Numan referred to himself as little more than 'an arranger of noises' (Malins 2001: 5). Its strict dancefloor beats can also be seen as a step towards the eventual partial hegemony of dance in the 1990s, although many would argue that synthpop did not eschew melody or personality to the same extent in its quest for success.

Historical roots and antecedents

As indicated in our overview, the roots of synthpop were diverse. The initial musical impetus for synthesiser music lay in the avant-garde or neoclassical work of composers such as Walter (Wendy) Carlos, Steve Reich and the *musique concrète* of Pierre Schaeffer, or from institutions such as the BBC. Within the popular music field, the synthesiser's exclusivity and expense excluded it from all but a handful of artists until the early 1970s. By the middle of that decade, synthesiser use was infiltrating mainstream pop. Many synthpop musicians drew upon the work of Roxy Music's Brian Eno, a truly ground-breaking conceptual artist more interested in ambience than chord progressions. The Roxy Music influence also encompassed the clothing style of lead singer Bryan Ferry. Sequencers, featuring a programmable memory that could play-back, mix sounds and adjust tempo, had also made their appearance on works such as The Who's *Who's Next* and Pink Floyd's *Dark Side Of The Moon*. In particular, *On The Run*, from the latter work, can be seen as a blueprint for subsequent genres such as synthpop and techno. Drum machines and electronic drum kits had also begun to be employed in popular music, in genres as diverse as funk (Sly and the Family Stone's *There's A Riot Goin' On*), progressive rock (Kingdom Come's *Journey*), and proto-techno (Suicide's eponymous debut album and Kraftwerk's 1970s' output). The possibilities and limitations of all these new technologies at least partially determined the structure and feel of much synthpop.

In many ways, synthpop's immediate predecessor punk rock was a major influence on the genre, but only in the sense that synthpop was a reaction to, rather than a continuation of, punk rock. Punk's DIY ideology did not encompass the use of synthesising technology (a reaction against its dominance in progressive rock), preferring to believe that the roughly played and untuned guitar was the most authentic 'voice' of musical alienation. Peter York would certainly agree, suggesting that the reasoning behind New Romantic's fetishism of synthesising technology was as a reaction to the 'modern Luddism' and 'formalized primitivism' of punk rock, which was itself a reaction against 'the boring pretensions' of keyboard-based progressive rock (York 1980: 164). A further crucial difference between punk rock and synthpop was that musicians working in the latter field had little of the 'authenticist' snobbery of the rock world. Indeed, many revelled in the seemingly artificial nature of synthesisers. The Human League adopted a strict 'synthesisers only' rule in their early days to avoid 'musicians' taking control away from them (Rimmer 1985: 18).

The so-called foundations of popular music, be they jazz, blues, folk or soul, had little influence upon the synthpop genre. Instead, critically derided forms such as disco and glam rock provided much of the blueprint for synthpop, summed up as using 'modern-sounding electronic instruments to play good old-fashioned pop songs' (Rimmer 1985: 55).

With these forms, synthpop shared an interest in accessibility, dance beats and melody, filtered through the possibilities offered by new sounds and textures. A figure such as David Bowie, one of very few musicians to garner both widespread artistic credibility and commercial fame in the 1970s, was crucial to the synthpop scene, with musicians such as Gary Numan, Gary Kemp of Spandau Ballet, John Foxx (Dennis Leigh) of Ultravox and Duran Duran's Nick Rhodes (Nicholas Bates) evidently in his debt.

If Bowie was the principal British role model for synthpop, then the debt owed to Kraftwerk cannot be overlooked. From avant-garde beginnings, the group honed and minimalised their sound by the time of their commercial breakthrough with *Autobahn* in 1975. This album, along with *Trans Europe Express* and *The Man Machine*, alerted musicians to the opportunities made available by technologies that were very rudimentary by later standards. In particular, Bowie's work on *Low* and *Heroes* adds a sheen of visual appeal and accessibility to the somewhat foreboding appearance and delivery of Kraftwerk.

The final major contribution to synthpop lay in the ground-breaking Euro-disco sound popularised most effectively by Donna Summer and her producers/writers Giorgio Moroder and Pete Bellotte. By fusing 'soul diva' vocals with a backing track built upon a combination of synthetic and traditional instruments (albeit played as though by machines), this team of musicians operating in the unlikely setting of a studio in Munich achieved huge commercial and critical success with tracks such as *I Feel Love*. The rigid 4 : 4 drive of the disco beat fuelled most synthpop tracks and its huge legacy remains widespread to this day. More conventional soul/disco acts such as Chic also influenced synthpop. A track such as Duran Duran's *Careless Memories* is a classic hybrid of Euro-disco, new wave guitar pop and Bowie/Kraftwerk, topped off with the teen appeal imagery and classic song structure and melody of commercial pop.

Social and political context

The synthpop scene occurred shortly after the transformation of punk rock into the more marketable 'new wave'. New wave still shared a common set of values with its progenitor based around aggression, authenticity and the power of rock as an agent of social change. In spring 1979, at the height of popularity for new wave, Britain returned the Conservatives to power after a five-year absence, and in doing so elected Britain's first female Prime Minister, Margaret Thatcher. The effects of the Conservative Party's shift to the right were soon seen with a marked increase in unemployment and the development of a significant polarisation in both society and politics.

Unlike the contemporaneous movement based around a British ska revival (as epitomised by The Specials and their 2-Tone record label), synthpop chose not to deal explicitly with the continuing social issues of high unemployment, the decline of traditional industries and a burgeoning revival in right-wing politics, and instead chose flamboyance, overt commercialism and escapism as its central tenets. As such, synthpop was seen as a reaction against the perceived greyness of British culture and the visual and stylistic straightjacket of punk. The greyness of British culture was itself seen as an effect of the slow collapse of the postwar settlement. With Thatcherism's clean break from consensus politics, we therefore have what those on the right wing of British politics saw as a 'brave new world' of individualism, entrepreneurialism, consumerism and self-reliance.

The new decade saw elements of youth culture self-consciously embrace the new consumerism in order to gain success. 'Style' became a transcending signifier, aided by the shift in music journalism from the weekly 'inkies' (*New Musical Express*, *Sounds*, *Melody Maker*) to the recently established fortnightly or monthly 'glossies' (*The Face*, *i-D*, *Smash Hits*). Concepts such as design, marketing and image became central to the star-making machinery. There was nothing altogether new in this process, but they now became more overt, blatant and significant elements. After the monochrome blacks and greys of punk/new wave, synthpop was promoted by a youth media interested in people who wanted to be pop stars, such as Boy George and Adam Ant, and who 'looked good in colour: Numan . . . Toyah' (Rimmer 1985: 19).

Synthpop's focus on fashion and individualism, along with its new business-friendly approach, would have been anathema to the previous punk generation. This led certain commentators to suggest that whereas punk was oppositional, synthpop fitted neatly into the new political discourse formed by Thatcherism. This can be seen most clearly with the career of Gary Numan. Numan's career was kick-started by his parents, who invested their savings to enable him to develop a career. Numan, an avowed Conservative, also employed various members of his family to complete 'backroom' tasks (mirroring Thatcherism's 'family values') while investing the profits from his hits in a variety of different business ventures. As Numan stated in 1979, 'originally I wanted to be famous like I wanted to breathe, now I just want to be rich' (quoted in Rimmer 1985: 18–19).

In many respects, this 'artist as entrepreneur' figure was also seen in a variety of early 1980s' pop bands, including ABC, Culture Club and

Spandau Ballet. Simon Reynolds cites ABC's Martin Fry as talking of 'choice and change and value – almost just a vision of better, more exciting and efficient consumer capitalist' (Reynolds 1985). Culture Club were equally entrepreneurialist. While Boy George (George O'Dowd) appeared to be the driving force behind the band, in many respects Culture Club's mid-1980s' reign was managed by band member Jon Moss, who is described by Dave Rimmer as 'an entrepreneur in the classic free enterprise mould; someone whose talent is in organizing the talent around him to make something happen' (Rimmer 1985: 76). At the height of Culture Club's success, Moss could be seen to be acting more as an entrepreneur rather than as a musician, and once suggested that 'we're not in the music business anymore. We're in the commodities business' (Rimmer 1985: 141). However, like Thatcherism, Moss' entrepreneurial politics were accompanied by a strong moral code that became prevalent in band interviews. This mixture of entrepreneurialism flavoured with moralism can also be seen in those artists of the mid-1980s who were avowedly anti-Thatcherite. For example, The Jam and The Style Council's Paul Weller also employed family members to run his musical business, and invested profits in his own Solid Bond Studios in London's desirable Marble Arch area. (Weller eventually sold the studio once The Style Council folded – see Ingham 2000.)

As is often the case, the ideological content of New Romantic synthpop was at its most powerful when it appeared to be apolitical. If we were to narrow the synthpop genre to the music of the New Romantics, this argument is strengthened greatly. The 1980s' style theorist Peter York went as far as suggesting that the New Romantics and the New Right were effectively opposite sides of the same coin (see York and Jennings 1995). These similarities are therefore worth exploring.

New Right:
- A 'radicalism' that rejected 1970s' 'strife'
- An individualism that rejected the 'statism' of the postwar settlement
- A focus on 'individuals and their families' rather than the class politics of the previous epoch
- Monetarism rather than Keynesianism
- Entrepreneurialism
- The creation of individual wealth.

New Romantics:
- A 'futurism' that rejected the 'grey' 1970s
- An individualism that rejected the 'conformism' of punk

- A focus on apolitical hedonism as a replacement for the political commitment of punk
- Business plans rather than gestural politics
- Entrepreneurialism
- The celebration of individual wealth.

The connection between Thatcherism and the New Romantics can be seen most clearly in the music and style of Spandau Ballet. The band formed their own record label and publishing company, but not to gain 'independence' as the punks did, but as part of a long-term strategy to sign a lucrative deal with a major label. Manager Steve Dagger, whose central role in the group was to make them successful, monitored the band's progress carefully. The designs of Spandau Ballet's records were carefully constructed to form a 'corporate identity'.[1] Even though Gary Kemp, the songwriting force behind the band, was always keen to emphasise his working-class credentials, this merely served to emphasise the connection to Thatcherism rather than disguise it. As Stuart Hall has noted, Thatcherism was equal parts populism and authoritarianism – a heady mix designed to appeal as much to the upwardly mobile working class as to so-called 'middle England' (see Hall 1980). One of the emblematic symbols of the period, the yuppie, was much in evidence in the New Romantic scene, and was immortalised in Spandau Ballet's song *Gold*, a near hymn to the power of individual wealth, with lyrics that valorised 'the man with the suit and the pace'.

While the individualism of synthpop remained dominant in the early 1980s, there were some signs in the mid-1980s that 'protest' music was about to return, albeit in a different form. Whereas a playful postmodern irony could be seen to be at work in synthpop, the return to 'authenticity' and protest was signalled by the 'political pop' of the mid-1980s (see Redhead 1990: 12–23). Acts such as The Style Council, Madness, Tom Robinson and Billy Bragg rallied around the Labour Party and on 21 November 1985 formed Red Wedge to campaign for a Labour Party victory at the next General Election. Equally, the famous Band Aid single of Christmas 1984 and Live Aid concert of 13 July 1985 signalled a return within popular music towards overt politics (as opposed to escapism) and a progressive lyrical message. What is also notable is that the music changed along with the lyrical message. Out went the 'inauthentic' synthesisers to be replaced by guitars, often the favoured instrument of the self-consciously politically aware. Even Gary Kemp retreated from both the formal electronic experimentation of early Spandau Ballet singles and the Thatcherism of *Gold* with his performance on an acoustic guitar at various Red Wedge concerts. Steve Redhead also cites Paddy McAloon (Prefab Sprout), Roddy Frame (Aztec Camera) and Lloyd Cole (of Lloyd Cole and the Commotions) as being part of this return to the traditional 'protest singer with guitar' format (Redhead 1990: 16).

The musical texts

While there were some notably high-selling synthpop albums, it was in the field of single releases that synthpop had most of its success. This section will therefore be dedicated to a textual analysis of ten key synthpop singles (listed in order of release). In doing this, we hope to draw a picture of the stylistic and formal conventions of the synthpop genre.

TUBEWAY ARMY (1979) *ARE 'FRIENDS' ELECTRIC?*
5 : 23, released May 1979, sixteen weeks on UK chart, spending four weeks at No. 1

The first synthpop hit. Starting with a distinctive four-bar pattern, featuring a sustained synthesiser, bass, and drums emphasising the second and fourth beats of the bar, the vocals for this track begin during the ninth bar. Interestingly, there are some offbeat elements to the rhythm, which is unexpected in a 'technologist' genre that would subsequently emphasise a perfectly sequenced crotchet beat. A further aspect to note is the remarkably slow tempo of this track (94 beats per minute), which, combined with the sustained synthesiser riff, lends a dirge-like quality. Typically self-referential, the song focuses upon the lyricist's (and narrator's) alienation from his former friends now that he is a *bone fide* pop star (see Savage 1979).

JAPAN (1980) *GENTLEMEN TAKE POLAROIDS*
3 : 28 [single edit], released October 1980, two weeks on UK chart, reaching No. 60

The first notable aspect of Japan's first hit is the use of oriental-sounding melodies submerged beneath a keyboard-driven arpeggio. Whereas most tracks within the genre draw upon a mythically European 'technological' sound, Japan's complex layered sound also draws upon 'Eastern' sources. This is accentuated by the track's use of a saxophone between the first chorus and second verse, and the use of a guitar solo between the second and third choruses on the seven-minute-long album version of the track.

VISAGE (1980) *FADE TO GREY*
3 : 54, released November 1980, fifteen weeks on UK chart, reaching No. 8

This track starts with four bars of indistinct electronic percussion with ambient 'padded' chords before the song's trademark sustained keyboard riff begins. From here on in, while there are some structural changes (for example alteration on bars nine and ten and a key change when the lyrics start), this synthesised riff remains a prominent feature of the track from beginning to end. Lyrically the track emphasises the individualism prominent in the New Romantic scene that Visage were a part of ('one man on a lonely platform'). Like *Are 'Friends' Electric?* the track also features spoken vocals (on the second and third choruses), but the use of French vocals and a female vocalist add a feeling of European sophistication to the track. One can surmise that the track enunciates an English suburbanite's dream for a more glamorous European existence.

ORCHESTRAL MANOEUVRES IN THE DARK (1980) *ENOLA GAY*
3 : 26, released November 1980, fifteen weeks on UK chart, reaching No. 8

Like *Fade To Grey*, *Enola Gay* begins with some light electronic percussion, but perhaps to jolt the listener the melody appears approximately halfway between the first and second beats of the second bar. For the next eight bars we have a strict crotchet beat, followed by a drum roll, which sounds somewhat 'rockist' when placed immediately before the next four bars of simple synthesised melody. It is at this point that the lyrics start, thirty seconds into the track. After a four-line first verse, the distinctive synthesised melody reappears for four bars before the second verse of four lines. The melody pattern is then repeated for eight bars, but there has been a key change and instrument change, away from the relative clarity of the original melody towards a more fuzzy and distorted synthesiser sound. A chorus follows this. Unlike the first two verses, which have an AABA format (where the last syllable of the first, second and fourth lines rhyme), the chorus has an AABB structure. Following this chorus (approximately two minutes into the track), the track breaks down to the percussion for four bars alongside a second less prominent melody that has featured earlier in the track. The dominant melody returns for four bars, prior to another AABA verse, which is immediately followed by two further choruses. The track ends with the same electronic percussion loop with which it began, accompanied by a sustained chord gradually decreasing in volume.

As a commentary on the American bombing of Hiroshima in World War Two (the Enola Gay was the name of the B-29 Superfortress plane that dropped the atomic bomb), this track is one of the few explicitly political synthpop tracks, although the precise nature of the political message of the track is not entirely clear.

HEAVEN 17 (1981) *(WE DON'T NEED THIS) FASCIST GROOVE THANG*
4 : 06, released March 1981, five weeks on UK chart, reaching No. 45

The synthpop/funk crossover. This track is recorded at a much higher tempo (146 beats per minute) than seen elsewhere in synthpop, although the emphasis on two beats of the bar make the track seem slower. Like *Gentlemen Take Polaroids*, this track makes use of an arpeggio, only here it is used to provide an almost percussive sound. Unlike *Enola Gay*, the politics of this track are far more explicit, with its direct accusation that Ronald Reagan (American President in the 1980s) held fascist views. In general, this track is an attempt to provide a warning regarding the rightward shift in Western politics in the early 1980s.

SOFT CELL (1981) *TAINTED LOVE*
3 : 44, released July 1981, sixteen weeks on UK chart, spending two weeks at No. 1

Like Eurythmics and Yazoo, Soft Cell conformed to the archetypal synthpop band make-up of flamboyant vocalist and esoteric keyboard player. While *Tainted Love* was originally recorded by Motown artist Gloria Jones in 1964, the poignancy of the song's lyrical content is merely emphasised here by the fact that Soft Cell vocalist Marc Almond was an 'out' homosexual man when the duo's version was released in 1981. Like the Heaven 17 track above, the fast tempo of this track (150 beats per minute) is hidden by an emphasis on alternate beats. This can be seen at the very beginning the track, where a kick drum knocks out a rigid crotchet beat, and where a snare is used to emphasise the second and fourth beats of the bar. However, like other synthpop tracks, the defining feature of *Tainted Love* is not its tempo, rhythm or percussion, but its trademark synthesised melody. Rather than the sustained notes of *Are 'Friends' Electric?* or *Fade To Grey*, this melody consists of a simple arrangement of distinctive keyboard stabs.

DEPECHE MODE (1981) *JUST CAN'T GET ENOUGH*
3 : 36, released September 1981, ten weeks on UK chart, reaching No. 8

Again, it is the distinctive nature of the keyboard melody of this track that is at the centre of its appeal, making the track instantly recognisable. Like much synthpop, innovation within *Just Can't Get Enough* is at the level of instrumentation rather than at the level of structure which remains relatively traditional. Lyrically simplistic ('just like a rainbow, you know you set me free'), the keyboard motif is enough to allow consideration of this track as a classic of the genre.

THE HUMAN LEAGUE (1981) *DON'T YOU WANT ME*
3 : 58, released November 1981, thirteen weeks on UK chart, spending five weeks at No. 1

Like *Fade To Grey* and *Are 'Friends' Electric?* The Human League's track also employs spoken lyrics, but the narrative intrigue of the track is provided by the fact that alternate verses are spoken by two separate narrators (one male, one female). The simple device of providing two separate perspectives on a universal romantic theme, set against the backdrop of boy meets girl in a cocktail bar, certainly led to its huge success. Again, the structure of the song is resolutely traditional (verse, two choruses, second verse, chorus repeated four times and fade). Electronic beats at 118 beats per minute knock out a simple crotchet beat, while a prominent synthesised bassline provides 'groove'.

EURYTHMICS (1983) *SWEET DREAMS (ARE MADE OF THIS)*
3 : 34, released January 1983, fourteen weeks on UK chart, reaching No. 2

Again, a strict crotchet beat provides the bedrock of this track, with hi-hats or an emphasis on alternate beats being used at certain key points in the song. Stereo panning is also used to good effect. The song contains three identical verses, with variation provided by the rhythmic and melodic backdrop (for example during the final verse the rhythm is stripped down to a kick drum providing a simple crotchet beat). While the main vocals and the repetition of the single verse and chorus fit into synthpop's technological aesthetic of repetition, the backing vocals provide a hint that certain key players in the genre (including Eurythmics) would move away from synthpop's 'Europeanness', and return to a more traditional (and some would say Americanised) 'soulful' sound.

SPANDAU BALLET (1983) *GOLD*
3 : 50, released August 1983, nine weeks on UK chart, reaching No. 2

While not really a synthpop track, the inclusion of Spandau Ballet's *Gold* in this selection emphasises how many working within and around the synthpop genre retreated from austere electronic modernism, replacing it with a more traditional 'soulful' and 'funky' sound. Or, as Dave Rimmer puts it, 'after their first couple of hits, Spandau Ballet ditched numb Euro-disco electronics, which they'd never been very good at anyway, and set about trying to make a funk record' (Rimmer 1985: 54). In many respects this shift in Spandau Ballet's sound was part of a wider 'move back to "authenticity" after the self-conscious "play" of the New Pop era' (Redhead 1990: 14). While Redhead cites the more explicitly political elements of mid-to-late 1980s' pop, this move can also be detected in certain 1983 releases. In particular, Duran Duran made use of funk percussion on *Union Of The Snake*, and even arch-technologists The Human League drew back from electronic minimalism with the use of a synthesised brass sound on *(Keep Feeling) Fascination*.

Whereas the dominant sound of earlier Spandau Ballet tracks such as *Muscle Bound* was a slow, heavily reverbed, crotchet beat that emphasised the second and fourth beats in the bar (not unlike Soft Cell's *Tainted Love*, but at a much slower tempo), *Gold* draws back from this percussion-led minimalism, emphasising 'real' drumming. Equally, while early tracks such as *Muscle Bound* and *Chant No. 1 (I Don't Need This Pressure On)* featured spoken vocals, chants and group-sung lyrics that follow the rhythm, *Gold* is dominated by the bombastic vocal style of Tony Hadley. Furthermore, while earlier synthpop tracks more often than not ignored politics entirely, *Gold* is a clear espousal of unadulterated Thatcherism.

Visual aesthetic

As suggested in the introduction, the term New Romantic was used to describe a particular club scene and fashion sensibility that came to be associated with synthpop bands in the late 1970s and early 1980s. With its playful flamboyance and individualism, New Romanticism was in many ways the sartorial expression of the synthpop aesthetic. This section will therefore focus upon the individualism inherent in the clothing styles of those members of the synthpop order who could most closely be labelled 'New Romantics' (Spandau Ballet, Duran Duran and Visage).

In emphasising the role of individuality in New Romanticism (itself drawn from the growing mood of neo-Thatcherite individualism prevalent in the late 1970s and early 1980s), we are necessarily downplaying the role of the fashion industry in constructing this style. As Peter York suggests, this is not surprising, as the late 1970s saw 'a crisis in the fashion industry . . . The fact was that style *fragmentation* followed mass youth fashion in a sophisticated economy as inexorably as the call for devolution followed total planning' (York 1980: 11). Here York is suggesting that while the clothing industry clearly made a profit from the sale of clothes to young people in the late 1970s and early 1980s, it was no longer able to dictate (or even follow) rapid changes in youth style. This was because the linear (diachronic) progress of youth fashion had been so resolutely disrupted by punk (which was, in many ways, a form of 'anti-fashion' designed to disrupt conventional notions of fashionability). Following the immediate aftermath of punk, the 'grammatical repertoire' of youth style had been so disrupted that any item of clothing could be combined with any other, and this 'mix and match' aesthetic (a feature of postmodern cultures) had eroded the traditional paradigmatic choices and syntagmatic combinations of early youth fashions.[2] Or, as Peter York put it, 'the old laws are clearly being mucked about with something criminal' (York 1980: 42). York goes on to suggest that

> The repertoire of teen style is now pretty much open to *anyone*. Above all, the jumble sale habit, once something that one never saw below the *Time Out* middle-class waterline of bohemia, has gone down to ordinary teenagers with a vengeance, and they're picking up the strangest things and changing the meanings of what they wear. (York 1980: 42–3)

New Romantic fashion can therefore be seen as both an extension of this aesthetic (in that it 'mixed and matched' a variety of different items of clothing) and a reaction to it (whereas the 'jumble sale habit' is inherently democratic, New Romantic clothing styles were elitist).

Within the mix and match aesthetic, there were dominant themes. One of these was 'gender bending', cross-dressing and the wearing of make-up for men. We can see examples of this style in Divine (Harris Milstead), The Human League's Phil Oakey, Culture Club's Boy George, New Romantic 'face' Marilyn (Peter Robinson), Duran Duran's Nick Rhodes, Japan, and Depeche Mode's Martin Gore. While Gary Numan also wore make-up, he avoided the New Romantic tag through adherence to a much more futurist look that also incorporated a leather jacket (rarely seen on New Romantics, presumably due to its 'rockist' connotations). Other 'frilly' and occasionally effeminate clothes were also worn by Adam Ant (Stuart Goddard), Spandau Ballet, and Visage's Steve Strange. Savage suggests that this focus in cross-dressing was part of a wider cultural interest, citing the film *Tootsie*, the television comedy characters *Hinge and Bracket* and 'a transvestite Prime Minister – Mrs Thatcher is more of a man that you'll

New Romantics. Glamorous looks for the post-punk era.

ever be' (Savage 1983). In a suitable reversal of this dominant trend in male pop star fashion, Eurythmics' singer Annie Lennox wore a particularly masculine pin stripe suit for the *Sweet Dreams (Are Made of This)* video.

Other themes were taken from clothes worn by David Bowie in the 1970s (particularly the silver futurism of 'Ziggy Stardust' and the austere clothing of his Berlin period) and Bryan Ferry. With bands such as Spandau Ballet and Adam and the Ants we also see the entire band dressing up in themed clothing. Jon Savage dubbed Spandau Ballet's use of tartan as 'Culloden chic' (Savage 1981), while early New Pop band Adam and the Ants preferred pirate clothing, which briefly became popular.

As outlandish as the clothes and make-up were the haircuts. Whereas various members of Spandau Ballet, Japan, ABC and Duran Duran opted for bleached or dyed 'wedges' or 'mullets', others such as The Human League's Phil Oakey, A Flock of Seagulls' Mike Score, and Depeche Mode/Yazoo's Vince Clarke went to ludicrous extremes in hairstyling.

Those synthpop artists who rejected the New Romantic clothing style nonetheless adopted a coherent 'look'. In particular, suits were remarkably prevalent. Kraftwerk, Heaven 17 and Ultravox wore suits and ties on the covers of *Trans Europe Express*, *Penthouse And Pavement* and *Vienna* respectively, while various members of The Human League, Duran Duran and Orchestral Manoeuvres in the Dark also wore suits on promotional photographs. Dave Ball, the 'straight' (both sexually and sartorially) member of Soft Cell, also wore a suit on the cover of their *Non-Stop Erotic Cabaret* album, which contrasted with Marc Almond's leather jacket. Elsewhere, Almond wore more risqué clothing (such as black leather and arm bracelets during a *Top of the Pops* television performance) that emphasised his homosexuality. Despite his statement that 'I'm not into politics or making stands' (Savage 1982), this flaunting of gay fetish wear was an important statement in 1981. Also adopting the leather fetish look were Frankie Goes To Hollywood, who, along with their producer Trevor Horn, took up the mantle of synthesised music once the original early 1980s' synthpop acts had retreated into soulful pop.

Even when synthpop band members looked 'normal', this invariably reflected their position within, or the outlook of, the band. For example, contrasting with Phil Oakey's 'gender bending' make-up and haircut (allegedly styled on Veronica Lake), The Human League vocalists Susanne Sulley and Joanne Catherall adopted a restrained and traditionally feminine 'Saturday night' image. This merely emphasised the suggestion that Sulley and Catherall were 'ordinary' teenage girls plucked from the obscurity of a Sheffield nightclub by bandleader Oakey. Thus we have another example of how there is a homology between the central meaning of clothing styles and musical texts in the synthpop genre.

Subsequent generic developments

As previously indicated, the basic nature of musical technology in the synthpop era partially determined the music produced. Synthesisers around 1981 were usually monophonic and featured a relatively small number of pre-set sounds. Drum machines were rudimentary and often did not allow for a programmable tempo setting. When Depeche Mode first recorded in 1980 they utilised a Dr Rhythm drum machine, basic analogue synths and an analogue sequencer. There was no polyphony and, as with punk rock, whole tracks were recorded and mixed in one day (Malins 2001: 22).

When performing live, groups such as The Human League and Orchestral Manoeuvres in the Dark (later abbreviated to OMD) were reliant upon backing tracks on tape, with all the inherent limitations implied. Indeed, when producing *Dare*, The Human League had entered the information in step-time into sequencing equipment rather than recording it in the accepted sense of the word. All of these dimensions encouraged the production of strict-tempo dance-beat pop tunes with an endearingly 'naive' feel and a narrow sound palette.

During the early to mid-1980s, technology improved rapidly, encompassing digital recording and instrumentation, sampling and polyphony. Perhaps more importantly, elements such as 'feel' and all the small variations in tempo and timbre previously associated with live playing were now programmable, resulting in a more lush, less robotic feel to synth-based music. In addition, traditional instrumentation began to augment rather than be totally superseded by newer sounds (Depeche Mode, The Human League). This resulted in a number of developments. It allowed The Human League to be totally assimilated into the pop mainstream, losing the last vestiges of their earlier experimental 'austerity' in the process, as tracks such as *The Lebanon* (1984) and *Human* (1986) demonstrate. Conversely, Depeche Mode, while remaining a Top 40 chart act, managed to develop a darker-textured sound based on the richer timbral opportunities made possible by a wider range of instruments and, crucially, new sampling technology. The textural and artistic leap between their first album *Speak and Spell* (1981) and *Construction Time Again* (1983) is immense. Subsequent albums, such as 1986's *Black Celebration*, 1987's *Music For The Masses*, and 1990's *Violator*, show a continuing 'darkening' of Depeche Mode's sound in their steady progress from synthpop to electro-goth.

For other acts such as the Eurythmics, the development was more retrogressive, resulting in something of a retreat from the minimalist and unsettling Euro beats of *Love Is A Stranger* (1982) and *Sweet Dreams* (1983) to the more comforting stadium-rock sound provided by *Would I Lie To You* (1985) and *Thorn In My Side* (1986). Other acts such as Duran Duran and Spandau Ballet honed their sound to embrace the pop mainstream more fully. This involved jettisoning the electronic-led melodies and percussion of their early singles in favour of a fuller, more traditional sound that foregrounded 'real' instruments such as pianos, drum kits and guitars.

Genres sometimes far removed from synthpop were heavily influenced by its rationale and techniques. Rap, in its earliest commercial manifestations, consisted of a musical backing track often lifted *verbatim* from a disco hit, as in the case of The Sugarhill Gang's *Rapper's Delight* containing the bassline from Chic's *Good Times*. However, the influence of synthpop and Kraftwerk heavily influenced the rap subgenre known as electro, which was hugely successful in the early 1980s, and has given us such classics as Afrika Bambaataa's *Planet Rock* and *Looking For The Perfect Beat*.

British soul and funk, hitherto discounted as inferior to the American model, utilised the synthetic textures of synthpop to some success. Acts such as Linx, Imagination and Junior Giscombe took British dance music beyond the constraints of disco-influenced dance with a more contemporary sounding mix. Indeed, dance music as a whole was affected by synths and drum machines. Compare the disco hits of Shalamar, such as *That To The Bank*, with the crossover synth/dance textures of *Disappearing Act*, and the influence is very apparent.

The dancefloor opportunities inherent within sequencer and synth technology were made use of by a variety of acts in the early 1980s. The seemingly oppositional styles of funk ('hot') and synthpop ('cold') were brought into fruitful contact by acts such as A Certain Ratio and Heaven 17. Certainly, synthpop played its part in the rehabilitation of dance music for the 'mainstream' and 'specialist' audience, following the rigid demarcations set up between genres such as punk rock and disco. Dance genres such as house and, in particular, techno were also influenced hugely by synthpop. Seminal techno producers such as Derrick May and Juan Atkins have testified to its importance. Another American innovator Kevin Saunderson went as far as to term Depeche Mode's *Get The Balance Right* 'the first ever house record' (Malins 2001: 140). More recently, the European and New York 'electroclash' scenes, including acts such as Ladytron (see Chapter 10), have fashioned a sound that returns us to elements of the synthpop template. After years of breakbeat-based rap and jungle, highly syncopated house and music that features samples of 'real' instruments, the much-vilified 'robotic, cold' rhythms and timbres of the early 1980s have been reappraised. Even a figure such as Gary Numan, in the past treated as almost a joke by the music press in the UK, finds tribute albums, renewed success and name-checking by the likes of Moby now commonplace.

Notes

1. This was taken to ridiculous length by Heaven 17, who appeared in publicity shots wearing bowler hats, and carrying briefcases and copies of *The Financial Times* (see Rimmer 2003: 122).
2. In his book *Système de la Mode [The Fashion System]*, Roland Barthes analyses fashion as a system analogous with language. Within such an analysis, individual items of clothing are selected from a 'paradigm' of clothes and combined 'syntagmatically' so as to produce a coherent statement concerning the wearer and his or her social status (Barthes 1985). This type of analysis is particularly applicable to the study of New Romantic fashion, as the New Romantic mode of dressing involved a higher degree of individual choice and selection than previous youth styles.

Recommended reading

Buckley, D. (1999) *Strange Fascination: David Bowie, the Definitive Story*. London: Virgin.

Cunningham, M. (1999) *Good Vibrations: A History of Record Production*. London: Sanctuary.

Flur, W. (2000) *Kraftwerk: I Was a Robot*. London: Sanctuary.

Malins, S. (2001) *Depeche Mode: A Biography*. London: André Deutsch.

Prendergast, M. (2000) *The Ambient Century*. London: Bloomsbury.

Rimmer, D. (1985) *Like Punk Never Happened: Culture Club and the New Pop*. London: Faber & Faber.

Rimmer, D. (2003) *New Romantics: The Look*. London: Omnibus Press.

Savage, J. (1997) *Time Travel: From the Sex Pistols to Nirvana: Pop, Media and Sexuality, 1977 96*. London: Vintage.

Tamm, E. (1989) *Brian Eno, His Music and the Vertical Color of Sound*. London: Faber & Faber.

York, P. (1980) *Style Wars*. London: Sidgwick & Jackson.

York, P. and Jennings, C. (1995) *Peter York's Eighties*. London: BBC Books.

Recommended listening

Antecedents

Bowie, D. (1977) *Low*. RCA.

Kraftwerk (1977) *Trans Europe Express*. EMI.

Donna Summer (1977) *I Remember Yesterday*. Casablanca.

Ultravox (1977) *Ha!Ha!Ha!* Island.

Generic texts

Depeche Mode (1981) *Speak And Spell*. Mute.

Duran Duran (1981) *Duran Duran*. EMI.

Heaven 17 (1981) *Penthouse And Pavement*. Virgin.

The Human League (1981) *Dare*. Virgin.

Japan (1980) *Gentlemen Take Polaroids*. Virgin.

Orchestral Manouevres in the Dark (1980) *Architecture And Morality*. Virgin.

Tubeway Army (1979) *Replicas*. Beggar's Banquet.

Soft Cell (1981) *Non-Stop Erotic Cabaret*. Some Bizarre.

Spandau Ballet (1981) *Journeys To Glory*. Chrysalis.

Various Artists (1981) *Some Bizarre*. Some Bizarre.

Subsequent generic developments

Depeche Mode (1983) *Construction Time Again*. Mute.

Ladytron (2001) *604*. Invicta Hi-Fi.

Various Artists (1988) *Techno! – The New Dance Sound Of Detroit*. Virgin.

CHAPTER 8

Heavy metal: noise for the boys?

An overview of the genre

Despite ongoing contestation by both fans and musicians as to what constitutes the genre and which acts should be included under its banner, heavy metal and its close derivatives have been a vibrant, successful and influential musical genre for over thirty years. Unlike many of the other musical forms in this book, heavy metal (henceforth 'metal') has at least partially subverted the vagaries of fashion and 'coolness' by being a consistently successful commercial genre. In 1989, *Rolling Stone* magazine termed heavy metal 'the mainstream of rock and roll' (Walser 1993: 3).

The musical roots of metal lie chiefly within blues rock and psychedelic rock. From these two genres, metal drew upon such elements as the constructed notions of 'roots' and 'authenticity', as well as an interest in virtuosity and timbral intensity achieved through new production techniques, effects, structures and playing styles.

In the main, the earliest manifestations of metal in the mid to late 1960s (and known at the time as 'rock' or 'hard rock') can be found in the work of groups such as The Yardbirds, Cream and The Jimi Hendrix Experience in Britain, and Blue Cheer, Steppenwolf and Vanilla Fudge in the US. In particular, the centrality of the distorted guitar riff and the powerchord, in songs such as Cream's *Sunshine Of Your Love* and Blue Cheer's *Summertime Blues*, set the tone for probably the most important textural element in most subsequent metal recordings.

The audience for metal, certainly until the early 1980s, was overwhelmingly male, white and working class (or in US parlance, 'blue collar'). In Britain, its most fervent devotees were often found in regions historically associated with heavy industry – South Wales, the Midlands and the North East. Similarly, in the States, industrial cities such as Cleveland and Detroit became known as 'rock cities' – as did whole tracts of the urban Mid-West. This geographical determinant is seen as an important element by many critics – for Robert Walser 'that heavy metal bands now labor in spaces abandoned by industry is particularly appropriate for a music that has flourished during a period of American deindustrialization' (Walser 1993: x).

The nature of the music, its lyrical subject matter, and its core audience all contributed to a widespread antipathy towards metal, both within the industry itself and in 'polite society' as a whole. In the US, metal has been the catalyst behind moral panics, particularly regarding so-called Satanist tendencies (see Moynihan and Soderlind 1998). Indeed, the music has achieved the remarkable feat of uniting conservatives, religious fundamentalists and left-wing liberals in their condemnation. Joe Stuessy (Professor and Director of the Division of Music at the University of Texas at San Antonio), testifying about metal to a US Senate Committee, suggested that 'it contains the element of hatred, a meanness of spirit. Its principal themes are . . . extreme violence, extreme rebellion, substance abuse, sexual promiscuity, and perversion and Satanism' (Stuessy, quoted in Weinstein 2000: 1–2). It is fair to say that only rap and punk have garnered such a negative critical press as metal, but not for such a long and continuous period. Unlike rap and punk, it could be argued in the broadest terms that metal's 'rebellion', shared to an extent with prog rock (see Macan 1997: 173), is more typically manifested through escapism and fantasy rather than an engagement with the political realities of social circumstances, although there are important exceptions to this generalisation.

Traces of this widespread animosity towards metal remain until the present day, although the last few years have seen such a remarkable upsurge in metal (and indeed guitar music in general) that the form has become possibly the dominant youth music genre among certain age groups and social strata. The music audience for metal is now mixed-gender, although still overwhelmingly white (see Walser 1993: 16–19).

One of the reasons for metal's longevity, in addition to its perennial appeal for 'rebellious youth' (while still connecting with older generations), has lain in its ability to mutate and develop subgenres. Although its core elements remain largely unaltered, the metal of any historical period possesses a certain specificity, and does reflect or comment upon prevailing technologies or social patterns. Since its beginnings as a named genre, metal has slowly moved away from its blues and psychedelic roots to engage with other styles such as prog, glam, mainstream pop, classical, punk/hardcore, synthpop, rap, even disco, its supposed antithesis. In addition, metal is now a global phenomenon, with huge markets in areas such as South America developing since the 1980s, aided by the exponential growth of music television which the visual excesses of the genre are ideally adapted to. Some of the genre's most popular acts have emerged from countries as diverse as Germany (the Scorpions, Rammstein), Brazil (Sepultura) and Australia (AC/DC).

For metal devotees, the music is just one element in a 'whole way of life' encompassing dress, social activities, hobbies and collecting, and implied values. This can, of course, be the case within any musical/subcultural group, but is particularly intense – matching the music – in metal (see Arnett 1996). While all the classic clichés to the effect that you 'either love this music, or you hate it' are not completely true, the music and associated lifestyle do ensure that it is difficult to remain neutral in relation to metal. However, part of metal's huge constituency does consist of more peripheral audiences who engage with only certain elements of the style at certain periods or not exclusively. On several occasions over the past thirty years, when the devotees and the more detached followers of the style have merged, metal has moved from the relative margins into the market mainstream.

This phenomenon has particularly happened during the following periods:

- Classic metal (early 1970s) – Black Sabbath, Deep Purple, Led Zeppelin
- US stadium metal (late 1970s) – Kiss, Aerosmith, Boston
- New wave of British heavy metal (late 1970s) – Judas Priest, Def Leppard, Iron Maiden, Motörhead
- Video-influenced metal (early to mid-1980s) – Twisted Sister, Poison, Mötley Crüe
- Thrash metal (early to mid-1980s) – Metallica, Megadeth, Anthrax, Napalm Death
- Grunge (early 1990s) – Nirvana, Pearl Jam, Soundgarden
- Nu metal (early 2000s) – Limp Bizkit, Slipknot, Linkin Park.

Throughout this whole period metal has been a constant noisy element in the world of popular music genres, whether in or out of fashion, or ignored, reviled or, less often, revered by critics.

Historical roots and antecedents

From its main roots in blues rock and psychedelic rock, what became known as metal – what we might term 'proto-metal' in the period 1968–70 – was in some respects a distillation of certain basic attitudes and timbral tendencies already present in aggressive, 'masculine' or 'proletarian' styles. Added to these new elements were new sounds and production techniques made possible by both creative innovations and new technologies. As is often the case, even if the will to produce metal had been present in the early 1960s, other factors would have mitigated against the style coming to the fore any earlier than it did. American 'garage rock' bands such as the Sonics were producing a fairly raucous and distorted sound as early as 1965, but still within the huge limitations posed by the technology of the day.

Central to the development of metal were effects pedals such as fuzz-tone, and hugely powerful amplifiers and speaker cabinets most importantly associated with the Marshall Company. Whereas The Beatles played huge stadium venues in 1964–5 with their small 30-watt and 50-watt combos drowned out by the screams of the crowd, by 1968 bands such as The Who were generating thousands of watts of power from what was, and remains, the classic rock 'back line' – banks of four-by-twelve speaker cabinets powered by amps and slave amps. As well as this equipment offering sheer volume, valve and harmonic distortion became controllable components, resulting in the classic metal powerchord being made sonically complex by overtones and feedback. For Walser, metal is fundamentally about this 'musical articulation of power' (Walser 1993: 2). As well as the immense amount of latent power within guitar capability, the increased physical presence of bass and drum elements increased the overall 'attack and sustain' of the metal line-up, although the lead guitar and its riffs were, and continue to be, the most important component in the genre.

Studio production techniques, particularly multitracking and the over-dubbing of identical guitar parts or vocal lines, made albums sound more powerful than hitherto. By 1969 many musicians, such as Led Zeppelin's Jimmy Page and John Paul Jones, had already served a long apprenticeship, both live and in the studio, and were symbolic of the move towards musicians having greater technical knowledge and creative input over recordings. Indeed, Page produced all of Led Zeppelin's work. The members of the group came from a wide variety of musical backgrounds, and this eclecticism was always an important part of their sound, allowing them to move between slow blues (*Since I've Been Loving You*), rock ballads (*Thank You*), modal North African folk (*Kashmir*) and progressive rock (*Stairway To Heaven*) structures at will. This is one reason why, despite their huge impact upon the genre, Led Zeppelin was arguably a band that played metal, rather than was metal. Their lead vocalist Robert Plant said of the group's first album 'That was not heavy metal . . . It was ethereal' (Plant, quoted in Walser 1993: 6). Many of their devotees would disagree.

The band whose sound was arguably more influential upon metal and whose own songs more typically lay within its terrain was Black Sabbath. From their beginnings as a British blues-boom outfit called Earth (blues elements were still present on early tracks such as *Evil Woman*), Black Sabbath developed their sound and found their name when they began composing lengthy gothic dirges such as *Black Sabbath* (1969). The opening of this track from their debut album set the sonic blueprint for myriad subsequent developments. *Black Sabbath* promoted an air of brooding menace, with virtual 'slabs' of guitar, lyrics and album cover design all symbolically connecting with literary texts by Poe and Shelley and associated concepts of the sublime and the Satanic. Deena Weinstein sees most heavy metal lyrics falling into two 'clusters defined by a binary opposition: *Dionysian* and Chaotic' (Weinstein 2000: 35). Classic pop tropes such as romance, dating and courtship rituals are noticeably absent in metal narratives.

By 1970, what became known as metal was a huge commercial success in both Britain and the US. In particular, Led Zeppelin were playing large venues in the States and setting the terrain for what became known as 'stadium rock'.

During this same period a third major British proto-metal act came to the fore. Again, from an eclectic range of backgrounds, Deep Purple shifted their attention to a more aggressive and driving sound with *In Rock* (1970) and *Machine Head* (1971), having had some success as both a mainstream rock act and in their work with a symphony orchestra. Deep Purple brought classically influenced virtuosity to metal in the form of the guitar and keyboard work of Ritchie Blackmore and Jon Lord. The speed and complexity of their playing styles, built as much on the precise arpeggiation of Bach's Toccatas as upon the blues tradition of note-bending and soloing, have proven to be a lasting influence upon metal. Love Sculpture's reworking of Khachaturian's *Sabre Dance*, released in November 1968 in the UK, shows very early manifestations of this crossover between orchestral music and proto-metal. Later virtuoso guitarists such as Eddie van Halen and Yngwie Malmsteen refined this tendency in a much more extreme, and some would say vacuous, manner. Certainly, one of the most creative tensions within metal has continued to be between its 'lumpen' and virtuoso dimensions, with the heroic transcendence embodied by the guitar hero/solo escaping the confines of the more pedestrian rhythm section. For a resolutely 'low art' form, virtuosity is an important, if somewhat paradoxical, feature of the genre. According to Walser, 'many heavy metal guitarists . . . have a much better grasp of harmonic theory and modal analysis than do most university graduates in music' (Walser 1993: 98).

As it was rooted more directly and extensively in the blues, early American metal tended to lack the purist singularity of the likes of Black Sabbath. This is a factor in judging the music of Steppenwolf, Vanilla Fudge and Iron Butterfly as simply 'heavy' or 'hard rock' rather than classic metal. In the early 1970s' bands such as Aerosmith, Blue Öyster Cult and Kiss released their first albums. All these bands achieved huge and lasting success with music that was driving, intense and aggressive – all classic metal traits – but without ever entering the pantheon of 'classic metal' acts. Aerosmith, for instance, fashioned a Rolling Stones-influenced sound built around R&B and funk guitar motifs rather than 'sledgehammer' riffs.

Metal's early 'classic' era can be seen to stretch from around 1970 to 1976, during which period all the aforementioned British acts produced their best work. During the punk era a different form of aggression rendered the 'old guard' of metal at least temporarily redundant in the eyes of some of its former devotees. Members of Deep Purple and Led Zeppelin were, for reasons of commercial success and longevity, seen as part of the musical 'establishment'. Although metal continued to sell, its critical capital, never very high, was certainly diminished in this period. In the conservative and slow-moving market of the US, early 1970s' hard rock mutated effortlessly into 'stadium rock', and America's own 'take' on punk rock happened later with the 'hardcore' of the likes of Black Flag and, to an extent, within grunge. But as David Handelman argues, metal seemed to suit America's relatively affluent youth more than other musical forms, articulating the fact that they were 'more bored than angry' (quoted in Weinstein 2000: 119).

Punk was never a dominant musical force in terms of mass audiences or the record charts (other than the occasional mixed-media 'spectacular', such as Sex Pistols' *God Save The Queen*), and in the late 1970s metal resurged in Britain, aided by a less flamboyant style that, at times was closely linked to the more rocky tendencies within punk. This gave Motörhead, Saxon and Judas Priest their commercial breakthrough, aided by sections of the UK rock press (particularly titles such as *Zig Zag* and *Sounds*) championing the style under the banner of the new wave of British heavy metal (see MacMillan 2001). In particular, Motörhead's sound was influential upon 1980s' offshoots such as speed metal and thrash metal, the style of which was aptly described within those titles.

From the early 1980s, metal has grown as much through mutation as it has through the opportunities offered by new media such as niche publications, music television (in 1986 MTV launched its first programme dedicated to metal – see Walser 1993: 13) and the commercial video market. Certainly, over the course of time metal's blues and psychedelic roots have diminished in relative importance, to be super-seded by elements of electronica, glam and rap. Indeed, significant elements of the most successful neo-metal in the 1990s (Red Hot Chili Peppers, Living Colour) clearly drew upon a 'hardcore rap' influence (Rage Against the Machine's metal/funk/rap hybrid sound being hugely influential), which itself is still most clearly associated with African-American traditions (see Porter 2002). At the same time, other elements in metal had very little to do with anything other than metal itself, often suffused with a strong undercurrent of European classical or folk influences.

Social and political context

Many commentators and participants have argued that early metal emerges as something of a 'backlash' against the received values and characteristics of the hippie subculture. Despite its virtuoso tendencies, particularly within guitar solos, metal was often resolutely accessible; its key elements were established by the early 1970s and remain largely unchanged. This allowed for large elements within the popular music market to identify with the music and associated subculture. In both Britain and the States metal devotees tended to come from a working-class non-university background. They were, and remain, overwhel-mingly white, and were, until the early 1980s, largely males between the ages of fifteen and twenty-five. They possessed few of the ideological and countercultural beliefs of the hippie subculture, often using the music as an escape or an alternative domain.

In common with other overtly aggressive or macho musical subcultures (such as Oi!), the metal domain is, to a large extent, a male-dominated one. Particularly in the early years of the genre, women inhabited a very marginal position, both as musical participants and as members of the fan base. Walser's work does much to articulate many of the contradictions that result, relating notions of display, homoeroticism and patriarchal control central to the genre. In particular, Walser suggests that

> metal replicates the dominant sexism of contemporary society, but it also allows a kind of free space to be opened up by and for certain women, performers and fans alike. Female fans identify with a kind of power that is usually understood in our culture as male . . . Yet women are able to access this power because it is channelled through a medium, music, that is intangible and difficult to police. (Walser 1993: 131–2)

There have always been female musicians working within the field (in the 1970s Fanny, Birtha, Girlschool). As these band names suggest, a degree of self-consciousness is evident among these musicians. As within some rap, the dilemma for female metal musicians has always been whether they should try and 'out rock' their male counterparts, thus validating their position in the genre, or whether they should deliver an alternative, 'feminine' take on the genre – in the process possibly subverting its mores. In terms of critical acclaim and sales, it is fair to say that no all-female metal act has achieved great success. Instead, other genres allied to metal in terms of their sonic and timbral characteristics, such as punk and post-punk forms (riot grrrl and queercore), and more recent 'alternative' rock forms have proven to be a more fertile terrain for female musicians.

Female role models such as Chrissie Hynde, Janis Joplin, Patti Smith (Patricia Lee Smith) and Joan Jett have had a great impact upon the likes of Tanya Donelly of the band Belly, Kim Gordon of Sonic Youth and D'Arcy Wretzky-Brown of Smashing Pumpkins, as well as bands such as Hole, L7, Babes in Toyland, Bikini Kill and Huggy Bear. However, the generic connections between these examples and metal are few. 'Quintessential metal' has been, and continues to be, quintessentially male. Women's roles in this more 'purist' field exist as the inspiration for lyrical subject matter, or more recently as fans.

Unlike the 1970s, today's metal fan base is more evenly divided in terms of gender. Subgenres of metal such as stadium rock or glam metal have long appealed to both sexes. The demographic has also broadened, with the appeal of a band such as The Darkness, whose sound is an updated version of acts such as Queen and Thin Lizzy, broad enough to grant them both credibility in the specialist press and frequent appearances on chart shows and mainstream television.

Because of the longevity of the genre, it is not possible to talk of a specific set of associated political circumstances. Certainly, metal emerged in opposition to the hippie subculture and with few overtly political trappings. Alice Cooper saw its historical emergence at the very end of the 'love decade' as deeply symbolic, and described the music as a kind of proletarian, 'junk food' antidote to the values of the Woodstock generation, adding that the band were more interested in comic books and drinking beer than spiritual pursuits.

> We were really the epitome of the American culture-less society . . . instead of being dopers we all drank beer . . . we were All-American! . . . we were the dagger in the heart of the love generation . . . we were right at the end of peace and love and all of a sudden was this shiny new horrible monster [sic]. (Quoted in Conefrey 1996)

It would be wrong to entirely identify metal and its followers as merely escapist and hedonistic. Metal did deal with issues, social conditions and particularly individual states of mind, but often in a fatalistic and pessimistic manner that saw no solution or one that eschewed direct political action. In this, it did make very relevant connections to those lacking political or cultural capital – the young, the working class, the unconventional, the lonely. In addition, metal offered an alternative identity to many ostensibly 'sensible' members of society who sought some kind of release or fulfilment within its social codes. There has always been a 'carnivalesque' dimension within metal. This dimension is not contained by any historical period or set of social circumstances, and may partly account for the genre's longevity.

The musical texts

In this section we will attempt to provide an overview of metal, with particular reference to a small number of tracks exhibiting considerable diversity in historical, musical and cultural terms. In common with prog, metal was an album form rather than one built upon singles or tracks. However, these examples do allow for an analytical extrapolation of the bands under scrutiny, and the genre as a whole, without ever being completely archetypal.

Classic Metal

BLACK SABBATH (1971) *AFTER FOREVER*
This track, from Sabbath's third album, *Master Of Reality*, demonstrates both the indebtedness of metal to prior musical models, but also its singularity of intent and affect. The track shares with prog and psyche-delia a structure built upon chain-link sections, rather than the more organic flow of the pop model, although some pop conventions do remain. The track has no chorus, with a guitar-led major key instrumental section effectively replacing the 'resolution' of a vocal/harmony song. However, there is a clear B section, or middle eight (although not eight-bar length), built upon key changes and a rhythmic shift that is more germane within pop song structures as a whole.

The track commences with a fade-in section consisting of a backwards tape-loop reminiscent of psychedelic production, before the chorus substitute section begins, acting as a bright and cheery (G major) mood-lightener unusual in metal. This section then segues into a much more menacing four-chord descending riff over which the first verse is sung. In classic metal style, the vocal melody is seemingly adapted to the more important element – the guitar-led riff, at least two guitars playing almost identically, reinforced by the bass following an octave below – rather than the riff or chords providing a backing to the melody. This is one of the key sonic signifiers of metal. At 1 : 04 the chorus section returns (with slight phasing, another classic psychedelic device), followed by a second verse. At 1 : 55 the B section commences, itself broken into two parts but slower than the main body of the song and with two key changes encouraging a higher vocal melody. The complexity of the shifts between the sections of this track are more similar to the techniques and engendered moods of prog.

After another chorus section and a third verse there follows a different B section at 3 : 26 that incorporates a guitar solo that is relatively clean sounding and not backed by a bank of rhythm guitars. It closely resembles the blues rock style of the late 1960s, although the skilful panning of the solo, gradually speeding up as the solo climaxes, is most typical of psychedelic rock. After a fourth chorus-and-verse section, the track runs out on a final chorus pattern, with a sustained G chord being reinforced by a fast-repeating high-G note on the bass, leading to the same looped section heard at the beginning of the track. At 5 : 27 the track is rock rather than pop length, but it is the complexity and variation of engendered moods with heavier, 'doomy' sections set against atypical 'jolly' sections that give the track its structural interest. At the same time, such tracks argue against the assumption that metal is monolithic in terms of structure or timbre. Equally, the lyrics, for the most part, argue for the moral ascendancy of religious faith over evil. Sabbath and their ilk were often dismissed as 'devil worshippers'. In actual fact, their lyrics, as a corpus, often unambiguously suggest the opposite view.

Virtuoso metal

VAN HALEN (1978) *ERUPTION*
At 1 : 45 this largely solo guitar piece signalled a seismic shift for metal, showcasing the remarkable dexterity and sheer speed of guitarist Eddie van Halen on the band's debut album. After a minimal rhythm backing against which van Halen initially establishes his 'rock god' credentials, the backing track fades out at around twenty-two seconds, leaving just one solo instrument to carry the sonic load. For the next eighty seconds we are treated to a solo fashioned without extraneous effects. Fast flurries of notes and rapid fretboard runs are interspersed with some slow slurs that also utilise the tremolo arm to great effect. Early on in the solo the style is very similar to the blues-based solo style of Hendrix on tracks such as *Voodoo Chile*. From around fifty seconds the style shifts to a more

European orchestral mode ('hyper-baroque'), carrying echoes of composers such as Bach and Scarlatti. Perhaps the most remarkable section in terms of its technical brilliance happens between 0 : 58 and 1 : 25, where van Halen makes great use of 'tapping', wherein a high amount of distorted 'gain' allows for rapid notes to be achieved without plucking or picking with the right hand (for a right-handed player). Instead, arpeggiated patterns are fashioned by merely tapping strings against the fretboard.

Eruption carries the virtuosity of both the blues-based players such as Hendrix and Jimmy Page and the hyper-baroque style of Deep Purple's Richie Blackmore to a new level of dexterity and complexity, and allows for a whole slew of similarly endowed guitarists (Yngwie Malmsteen, Joe Satriani, Steve Vai) to fashion successful careers. However, dexterity and rapid-fire brilliance became an end rather than a means in many cases, and merely allowed metal's detractors another avenue for their dismissal.

European metal

RAMMSTEIN (2002) *ICH WILL*

Rammstein, long popular in their homeland of Germany, broke through internationally with their 2002 album *Mutter*, accompanied by some inventive videos given heavy rotation on dedicated metal channels such as *Kerrang!* Some elements of the band's sound connect more closely with thrash metal (gothic or European overtones, minor key or folk/modal riffs and chord progressions, growling or guttural vocal styles) as opposed to the more 'crossover-friendly' stadium metal built upon harmony vocals and photogenic men-in-tights. However, without the high tempi and relentless, rapid riffing of thrash, tracks such as *Ich Will* inhabit a different terrain to both stadium and thrash modes of metal.

The key to Rammstein's sound is the often-understated incorporation of elements and timbres eccentric to blues-rock-influenced metal. On this track these elements consist of choral and solo (female) vocals more typical of opera or religious works, ethereal synth-string sounds and also the sine wave type of sequencer pattern most commonly associated with European dance forms such as techno or trance. These elements are brought into close contact with the riffs, the basic 4 : 4 rock beat and the growling, often spoken-word style of the singing. The band seem to exploit linguistically, historically and culturally the connotations that the German tongue and identity imbues. On other tracks they use elements such as sirens and marching feet. The vocals often resemble military orders, at least to our ears. This places the sound within the European (more specifically North or Anglo-Nordic rather than Latin or Hispanic) terrain, with almost all elements acting to ignore or eschew North American or African-American modes of expression and affect. Interestingly, totally or largely American bands such as Anthrax and early Metallica only hold a tenuous link to their 'home idioms', acting to define various forms of metal as at least partially grounded in the European folk/classical/pop traditions.

Fusion metal

RAGE AGAINST THE MACHINE (1992) *BULLET IN THE HEAD*

As previously indicated, this band were a key bridging point for hitherto diverse genres such as funk, rap and metal, and did much to influence the subsequent subgenre of nu metal that has proven to be one of the biggest worldwide commercial successes over the most recent period. On tracks such as *Bullet In The Head*, the band achieve what many would have thought impossible, by fusing the polemical, spoken-word delivery of rap associated with Ice-T and Public Enemy with the staccato funk of the likes of James Brown, and the distorted riffing of metal acts such as Black Sabbath. These diverse generic elements and textures allow for a track that connotes political engagement and anger, yet is partially constrained by the tension of funk. Early on in the track, during the verse section, this tension is manifested through the use of gaps and dynamics, with the bass playing slap-style, while the guitar eschews riffs for 'wah-wah chops' and atonal squeals. This is then released during the choruses by the temporary resolution of powerchords before again reverting to a funkier terrain. Towards the end of the track, our 'patience' is rewarded when we are offered a full-blown metal 'rock-out' in the conclusion of this track, which breaks out of its deliberately paced funk rhythm to double the beats per minute until the track's atonal powerchord finale. This structural and sonic template (restrained, funky elements interspersed with fuller and more noisy sections) has proven hugely influential, being widely employed by Nirvana in particular, and essentially providing us with the model for much contemporary or nu metal.

Visual aesthetic

The fans

Dress codes within metal communities developed away from the more showy and androgynous tendencies within late-1960s 'alternative' styles towards the more down-to-earth denim and long hair mode during the 1970s. This was often augmented by materials associated with 'macho' lifestyles, particularly the 'biker' or 'Hell's Angel' look of leather jackets, studded belts and sleeveless denim jackets covered in patches. Religious iconography, such as large crucifixes, was widespread. Unlike punk, where fans often dressed more flamboyantly than the musicians, within metal, the fans were often relatively nondescript in comparison to performers, many of whom wore their hair extremely long, and whose dress and stage manner often harked back to Eastern/hippie styles, or bordered on the androgynous (see Robert Plant, David Lee Roth of Van Halen or Aerosmith's Steven Tyler, for example). As Blake argues, this provides metal with a representative terrain that makes great use of the 'Orpheus problem':

> Orpheus must display supreme musicianship, including the public display of emotion. This outpouring, however, will destabilise his masculinity. HM, there-fore, for all its patriarchal posturing, is threatened; a threat often underlined/self-parodied by the dress and stage behaviour of the performers, in which gender codes are routinely mixed. (Blake 1997: 138)

Not only did gender tension exist as the result of such representation/textual dichotomies, but also much humour, both unwitting and ironic, resulted. In fact, metal was, and remains, one of the few popular music genres to generate humour, often through the medium of video.

After the reappraisal of metal in the post-new wave of british heavy metal era, metal fans' dress codes shifted, with drainpipe jeans and sneakers replacing the flares and platforms of the early 1970s, although long hair remained *de rigueur*. During the early 1980s a goth sensibility entered the subculture, mirroring the music and image of bands such as The Cult and Killing Joke, who formed a bridge between gothic punk and metal. At this point the importance of the colour black was established. Twenty years later, metal audiences still confirm the suspicion that 'metal is black', at least sartorially (and frequently musically, in affective terms).

At the same time that goth was making an impact upon dress codes, many bands working within what has been termed 'lite metal' adopted a more androgynous or glam persona. Central to bands such as Def Leppard, Poison and Bon Jovi was figure-hugging spandex and elabo-rately coiffured 'big hair' that gave the subgenre the often-used epithet 'poodle rock'. It was this visual shift, added to the move towards romantic narratives and less exaggerated vocal styles, which aided metal's overall move into the musical mainstream (see Weinstein 2000: 46).

Over the last decade, with the visual impact of hip-hop, grunge and punk all proving influential, metal dress codes have mutated. Most recently, popular music and its subcultural tribes have become more divided, with a variation of the historical binary opposition between 'rock' and 'pop' being reactivated. But certainly, many metal concertgoers in the early twenty-first century do closely resemble goths, updated punks or rap fans in some respects. The perennial baggy, black T-shirt replete with suitable band name and logo has been in fashion in metal almost to the point of timelessness.

More recently, the importance of 'extreme sports' upon musical styles and dress codes should not be underestimated, with the baggy 'industrial' and three-quarter-length shorts 'chic' of skateboarding, rollerblading and mountain biking being widespread, even global. Hair can be long and 'classic metal', or spiky and dyed or bleached 'Mohican-style'. Footwear can resemble 'body armour' or can be 'name brand trainer', although dark colours usually predominate (among British metal fans, white trainers are a clear style indicator of a 'scally' or 'casual' – a chart or dance music fan).

Acts such as American nu-metallers Linkin Park more closely resemble rap crews than 'metalheads' in their dress, with classic signifiers of rap such as baseball caps worn backwards symbolising the impact of the subculture and lifestyle. This was also clearly indicated in the title of their hugely successful album *Hybrid Theory*. Metal has achieved the great sonic and sartorial balancing act by combining the familiar and the archetypal with the developmental and the hybridised to long-lasting effect.

Album covers/artwork

Metal usually exhibits a consistent, if historically shifting homology across different elements. The look of the fans seems to intrinsically match the names of the bands, the sound of the music and the subject matter of the lyrics. Equally, visual iconography from the micro (typefaces) right through to the macro (concert settings, videos) is often extremely consistent and, within its 'alternative' parameters, largely standardised.

As Weinstein argues, regular typefaces or logo letterings are unsuitable for metal, particularly the more 'purist' forms, as they connote 'neutrality, efficiency, and order, all of which are antithetical . . . typefaces are more elaborate . . . some resemble runic, teutonic lettering. Others have a menacing, armor-breaking mace or sawtooth appearance' (Weinstein 2000: 28). This visual component is reinforced by many band names – Poison, Megadeth, Anthrax, Manowar, Slayer, etc.

Album cover art is diverse but within clearly defined limits. Dark fantasy of the 'dungeons and dragons' variety and gothic scenarios are widespread. Exaggerated macho archetypes such as warriors, devils or living skeletons are similarly legion.

As we have argued, metal's consistency allows for many elements within the music and lifestyle to transcend its immediate circumstances. The genre can be seen, to an extent, as a set of 'transcendental signifiers' – sign systems that are relatively unchanging yet welcoming to successive generations of fans who, paradoxically, find comfort and subcultural stability in its 'violatory' dimensions.

Subsequent generic developments

Because of metal's longevity, no musical form can be said to have superseded it in the historical sense, but during the course of the last three decades, many other genres have been influenced by it. Principal among these have been genres such as punk, 'industrial', funk, rap and various extreme forms of dance such as techno and jungle.

Punk, for all its revolutionary rhetoric, was often little more than basic hard rock. A comparison between the backing tracks of The Damned's *Love Song* and Motörhead's *Ace Of Spades* bears out this judgement. The chief distinction often lies in the vocal style. Without Lydon's distinctive voice, Sex Pistols tracks such as *Anarchy In The UK* and *Bodies* do border on metal, both in the prevalence of riffs and particularly during the guitar solo sections. Recent reunion live concerts by the Sex Pistols have shifted the balance even further towards the metal sonic template. Other punk acts such as The Saints and The Vibrators always exhibited similar tendencies. The aforementioned gothic punk acts operated in a parallel sonic terrain, but with an added vocal connection through subject matter, if not through vocal timbre. Hugely influential 'post-punk' acts such as Joy Division fashioned soundscapes influenced by punk, but strongly augmented by timbral textures, sound effects and white noise reminiscent of the avant-garde. In addition, the metallic riffs central to tracks such as *Dead Souls* and *Interzone* give them a further visceral dimension akin to metal. A 1980s' development known as 'industrial' (Ministry, Test Department, Einsturzender Neubauten) took experimental elements to extremes, employing the sheer physical assault of metal but not couched in the traditional song framework. This factor influenced the comparative and continuing marginality of this kind of music/noise.

Similarly atonal, acts such as the Gang of Four and the Pop Group did use guitar distortion and riffs as linking components connecting the disparate genres of punk and funk. Within funk itself, the 1980s saw performers such as Prince achieving huge crossover success by combining the accessibility of funk with that of guitar-based, neo-metal 'stadium rock' on albums such as *Purple Rain*, the second-biggest-selling album in the US during that decade. The biggest-selling album in the same period was Michael Jackson's *Thriller*, which replaced earlier albums' smooth disco-influenced textures with the distortion and virtuosity of Eddie van Halen's guitar on tracks such as *Beat It*.

Rap, from its early beginnings in disco, soul and funk, shifted into a more aggressive terrain during the 1980s with the incorporation of sampled elements such as white noise, distorted guitar riffs and drum loops. Beastie Boys' tracks such as *Fight For Your Right To Party* and *Rhymin' And Stealin'* built upon samples of the classic metal drum sound of Led Zeppelin's John Bonham are self-explanatory. Other rappers such as Ice-T went as far as to form a live 'band-within-a-band' known as Body Count, whose sound was literally metal topped by rap vocals. The Red Hot Chili Peppers have fashioned a long career from much the same sonic blueprint while adding funk-style slap bass and rock star lifestyle excess to the mix.

In the early 1990s, Rage Against The Machine emerged with a sound that seemed to draw equally upon the legacy of Black Sabbath, James Brown and Public Enemy. Their sound had the driving intensity and riffs of metal, the rhythmic groove of funk and the incendiary politicised lyrics of reality rap (see Chapter 9). Rather than alienating the followers of all three genres, they managed to unify them, appearing at such events as Lollapalooza, an 'alternative' annual festival. While metal garnered much greater critical capital as the result of such events, its influence was not always acknowledged. Members of Nirvana, the leading exponents of grunge in the same period, invariably distanced themselves from any links with metal, despite some sonic, subcultural and timbral evidence to the contrary. Weinstein stated openly that 'Grunge was not metal', while quoting Nirvana's Chris (*sic*) Novoselic who offered that 'we're heavy, but we're not heavy metal . . . Metal's searching for an identity because it's exhausted itself, so they're going to latch on to us' (quoted in Weinstein 2000: 278). Of course, drawing lines of generic distinctions is not an objective exercise, and we would disagree with Weinstein and Novoselic, arguing that grunge is a subgenre within metal not distinct enough to deserve its own separate genre heading. In addition, rather than metal exhausting itself in the early 1990s, it was more a case that the grunge offshoot of metal revitalised the whole genre, although in terms of the recent nu-metal form, the Rage against The Machine sound has, arguably, had at least as much impact upon metal as the Nirvana template.

As a final example of the impact of metal (at least, in terms of timbre and attitude, if not subculturally) upon other forms, what we have termed 'extreme' dance subgenres such as techno, drill 'n' bass and techstep should be mentioned (see Chapter 9). As well as possessing the 'nosebleed' tempi of speed/thrash metal, such forms commonly dealt with moods and topics well established in metal. Their relentlessly driving and aggressive sonic tendencies also encouraged physical responses among the largely male followers that closely resembled the 'mosh-pit' antics of metal concertgoers. The fact that such timbres were largely the result of samples and distortion rather than guitars should not detract from the affective similarities (this tendency in dance is further explored in Chapter 11).

Recommended reading

Arnett, J. (1996) *Metalheads: Heavy Metal Music and Adolescent Alienation*. Boulder, CO: Westview.

Blake, A. (1997) *The Land without Music: An Archaeology of Sound in Britain*. Manchester: Manchester University Press.

Christie, I. (2003) *Sound of the Beast: The Complete Headbanging History of Heavy Metal*. London: HarperEntertainment.

Davis, S. (1985) *Hammer of the Gods: The Led Zeppelin Saga*. New York: William Morrow.

Frith, S. and McRobbie, A. (2000) 'Rock and Sexuality,' in Frith, S. and Goodwin, A. (eds) *On Record: Rock, Pop and the Written Word*. London: Routledge.

McIver, J. (2000) *Extreme Metal*. London: Omnibus.

MacMillan, M. (2001) *The New Wave of British Heavy Metal Encyclopedia*. Berlin: Verlag Jeske.

Moore, A. (1993) *Rock: The Primary Text*. Buckingham: Open University Press.

Moynihan, M. and Soderlind, D. (1998) *Lords of Chaos: The Bloody Rise of the Satanic Metal Underground*. Los Angeles: Feral House.

Murray, C.-S. (1989) *Crosstown Traffic: Jimi Hendrix and Post-war Pop*. London: Faber & Faber.

Porter, D. (2002) *Rapcore: The Nu-Metal Rap Fusion*. London: Plexus.

Walser, R. (1993) *Running with the Devil: Power, Gender and Madness in Heavy Metal Music*. Hanover, NY: Wesleyan University Press.

Weinstein, D. (2000) *Heavy Metal: The Music and Its Culture*. Cambridge, MA: Da Capo Press.

Recommended music

Antecedents

Blue Cheer (1968) *Vincebus Eruptum*. Polygram.
Jeff Beck Group (1968) *Truth*. Premier/EMI.
Cream (1968) *Wheels Of Fire*. Polydor.

Fleetwood Mac (1995) *Live At The BBC*. Essential.
King Crimson (1969) *In The Court Of The Crimson King*. Island.
Love Sculpture (1999) *Forms And Feelings* [contains *Sabre Dance*, 1968]. EMI.
Steppenwolf (1968) *Steppenwolf II*. Beat Goes On.
The Stooges (1969) *The Stooges*. Elektra.
The Yardbirds (2002) *The Yardbirds Story*. Charly/Snapper.

Generic texts

Black Sabbath (1971) *Master Of Reality*. Vertigo.
Bon Jovi (1986) *Slippery When Wet*. Vertigo.
Deep Purple (1971) *Machine Head*. Harvest.
Def Leppard (1983) *Pyromania*. Bludgeon Riffola.
Guns 'n' Roses (1987) *Appetite for Destruction*. Geffen.
Iron Maiden (2002) *Eddie's Archive*. Sony.
Kiss (1975) *Kiss Alive*. Casablanca.
Led Zeppelin (1971) *Led Zeppelin* [also known as *4*, *ZOSO*, or *Four Symbols*].
   Atlantic.
Limp Bizkit (2000) *Chocolate Starfish And The Hot Dog Flavored Water*.
   Interscope.
Linkin Park (2000) *Hybrid Theory*. Warner.
Metallica (1988) *And Justice For All*. Vertigo.
Motörhead (1981) *No Sleep 'til Hammersmith*. Metal-Is.
Nirvana (1991) *Nevermind*. Geffen.
Rammstein (2001) *Mutter*. Universal.
Sepultura (1993) *Chaos AD*. Roadrunner.
Van Halen (1978) *Van Halen*. Warner.

CHAPTER 9

Rap: the word, rhythm and rhyme

An overview of the genre

The history of rap music is somewhat clearer than the history of many of the other genres discussed in this book. The aim of this section is therefore to present a simple chronological description of the key moments and texts in the development of rap music from its inception to the present day. The following section on 'roots and antecedents' will examine the more complex 'rhizome' of the diasporic traditions that rap drew upon and subsequently expanded, while the current state of rap music will be examined in the section entitled 'musical texts'.

Rap's story begins in the early 1970s with street parties in the Bronx and Harlem, inner-city areas of New York City.[1] At these 'block parties', mobile soundsystems supplied the music, with DJs such as DJ Kool Herc (Clive Campbell)[2] beginning to employ two record decks in order to mix records together. Of relevance is the fact that Campbell was a Jamaican immigrant, well schooled in the tradition of the Jamaican soundsystem, reggae deejay and 'selector'. Drawing upon the reggae soundsystem tradition, Campbell developed the use of two turntables and an audio mixer not merely to mix seamlessly two different records together,[3] but also to cut between two copies of the same record. The manual dexterity of Herc and other DJs such as Afrika Bambaataa meant that they could take a few seconds of a specific record and build several minutes of rhythm from it, playing and replaying the eight or sixteen-bar drum breaks found on specific soul or funk records. These drum breaks, subsequently termed breakbeats, formed the central musical component of rap music from this point until the present day, and have also come to dominate other genres such as jungle.

Some of the musical sources used by DJ Kool Herc, and rap music more generally, are familiar and unsurprising, others are more esoteric. In the former category is the most sampled artist in rap, James Brown, with

Herc being particularly well known for his use of the drum break from Brown's track *Give It Up Or Turnit A Loose*.[4] In the latter category is the influence of the early British beat combo The Shadows. The Shadows were an instrumental group whose first number one hit was *Apache*, the refrain from which can be heard on a number of rap tracks throughout the 1970s, 1980s and 1990s (generally sampled from the Incredible Bongo Band's cover version of the track). The hip-hop journalist and commentator Nelson George also cites other important early breakbeats, including Jimmy Castor's *It's Only Just Begun*, James Brown's *Sex Machine*, Baby Huey and the Babysitters' *Listen To Me*, Mandrill's *Fencewalk* and the Average White Band's *Pick Up The Pieces* (George 1998: 17).

Alongside the development of 'turntablism', we see the concurrent development of the rap, the lyrical accompaniment to the breakbeat. At the street parties of the 1970s an MC (Master of Ceremonies), or the DJ himself, provided rhythmically syncopated spoken vocals that matched the turntablist's vinyl manipulation. While Herc simply talked over his records, his partner Coke La Rock developed a way of reciting poetry and rhyming catchphrases in a particularly syncopated yet rhythmic style. It is here that we see rap music developing as a mixture of looped breakbeats and a modern take on the black 'vernacular' or oral tradition. Before long this potent combination was being taken from the streets of New York into recording studios, and by 1979 the nascent rap scene saw its first global hit with the Sugarhill Gang's *Rapper's Delight* (see Light 1999: 23–34).

The 1970s saw rapping combine with turntablism, graffiti art and breakdancing (literally 'dancing to breaks') to form the four central pillars of hip-hop culture, avidly consumed by the black and Hispanic denizens of New York. However, the arrival of digital technologies in music production meant that in the early 1980s the drum machine, and in the late 1980s the sampler, began to accompany and in many case replace the role of the DJ and band in the production of recorded rap music. Without sampling technology, the Sugarhill Band employed a bass player to replicate the bassline of Chic's *Good Times*, which formed an essential part of the rhythm on *Rapper's Delight*.[5] By the late 1980s, this process was completed more easily by a sampler, with the added bonus that a sampler did not need to be paid. A similar process occurred with DJing, whereby samplers could more easily loop a breakbeat than a DJ, or where a drum machine could be used to produce a newly programmed breakbeat. The use of such technology allowed Run-DMC to adopt a minimalist electronic aesthetic. For example, Run-DMC's first single, 1983's *It's Like That*, featured a B-side entitled *Sucker MCs* that contained nothing more than a MC and drum machine. In seeming opposition to this pared-down dualism, early pioneer Afrika Bambaataa had developed a far more expansive sound on the 1982 single and album entitled *Planet Rock*, which sampled electronic pioneers Kraftwerk, melding a European modernist aesthetic to the developing Afrocentricism of rap.

Along with the development of new percussive tools, the 1980s saw a dramatic shift in the central lyrical component of rap music. Whereas the raps of the 1970s featured braggadocio writ large, rapping in the 1980s shifted towards a mode of social and political commentary. This shift was first signalled by the success of Grandmaster Flash and the Furious Five's international 1982 hit *The Message*. While Grandmaster Flash is cited as a key figure in the development of the technical side of DJ mixing (see Ogg with Upshall 1999: 27), his other achievement was to allow rap to jettison its party image in order to reforge itself as a music of social commentary and explicit political intent. This movement reached its apotheosis in the late 1980s and early 1990s with the music of Public Enemy, whose complex sonic experiments were complemented by an aggressive and uncompromising lyrical style that prefaced resistance to the racism of mainstream white society, while also featuring separatist polemics inspired by both the Black Panthers and Elijah Mohammed's 'Nation of Islam' organisation.

In the 1990s this notion of rap as the radical voice of America's black community was disrupted by the arrival of so-called 'gangsta rap', which featured the violent and frequently misogynist fantasies of its flamboyant

Flavor Flav and Chuck D (Public Enemy) make some noize with Ice-T.

lyricists. Mirroring this structural reversal from political polemic to criminal fantasy and reportage was a shift in the core production site of rap music from America's north-east coast (New York) to its south-west coast of California (Los Angeles). Key 'playas' within this genre included NWA (an abbreviation of the guaranteed-to-be-controversial moniker 'Niggers With Attitude') and Ice-T, whose most controversial track *Cop Killer* was not even a rap track but was instead a rock track featuring a rap vocal, recorded and released by his heavy metal band Body Count.[6]

The continuation of an east versus west rivalry into the mid-1990s led to two high-profile casualties. 2 Pac (Tupac Shakur) from California's Death Row Records and the Notorious B.I.G. (Christopher Wallace) from New York's Bad Boy Records were both shot as the result of a so-called hip-hop feud, and at the time of writing their murders remain unsolved amid allegations of police corruption. By the end of the 1990s sales of gangsta rap had declined amid the shock of these two killings, and under the joint assault of major record corporations, moral spokespeople and a record-buying public keen to listen to something new (see Light 1999).

For some, this quest for something new led them to the white Detroit rapper Eminem (Marshall Mathers III). Eminem's verbal assaults are lyrically complex, and exquisitely delivered, and offensive in the extreme. As such, Mathers has taken the shocking core of gangsta rap and melded it with a delivery that is quintessentially rap, yet is as distinctive as any other singer in the world. Tricia Rose suggests that 'rap music is a black cultural expression that prioritises black voices from the margins of an urban America', and goes on to suggest that 'rap's stories continue to articulate the shifting terms of black marginality in contemporary American culture' (Rose 1994: 2–3). The fact that Eminem's music articulates the experience of a white American underclass, and the fact that Eminem has done this without attempting to ideologically recuperate black cultural resistance, questions this essentialism. This is not to deny the importance of rap for African-Americans, and conversely, this is not to deny the importance of African-American people in the development of rap. Rather what this emphasises is the truly global and inclusive nature of twenty-first-century hip-hop culture.[7]

Historical roots and antecedents

African diasporic traditions

Rose suggests that 'hip hop is propelled by Afro-diasporic traditions' (Rose 1994: 25). These traditions consist of two broad forms, the oral tradition and African folk music. Both these forms interact with American musical traditions due to the history of slavery and the subsequent settlement of Africans within the Americas. African languages and verbal modes of communication have a special importance within the African diaspora as they were a form of communication unknown to British and American slave owners, and were used by slaves to communicate among themselves. As we saw in Chapter 6, this led to certain slave owners banning the use of African languages by slaves, insisting upon the use of the slave owners' language. Slaves then turned to drumming, in particular the 'talking drum', as a way of passing secret messages between themselves, until drumming was itself banned. From this point onwards, Afrocentric forms of speech and African rhythms were seen to be synonymous with protest and African-American articulations of discontent in American society. Rap continues this process, with its 'use of cloaked speech and disguised cultural codes' (Rose 1994: 100). Rap often comments on and challenges inequalities in the societies in which both producers and consumers are situated. However, rap is not an entirely progressive force for it often reinforces social divisions, such as gender divisions, and frequently offers offensive and stereotypical representations of homosexuality, femininity and gender relations.

Blues

The blues was a form of music that allowed blacks in the rural southern states of America to articulate the experiences of endemic racism, industrialisation and urbanisation (see Baker 1984). Of particular importance to rap is the period during which the blues was 'electrified' using electric bass guitars, lead guitars and amplification equipment. The rawness, aggression and sheer volume of electric blues as played by Muddy Waters (McKinley Morganfield) and Chuck Berry was a major influence on the subsequent development of both rock 'n' roll and rap music.

Jazz

David Toop suggests that bebop jazz formed an essential antecedent for rap. In the 1930s and 1940s bandleaders employed MCs to introduce individual compositions and to form a link between the band and audience. These MCs began to be known for their 'jive talking' and rhyming couplets, while certain MCs such as Slim Gaillard interpreted jazz standards using a form of syncopated nonsense verse that he named 'vout'. Equally, bandleaders such as Cab Calloway (Cabell Calloway III) would conduct and sing at the same time, incorporating 'scat', a use of the voice as a rhythmic device, into their routines. Bandleaders such as Calloway and MCs such as Eddie Jefferson went on to influence those DJs who were at the forefront of the postwar expansion in American radio. Jive talk, scat and street slang began to seem like a natural accompaniment to rhyming DJ patter. With Toop quoting Dr Hep Cat's (Laveda Durst) couplet 'if you want to hip to the tip and bop to the top, you get some mad threads that just won't stop' (Toop 2000: 38), it is clear that radio DJs such as Daddy-O Daylie (Holmes Daylie) and Dr Hep Cat greatly influenced rapping.

Reggae

Many of the formal characteristics of the production and distribution of rap music can be found in reggae in Jamaica in the late 1960s. During this time, Jamaican record producers were producing remixed bass and rhythm tracks with few vocals ('dub plates') for playing on outdoor soundsystems that consisted of a bank of speakers, amplification equipment and twin record decks. In particular, dub plates were designed to be accompanied by the reggae equivalent of the rap MC, namely the deejay. Due to the popularity of soundsystem deejays, producers began to record deejay records, which featured the deejay's distinctive syncopated and rhythmic 'toasting'. This development pre-dates New York rap by several years. Some suggest that it is the arrival of Kool Herc from Jamaica, and Herc's subsequent immersion in New York street music, that led to the adaptation of the deejay and DJ format to form rap, only with soul and funk breakbeats forming the rhythm rather than the syncopated upbeats of rocksteady and reggae.

Soul

While rap's ideological or discursive influences are drawn from a wide range of music genres, the musical building blocks of the rap soundtrack, namely breakbeats, are more often than not drawn from soul music. As outlined in the introductory section of this chapter, the 'middle eights' of soul records were used by 1970s' DJs to produce a seamless mix of rhythm. What is perhaps less well known is the influence of soul vocals on rapping. Drawing influence from gospel and church spirituals, soul relied upon the oratory power of the vocalist to get its lyrical message across. In particular, Toop points to the role of 'soul rap' and gospel storytellers as predecessors of rapping, with The Soul Stirrers and Laura Lee employing a vocal style that is half-spoken and half-sung (Toop 1999: 47–53).

Social and political context

As Rose points out, rap music is the result of the interaction between the historical musical and political antecedents outlined above and the specificities of New York life in the 1970s (Rose 1994: 21–61). As such, it can be stated that the development of rap music from the 1980s until the present day is at least partly determined by the way in which the rap form developed in New York has been adapted and nurtured by African-Americans, white Americans and other ethnic groups throughout the world. This worldwide adaptation and nurturing was completed within an increasingly globalised music industry, yet the 'use' of rap music by different global groups has meant that it retains some of the localised specificities inherent in its original form. This will be dealt with in the section on 'subsequent developments' below.

De-industrialisation, globalisation and the rise of the New Right

In many respects, the shift from soul to rap mirrors the shift from the full employment and rising wages of postwar America to the globalised, de-industrialised, low pay, post-Fordist economy that began to emerge from the mid-1970s onwards. If the Fordist production methods of the great Detroit record label Motown embodied much of the ethos of the earlier epoch, the complicated relationships between rap music and a globalised record industry of the post-1970s' period are symptomatic of the latter post-Fordist conjuncture.

As in many European countries, the United States of the 1970s experienced the turbulent throes of globalisation, an economic recession partially related to the rising price of oil, and a shift away from welfare-state-oriented social policies towards a form of free-market economics that would soon become known as 'Reaganism'. In addition, the United States, like Britain, saw a general shift away from Fordist production towards a post-Fordist economy dominated by the service and communication industries. These political and economic shifts led to a decline in the availability and quality of employment, welfare benefits and social housing and an increased division between rich and poor. In New York, African-Americans were more likely to be employed in the newly emerging low-pay service sector than whites. African-Americans were also twice as likely to be unemployed as white Americans (Carroll 1990: 48). The gradual decline in welfare support and social housing, combined with policing widely seen as racist, meant that the African-American experience in New York was doubly oppressive.

Added to this fateful brew was a massive increase in the availability of heroin in the 1970s and crack cocaine in the 1980s and 1990s. While conspiracy theories abound as to the reasons for the sudden influx of these two drugs (many blame the CIA and other state agencies for encouraging or actually controlling the trade), the effects on a black underclass were deleterious, although a small minority within inner-city populations profited from increased drug use (George 1998: 34–41). This growth in drug use, drug crime and a consequent increase in incarcerated African-American males is intimately connected to the rise of rap music that reflects upon the negative effects of drug use (for example, Grandmaster Flash and the Furious Five's 1983 epic *White Lines*). Equally, some of the gangsta rap of the 1990s hyped the role of the black gangster, a glorification that was as intensely appealing to suburban whites as it was to certain urban African-Americans. Nelson George puts it baldly:

> Gangsta rap is a by-product of the crack explosion . . . suspicion of women, loyalty to the crew, adoption of a stone face in confronting the world, hatred of authority – all major themes of gangsta rap – owe their presence in lyrics and impact on audiences to the large number of African-American men incarcerated in the '90s. (George 1998: 42–4)

Hip-hop culture rose out of, and was directly determined by, the experience of African-American New Yorkers living amid these economic and political changes. A general philosophical shift towards individualism (which was already prevalent in mainstream American society) was contested by hip-hop's articulation of new forms of community and new forms of occupying the urban space bequeathed to African-Americans. George Lipsitz describes this process well with his comments on Afrika Bambaataa and his 'Zulu Nation' community organisation: 'Hemmed in by urban renewal, crime and police surveillance, and silenced by neglect from the culture industry, the school system, and city government, they found a way to declare themselves through music' (Lipsitz 1994: 26).

The musical texts

The raps

In *Rap Music and the Poetics of Identity*, Adam Krims suggests that there are three distinct modes of rapping. The 'flows' or rhythmed lyrics of the rapper (also known as an MC)[8] can be characterised as 'sung', 'percussion effusive' or 'speech effusive' (Krims 2000). Within 'sung' flows, rhythm and rhyme are used in a similar manner to rock and pop music, featuring rhythmic repetition, on-beat accents, regular on-beat pauses and couplet groupings. This style is epitomised by Grandmaster Flash and the Furious Five and the Beastie Boys. Within percussion-effusive and speech-effusive rapping there is a disruption of, and an extension beyond, the metre boundaries of the rhythm track, and an emphasis on staggered syntax, subdivision of beats, repeated off-beat accents, or any other way of breaking up and disrupting the 4 : 4 time of the rhythm track. Rap tracks that employ these styles have a polyrhythmic complexity not often found within other forms of popular music. Within the percussion-effusive style, a rapper uses his or her mouth as a percussion instrument. An extreme use of this is in 'human beat boxes', but in general, this style is used to emphasise 'counter-metric gestures'. Within speech-effusive styles, long sequences of syllables are rhymed. The percussive-effusive style often has its own predictable rhythmic patterns, with each syllable sharply detached or separated from the others, and with brief pauses in the middle of a line. On the other hand, speech-effusive styles are much closer to the spoken word and to earlier forms within the African vernacular tradition, and tend not to have an underlying metre (while also not necessarily matching the rhythm of the non-verbal tracks). This lack of metre does not mean that speech-effusive rapping is not rhythmic; rather that it is polyrhythmic and particularly syncopated.

The music

While rapping lies at the thematic centre of meaning within rap music, nonetheless an analysis of rap music would be incomplete without examining the music that accompanies rapping. As Rose suggests:

> Simply to recite or to read the lyrics to a rap song is not to understand them; they are also inflected with the syncopated rhythms and sampled sounds of the music. The music, its rhythmic patterns, and the idiosyncratic articulation by the rapper are essential to the song's meaning. (Rose 1994: 88)

While an initial examination of rapping might suggest that rap music is predominantly vocal-based, this is erroneous. The non-vocal aspects of rap are as distinctive as the vocal delivery of the rapper, and attention therefore needs to be paid to what Robin D. G. Kelly refers to as its 'sonic force' (Kelly 1997: 38). Only when combined do rap and rap music gain their full potency. This is confirmed by the renowned African-American writer Cornel West, who suggests that 'rap is unique because it combines the black preacher and the black music tradition, replacing the liturgical ecclesiastical setting with the African polyrhythms of the street' (West 1997: 407).

Structurally, rap music bears more than a passing similarity to the structure of reggae. In Chapter 6 we spoke of a 'version' and 'riddim'-based music where popular rhythms are re-used, re-edited and reconfigured over a period of years, with, on occasions, certain riddims, such as 'sleng teng', being used and re-used on hundreds of releases (see Goodman 2002). A similar process occurs in rap music, and as we will see in the final chapter of this book, in jungle music as well. Within rap music, soul

and funk breakbeats are sampled, edited, manipulated, treated and finally
looped to form a rhythmic backdrop recorded in 4 : 4 time and organised
into four-measure cycles.

Equally as important as the rhythm is the bassline, and again the
centrality and foregrounding of bass in rap music echoes the centrality of
bass to reggae. In recent years, melody has also become increasingly
prominent within rap. On rap releases in the 1980s, melody was often
hidden, or in the case of more minimal styles, eschewed altogether.
Within 1990s' rap tracks such Jay-Z's (Shawn Corey Carter) *Hard Knock
Life*, melody is brought to the fore and becomes integral to the structure
and meaning of the track. Equally, *Hard Knock Life* features a sung
chorus, a notable feature of many rap acts that 'crossed over' into the
mainstream pop charts in the late 1990s.

Once the rap musician has selected a breakbeat and edited and treated it
as he or she sees fit, and once a suitable bassline, melody and other elements
such as snatches of vocals or harmonies have been sampled or produced,
these fragments are then sutured together. Timbre plays an important part
in distinguishing between these layers, and allows the listener to separate
distinctive elements of each 'track'[9] within the overall 'song'.

Within rap music, elements that have a specific meaning within the
context of their original source are thus recontextualised and 'made to
mean' something. Andy Bennett uses the semiotic term *bricolage* to
describe this method of music production (Bennett 2001: 90). In employing this term, Bennett is suggesting that rap music is created largely from
fragments of previous songs and pieces of music, yet the meaning of these
musical fragments is often radically altered according to their newfound
position within a rap track.[10]

Having suggested that at the centre of rap music we find rapping,
breakbeats, foregrounded basslines and a *bricoleur* approach to sampling,
there are also clear distinctions within rap music between different
subgeneric styles. Krims is at the forefront of the analysis of these
differences. Outlining the state of rap music in the late 1990s, Krims
draws a distinction between old-school rap, 'hardcore' rap, 'commercial'
rap, regionally specific rap, party rap, mack/pimp rap, jazz/bohemian rap
and reality rap (Krims 2000).

Old-school rap

Employing a sung-rhythmic style, old-school rap has much sparser vocals
and instrumentation than modern styles. There are less rhymes within
sentences and more emphasis on end rhymes. The rhythm of the rapping
is particularly regular and the overall effect is more 'musical' than modern

styles. This style can be contrasted with modern raps that are faster and more complex, using multiple rhymes, internal rhymes, off-beat rhymes, multiple syncopations and what Krims refers to as 'overflows' and 'violations' of metre and rhythm (Krims 2000: 49).

Party rap

Prominent, foregrounded and regular fast rhythms are used, and there is little of the complex layering found in other styles. Unlike other styles there is less of a reliance on dissonance and more of a reliance on melody and harmony. 'Sung' flow is employed more so than on any other rap subgenre, resulting in prominent end rhymes and two- and four-bar groupings. Party rap often features traditional verse/chorus/verse meta-structures. Lyrical concerns often refer to parties, inebriation, dancing, celebration and romance, and are frequently light-hearted or humorous. Examples include The Sugar Hill Gang's *Rapper's Delight* and Naughty By Nature's *Hip Hop Hurray*.

Mack/pimp rap

Within mack rap, lyrical concerns focus upon sexual boasts, prowess and desire. Musically, there is a similarity with R&B, with formally delineated songs, a slow tempo, prominent keyboard melodies, jazz harmonies, and little of the disruptions of rhythm and harmonic dissonance found in other styles. Much mack rap is recorded using a band rather than employing samples, and as a result the rhythm conforms to a more regular metre than in other styles. There is also little of the intricate layering found in other styles. Krims cites LL Cool J's *Doin' It* and Ice T's *Who's The Mack* as particularly generic examples of this style (Krims 2000: 62–5). Krims also highlights a further subgeneric split within mack/pimp rap, which he refers to as don or Big Willy rap. Within this form, we have lyrical boasts of wealth, an anti-verisimilitude in which fantasy is prominent, and a particularly commercial employment of R&B-style music.

Jazz/bohemian rap

Using an eclectic range of samples and layered in a playfully postmodern manner, jazz rap is seen as being more cerebral than party or mack rap. Matching the playfulness and complexity of the sampling is a rapping style employing sung and effusive flows. Raps are often based on political consciousness, Afrocentricity and a general positivism, in sharp contrast to the 'ghettocentricism' of other styles. However, more abstract and complicated lyrics are also used. Krims suggests that this style of rap is close to beat poetry (Krims 2000: 69), and it is clear that this style draws upon Afrocentric forms of African–American speech. Examples of this subgenre include much of the work by De La Soul, A Tribe Called Quest and the Jungle Brothers.

Reality rap

This refers to rap that attempts to represent ghetto life. The nature of the lyrical focus of this form of rap also defines the features of a split between two further subgeneric divisions of reality rap. Within gangsta rap, lyrics are concerned with life as part of a criminal gang, and invariably explore the seedier side of American society in what George refers to as 'poetry of negation' (George 1998: 48). Within knowledge rap, we see the heavy influence of the Nation of Islam and Five Percent Nation organisations (who both preached racial separatism and black nationalism), as well as esoteric interpretations of black history, evolutionary theory, cosmology and numerology (as found on the releases of the Wu-Tang Clan).

In general, the reality form is rap at its most oppositional, transgressive and controversial. While jazz rap is often as didactic as reality rap, reality rap is far less likely to be as lyrically 'positive' as the jazz style. Musically, reality rap has shifted since Public Enemy almost single-handedly defined the subgenre in the mid to late 1980s. Krims suggests that through these changes an emphasis has always been placed on 'hardness', although what has connoted hardness in rap has shifted as time has passed. In the 1980s, the hardness of Public Enemy arose from the dense musical collages found on their records, with other Def Jam artists such as Run-DMC and the Beastie Boys making use of their producer Rick Rubin's ability to mesh breakbeat rhythms with heavy metal timbres. In the 1990s, Krims suggests that this hardness has meant a dominating and oppressive bassline, dissonant pitch combinations and samples that are obviously manipulated and 'deformed' (Krims 2000: 72). In general, reality rap is speech-effusive (or occasionally percussive-effusive) and sample based, and features extremely complex layers of a diverse range of sounds. Examples include the work of Bone Thugs 'N' Harmony, Nas' *Take It In Blood* and much of the work of the Wu-Tang Clan.

Visual aesthetic

Graffiti

In general, the defining features of hip-hop's graffiti subculture are the competitiveness of the individuals who produce graffiti pieces, the specifically urban spaces that are 'appropriated' by graffiti writers, the stylistic devices and formal properties of the graffiti itself, its illegality and the subsequent reactions of governmental authorities. Hip-hop's use of graffiti dates back to the 1970s and the spray painting or 'tagging' of subway trains, walls and other spaces and vehicles within inner-city New York (see Castleman 1982, and Cooper and Chalfant 1984). The very nature of this activity involved an element of criminality, be it trespass, breaking and entering or vandalism, and therefore hip-hop graffiti artists automatically came into conflict with city and town authorities. However, this should not lead necessarily to the suggestion that hip-hop graffiti is of little worth. In many respects hip-hop graffiti is as complicated, intricate and skilful as many other visual art forms. This is demonstrated by the genre of 'wildstyle' graffiti, which Nancy Macdonald defines as 'the subculture's most complex form, characterized by its angular inter-locking letters, distorted letter boundaries, accompanying arrows and extensive use of colour' (Macdonald 2001: 159). Such pieces are not only just found on city walls, trains, and buses, but have made their way into art galleries and specialist magazines, onto record covers and promotional materials produced for specific rap artists, and onto film. The first 'hip-hop movie', *Wild Style*, was the brainchild of film director Charlie Ahearn and Fab Five Freddie (Fred Braithwaite), an early graffiti artist who had featured on the video for Blondie's early rap homage *Rapture*. While Freddie went on to have a career producing videos that would subsequently help to define hip-hop's visual aesthetic ('band-identified geography, Afrocentric icons, and tribal imagery', George 1998: 100), *Wild Style* proved to be a catalyst for the production of a range of hip-hop-flavoured films.

Film and video
The rise of hip-hop film was significantly shaped by African-American film maker Spike Lee, who during the 1980s and 1990s directed several commercially successful hip-hop films, including *She's Gotta Have It*, *Do The Right Thing* and *Clockers*. Following Lee's success, the flood gates opened, and Hollywood produced a range of films that articulated central hip-hop themes, including *New Jack City* (starring Ice-T), *Boyz N the Hood* (starring Ice Cube), *Juice* (starring Tupac Shakur), *CB4*, *Menace II Society* and *Fear of a Black Hat*. More recently, Marshall Mathers III has starred and rapped in the film *Eight Mile*. As record companies, film studios and other media producers merge into global media conglomerates we can expect more of this kind of commercial synergy, whereby a musician or rapper stars in a film produced by a media conglomerate, while the film soundtrack and artist's album are also released by a separate section within the conglomerate.

Alongside the development of the hip-hop film, the 1980s and 1990s also saw the role for music videos in hip-hop increasing in importance. While early music video cable channels such as MTV initially operated a policy of refusing to play videos by black artists (Rose 1994: 8), other channels filled this gap in the market. In the mid-1980s *Video Music Box* programmed rap videos and broadcast to New York City, while *Friday Night Videos* was broadcast by NBC and *The Box*, a Miami-based network, played videos that were selected directly by viewers and therefore invariably programmed rap videos.

Since the mid-1980s rap has become one of the most popular and prevalent genres on music video channels such as *The Box* (now available in a UK incarnation). Notable videos during the 1980s included Run-DMC's collaboration with Aerosmith on *Walk This Way* (which Nelson George cites as the video that made rap 'MTV friendly'), a sequence of provocative and politically radical videos from Public Enemy and the equally controversial, but somewhat less overtly political, video for *Fight For Your Right To Party* by the Beastie Boys. By 1989, MTV had relented to commercial and political pressure and developed a show entitled *Yo! MTV Raps*. Fronted by Fab Five Freddie, *Yo! MTV Raps* meant that hip-hop video production was further stimulated by MTV's global distribution network.

George suggests that this is the point at which hip-hop culture became firmly embedded within American culture (George 1998). In particular, rap videos popularised certain forms of dress and visual style that were subsequently seen back on the streets in a mass-marketed form. As many of the early rap videos by New York rappers were shot in New York, New York's street aesthetic was seen across the nation. Mainstream fashion houses were not slow to see this trend, and hip-hop fashion can be seen to be split between two separate periods. Old-school hip-hop fashion from the early 1970s to the mid-1980s was largely improvised and individualised, and employed a *bricolage* aesthetic reminiscent of British punk, but with greatly different results. From the mid-1980s onwards fashion designers such as early pioneers Willi Smith and Stephen Sprouse made *couture* fashion that drew upon graffiti styles and day-glo colours (see George 1998: 157). It was not long before the big American fashion houses took note of hip-hop's emerging boutique culture, and following the success of their track *My Adidas*, Run-DMC's management company Rush Management signed a sponsorship deal with the sportswear manufacturer that was worth $1.5 million. The *bricolage* aesthetic gave way to a dialectic relationship between the major sportswear manufacturers, the fashion houses and the rap industry. Clothes and footwear by Nike,

Tommy Hilfiger, Timberland and Ralph Lauren became increasingly popular, with these major clothes designers producing items specifically aimed at the hip-hop market. The general look was baggy, colourful and flamboyant, touched with a hint of street menace.

In the 1990s, rap videos 'crossed over' from specialist programming into mainstream television. As this popularisation occurred, the form of content of rap videos began to settle around the articulation of what Rose considers rap's primary thematic concerns: identity and location. In particular, Rose suggests that

> rap video themes have repeatedly converged around the depiction of the local neighborhood and the local posse, crew, or support system. Nothing is more central to Rap's music video narratives than situating the rapper in his or her milieu and among one's crew or posse . . . Rap music videos are set on buses, subways, in abandoned buildings, and almost always in black urban inner-city locations. This usually involves ample shots of school yards, roofs, and childhood friends. (Rose 1994: 10)

Since the publication of Rose's analysis, a further aspect of African-American life has come to complement this concern with locality and neighbourhood, namely fantasies of wealth, fame and an escape from the rigours of inner-city life. The fact that fantastical imagery and portrayals of wealth and fame became more prominent during the 1990s when a range of rap musicians and entrepreneurs were experiencing unparalleled commercial success should come as no surprise. As rap moguls such as Puff Daddy/ P Diddy (Sean Combs) and Dr Dre (Andre Young) become increasingly successful, they necessarily become more distant from the streets that they previously inhabited. These 1990s' high earners began to develop a taste for the extravagant designs of Gianni Versace and the *haute couture* work of designers such as Giorgio Armani and Gucci. This style became known as 'ghetto fabulous', and when combined with the 'bling bling' of chunky gold jewellery (named after the sound of the jewellery when rattled), it symbolised the ethos of materialism that had come to dominate hip-hop culture. Escape from the streets had always been a central theme of hip-hop, so artists such as Diddy and Dre are celebrated for their wealth and success rather than denigrated for being out of touch.

Subsequent generic developments

Rap music is now a major seller in a range of different countries and across all continents. In Europe, rap has been 'inflected' with both European accents and sensibilities. For example, Bennett (2000) shows us how rap

music in Frankfurt am Main was first popularised by American Forces
Network radio (AFN), and then adapted by North Africans, Spanish,
Germans, South East Asians and Southern European ethnic minorities in
the suburb of Sachsenhausen. These groups 'reworked' rap music into a
form that they could use to reflect upon locally relevant issues. This was
completed through rapping in German, which, as Bennett suggests, allows
local rappers to obtain an 'ownership' of the rap form, thereby giving
German rap an authenticity prefaced on a 'more localised social experience
and linguistic representation' (Bennett 2000: 141). In particular, the rap
that Bennett observes attempts to counter dominant stereotypes of the
German *Asylbewerber* or asylum seeker, and the racism encountered by
non-white German citizens. Other forms of German rap offer a more direct
critique of mainstream German society, alongside the Afrocentricity often
found in global rap music. Equally, hybrid German and Turkish rap is
prominent in those German cities with a large Turkish population. This
Turkish rap is explicitly anti-fascist and anti-racist in direct response to
physical attacks upon German residents of Turkish descent.

   This pattern of local adaptation is to be found all over Europe, with
a range of Euro-American hybrids developing, including the Cuban-
oriented hip-hop act Orishas, who rap in Spanish and incorporate Afro-
Cuban Santeria drumming within their Latin-flavoured rap. Nelson
George also suggests that graffiti is particularly popular in the large
Spanish cities (George 1998: 203). In Sweden rap artists drawn from
ethnic minorities rap in English, the lingua franca of young people from
mixed ethnic backgrounds, and counterpose themselves against the right-
wing skinhead cult still prominent in Swedish youth culture (Bennett
2001: 96). In France, *le rap* is phenomenally popular, with French rap
receiving indirect support from the French state due to quota restrictions
on non-French singing on French radio. However, this popularity has not
been at the expense of French rap's radical politics, with rap being at the
forefront of youthful opposition to the rise of the far-right Front National.
Lyrically, French rap has avoided the mack raps of 'commercial' American hip-hop, while prefacing the concerns of inner-city poverty, with
successful French rappers such as Senegalese-born MC Solaar (Claude
M'barali) employing a particularly intellectualised lyrical style. Musically, French rap has also combined with French house music and African
musical forms, especially those from Francophone North and West
Africa. Some of the artists working within the latter sphere emphasise
their Islamic belief in both their rapping and accompanying musical
backdrops, with artists such as Kerry James avoiding the use of wind or
stringed instruments in accordance with Islamic beliefs.

In Britain, US rap has been popular since the old-school rap days of the early 1980s. Since then there has been a diverse range of acts who can be situated on a continuum of rap forms from American-centric styles which mimic gangsta and mack rap to artists whose music is based on non-rap rhythms but which also feature vocal deliveries that are clearly rap related. In the former category is the controversial Midlands rapper Mark Morrison, whose R&B comeback single, *Return Of The Mack*, reached number one in the singles charts in 1996. In the latter category are a whole host of artists working in a range of diverse musical fields including Pop Will Eat Itself, MC Tunes (Nicky Locket – 808 State) and Mr C (Richard West – The Shamen) who led the brief popularity of a techno rap hybrid in the late 1980s and early 1990s. Between these two extremes is situated Roots Manuva (Rodney Smith), whose albums *Run Come Save Me* and *Brand New Second Hand* feature a range of Anglo-centric lyrical concerns, delivered in a mixture of Jamaican patois and south London slang, and set to a rhythm track that could have originated on either side of the Atlantic ocean.

In Africa, rap has hybridised with local musics to form a bewildering array of Afro-rap styles. For example, since the early 1990s, 'hip life', a hybrid of 'high life' and rap music, has become ever more prominent in the Ghanaian music industry. With raps in English as well as the local languages of Twi, Ga and Hausahis, this musical form is particularly controversial due to its explicit sexuality. In South Africa, kwaito combines rap rhythms and house beats 'pitched down' to rap's sub-100 beats per minute tempo. This post-apartheid form focuses upon issues relating to South Africa's nascent multiculturalism, with vocals in English, Afrikaans and Zulu. More traditional hip-hop rhythms can also be found in South Africa, with artists rapping about a variety of subjects. For example, Cape Town is a rap stronghold, with local crews such as Black Noise, POC and Mr Devious taking part in local health awareness campaigns concerning HIV/AIDS. In Sierra Leone and Kenya artists such as Sir Prestige (Patrick Waweru – Kenya) maintain links between Africa and Europe, with British radio DJs such as Tim Westwood popularising East African hip-hop in Britain. In Uganda in Central Africa, rap music expanded following the collapse of the Idi Amin regime. Firstly, rap was popularised in Makerere University, before hybridising with ragga following the influence of Jamaican deejay Red Rat in the 1990s. In Northern Africa, a postcolonial dynamic is also evident. In Algeria, rap artists have maintained connections with Algerian émigrés living in France. Algerian rap also focuses explicitly on political and cultural repression in Algeria, with rap artists frequently attacked by the forces of the state. According to the continent's leading hip-hop website, rap music can also be found in Angola, Benin, Botswana, Cameroon, Cabo Verde, Congo, Gambia, Guinea, Ivory Coast, Liberia, Malawi, Mali, Mozambique, Namibia, Nigeria, Rwanda, Senegal, Swaziland, Tanzania, Togo, Zambia, and Zimbabwe (www.africanhiphop.com).

In Oceania, rap has also been reworked and refocused due to the dynamics of specific local contexts. Bennett draws upon work by Ian Condry in showing how rap music, so frequently a tool for the articulation of dissent against ethnic and racial oppression, is used by relatively affluent Japanese youth to articulate generational dissent to the authoritarian structures of Japanese society (see Bennett 2001: 100, and Condry 1999). Rap has also been used by a variety of social groups to 'signify' their presence within Australia and New Zealand. Tony Mitchell appropriates Roland Robertson's term 'glocal' (Robertson 1995) to describe the way that rap music has been adapted by Australian rap musicians. Mitchell gives the example of the group Koolism, whose rapper Boomstix uses an undeniably antipodean accent (Mitchell 1998). This notion of 'glocalism' is complicated by the Australian academic Kurt Iveson, who shows us how 'homegrown' Australian music is dominated by whites and how definitions of Australian music discriminate against musics produced by non-white and indigenous ethnic groups. In many ways Australian rap challenges 'dominant visions' of Australian national identity, and attempts to replace these 'visions' with a 'more genuine form of Australian multiculturalism' that incorporates the use of traditional Australian instruments, traditional Arabic music and a variety of different languages, including Greek, Italian, Lebanese and Vietnamese. Equally, New Zealand rap uses Maori music language to express local concerns and ethnic discrimination (Iveson 1997, Mitchell 1998).

Notes

1. See Lipsitz (1994), and Ogg with Upshall (1999), for a fuller examination of these early years of rap.
2. Rap musicians are rarely referred to by anything other than their pseudonyms. However, as in other chapters, we are also providing readers with the birth names of pseudonymous artists (where known).
3. While Kool Herc is often credited with being the first person to use a mixer and two record decks to extend manually the drum break of a specific record, the use of two record decks per se can be traced back to the 1920s where two gramophone record players were used to provide a seamless musical accompaniment to silent films (see Johnson 1927: 81 and Donnelly 2001).

4. For a brief analysis of the relationship between the music of James Brown and the form of rap music, see Rose (1994: 70).

5. Chic's original track was written by Nile Rodgers and Bernard Edwards who sued the Sugarhill Gang and obtained full songwriting credits and all ensuing royalties from the sale of the Sugarhill Gang's hit (George 1998: 94).

6. See Tricia Rose's examination of rap *Black Noise* for a brief examination of the relevance of this rock track to media discourses on rap music (Rose 1994: 130).

7. Andy Bennett analyses this double meaning of rap with his description of 'hip hop as a global resource', where 'young people of differing ethnic backgrounds in cities and regions across the globe have reworked the rap text in ways that incorporate local knowledges and sensibilities, thus transforming rap into a means of communication that works in the context of specific localities' (Bennett 2001: 93–4). Indeed, Bennett's own research on hip-hop culture in Frankfurt am Main and Newcastle upon Tyne, alongside Krims' analysis of a form of Dutch rap entitled *Nederhop* (Krims 2000: 152–97) goes some way to showing us how rap has been adapted by different ethnic and social groups (see Bennett 2000: 133–65).

8. A clear distinction should be drawn between the role of an MC in rap music and MCing in jungle music and UK garage. Within jungle and UK garage the MC's job is to provide a verbal accompaniment to a DJ's set in a club or rave, or occasionally on record or on radio. Within rap music the MC's raps are integral to the structure of the music and are not a 'post-production' addition as in jungle and UK garage.

9. Elsewhere the term 'track' is used to denote a song or a discrete instrumental piece. Within this context track is used to refer to each discrete instrument within an overall composition. For example, a kick drum, cymbals, hi-hats, basslines, rapping, backing vocals, keyboard melody and individual sound effects might all occupy a single track during the recording process before these eight tracks are 'bounced down' to a single final stereo mix.

10. A good example might be the aforementioned *Hard Knock Life* by Jay Z (Shawn Corey Carter). Jay Z's track *Hard Knock Life* is based on a song from the opening scene of the Broadway musical *Annie*. Within the musical the song is used to speak of the privations and cruelties of life for a group of homeless girls in an orphanage. Within Jay Z's track, the original *Annie* soundtrack is recontextualised and, alongside Jay Z's rap, is used to refer to African-American experiences of police brutality, crime, prostitution, inner-city poverty, poor educational opportunities and racism.

Recommended reading

Dyson, M. E. (1996) *Between God and Gangsta Rap: Bearing Witness to Black Culture*. Oxford: Oxford University Press.

George, N. (1998) *Hip Hop America*. London: Penguin Books.

Krims, A. (2000) *Rap Music and the Poetics of Identity*. Cambridge: Cambridge University Press.

Lipsitz, G. (1994) *Dangerous Crossroads: Popular Music, Postmodernism and the Poetics of Place*. London: Verso

Light, A. (ed.) (1999) *The Vibe History of Hip Hop*. London: Plexus Publishing

Ogg, A. with Upshall, D. (1999) *The Hip Hop Years: A History of Rap*. London and Basingstoke: Channel 4 Books.

Perkins, W. E. (1996) *Droppin' Science: Critical Essays on Rap Music and Hip-Hop Culture*. Philadelphia: Temple Press.

Potter, R. (1995) *Spectacular Vernaculars: Hip-Hop and the Politics of Post-modernism*. New York: State University of New York Press.

Rose, T. (1994) *Black Noise: Rap Music and Black Culture in Contemporary America*. Middleton, NC: Wesleyan University Press.

Toop, D. (1999) *Rap Attack #3: African Rap to Global Hip Hop*. London: Serpent's Tail.

Recommended listening

Antecedents

Gil Scott Heron (1974) *The Revolution Will Not Be Televised*. RCA.

James Brown (1970) *Funk Power 1970. A Brand New Thang*. Polydor.

Various (1998) *The Trojan DJ Box Set*. Trojan.

Generic texts

Afrika Bambaataa and the Soulsonic Force (1982) *Planet Rock* [single]. Tommy Boy.

Beastie Boys (1986) *Licensed To Ill*. Def Jam Records.

De La Soul (1989) *3 Feet High And Rising*. Tommy Boy.

Eminem (2000) *The Marshall Mathers LP*. Interscope.

Grandmaster Flash and the Furious Five (1982) *The Message* [single]. Sugarhill Records.

Notorious B.I.G. (1995) *Ready To Die*. Arista.

NWA (1988) *Straight Outta Compton*. Priority.

Public Enemy (1988) *It Takes A Nation Of Millions To Hold Us Back*. Def Jam Records.

Run-DMC (1984) *Run-DMC*. Arista.

The Sugarhill Gang (1979) *Rapper's Delight* [single]. Sugarhill Records.

Tupac Shakur (1994) *Thug Life*. Interscope Records.

Wu Tang Clan (1994) *Enter The Wu-Tang (36 Chambers)*. RCA.

Subsequent generic developments

Various (2000) *Best Of International Hip Hop*. Universal IMS.

CHAPTER 10

Indie: the politics of production and distribution

An overview of the genre

The term 'indie' rose to popularity in the British music industry during the post-punk era (1979–86) and was used initially as an abbreviation for 'independent'. As such, the phrase 'indie' referred originally to those record labels that were independent of 'the majors' (transnational record corporations such as the EMI Group).[1] However, as the 1980s progressed, it became apparent that the term indie was also being used to describe a musical genre.

In the period from the late 1970s to the mid-1980s, there was a range of successful independent record companies whose record releases also bore a musical similarity (see below). Many punk and new-wave bands set up labels to release their own records and often limited their output to small runs of seven-inch singles made for the punk and new-wave markets.

Punk and new-wave indies:
- 2-Tone, financed and run by the Specials prior to completing a production and distribution deal with Chrysalis in 1980 (see Marshall 1997, and Frith 1980).
- Zoo, based in Liverpool (see Cooper 1982).
- New Hormones, financed by Buzzcocks and based in Manchester (see McGartland 1995, and Rawlins and Diggle 2002).
- Factory Records, also based in Manchester (see Haslam 1999: 109–38).

In the early to mid-1980s, a second generation of post-punk indie labels began to share a different musical aesthetic while also remaining largely independent from the major record corporations. This musical aesthetic was particularly noticeable with the release by the *New Musical Express* of a free compilation cassette entitled *C86*, which featured so-called 'shambling' bands such as The Soup Dragons, The Pastels, Shop Assistants and The Wedding Present. (Strange Fruit subsequently released this compilation as a vinyl LP.) Other names for this indie subgenre included 'indie pop' and 'cutie'. Initially, the economic rationale of most mid-1980s' indie labels mirrored that of Rough Trade, who signed '50/50' deals with their bands whereby costs and receipts were split equally between band and label (as opposed to major-label deals which generally favoured the record company).[2]

1980s indie labels and bands:
- Postcard: Aztec Camera, Go-Betweens, Josef K, Orange Juice.
- Cherry Red: Blue Orchids, Everything But The Girl, Red Lorry Yellow Lorry, Television Personalities, Woodentops.
- Creation Records: Felt, Jesus and Mary Chain, My Bloody Valentine, Primal Scream, The Weather Prophets.
- Rough Trade: Scritti Politti, the Raincoats.
- Sarah Records: the Field Mice, The Orchids, The Sea Urchins, 14 Iced Bears.
- 53rd and 3rd: BMX Bandits, Shop Assistants, Tallulah Gosh, The Vaselines.

Other 1980s' indie bands such as The Smiths and The Cure were not attached to the C86 scene but nonetheless shared the shambling bands' penchant for short and traditionally structured songs and lyrics concerning loves lost and teenage discontentment. (The Smiths were signed to Rough Trade while The Cure were signed to Fiction Records and distributed by Polydor.)

As 1980s' indie bands became more successful, some signed deals with major labels yet retained an adherence to a generic form. This generic form is defined none too succinctly by Colin Larkin as 'post Sex Pistols music sometimes lo-fi or grungy played by creative on the edge artists who are often influenced by the Byrds, Velvet Underground and Blondie' (Larkin 1998: 3). Therefore, the late 1980s saw a split in the definition of indie between those records that conformed to this loose generic description, and those that were released and/or distributed by independent record labels and distributors (with some records falling into both camps).

While the musical genre of indie was taking root, it was becoming apparent that the relationship between independent and major record labels was becoming somewhat 'one way'. As David Cavanagh, author of *The Creation Records Story: My Magpie Eyes Are Hungry for the Prize*, puts it, 'the indies were finding the talent, and the majors were creaming it off' (Cavanagh 2001: 91). This process led to Rough Trade collapsing in 1991 (Harris 2003: 23). In many ways, this process had begun in the 1970s with bands such as Squeeze releasing their first single on Deptford Fun City Records before signing a deal with A&M. The situation was complicated in the 1990s when many independent record labels began to sign business deals with major labels for the rights to release records outside the UK ('licensing deals'), or who signed contracts with major record labels whereby the major label would distribute the independents' products. Equally, some independent record labels completed financing deals with major labels in order to receive capital investment in return for shares.

Early precedents for this include Stiff Records, who in the late 1970s released records by Elvis Costello, Ian Dury and the Blockheads and Madness that were distributed by EMI or, following EMI's late-1970s financial troubles, CBS (Muirhead 1983: 7). A more contemporary example is Creation Records, originally a fiercely independent record label founded in 1982 by the charismatic Glaswegian Alan McGee. In 1991, McGee improved Creation's parlous financial affairs by signing a deal with Sony, whereby Sony bought 49 per cent of Creation and controlled the production and distribution of many Creation artists outside of the UK. During this time, McGee famously signed Oasis, who went on to spearhead 'Britpop', an indie subgenre that harked back to British rock and pop of the 1960s. The Creation/Sony deal was renewed in 1996, but by the late 1990s it was apparent that McGee was becoming ever more discontented with the global record industry, and left Creation, which folded rapidly with their roster of artists falling into the hands of Sony. (McGee now runs a successful independent label called Poptones.) Ironically, following the collapse of the label, it became apparent that perhaps Oasis had never been 'signed' to Creation at all, and that Oasis had signed a deal with Sony's Licensed Repertoire Division and Sony then 'licensed' the band to Creation in the UK (see Cavanagh 2002, and Harris 2003: 131).

Oasis' main Britpop competitors were Blur, who were signed to the Food Records label throughout the 1990s. Founded in 1984 by ex-Teardrop Explodes keyboardist Dave Balfe, Food had a notable record for discovering talented groups who went on to achieve commercial success. However, this commercial success generally only came about after major record labels had lured the bands away from Food. In 1985 journalist Andy Ross joined Balfe, and, following this, Food came to the attention of EMI, who purchased a stake in the label in 1988. This deal allowed Food to maintain a hold over those bands that were becoming successful, using profits from these successes to fund up-and-coming acts. Had Food not completed a deal with EMI it is doubtful whether their most successful band of the 1990s, Blur, would have remained on the label following their early hits. Balfe finally sold the rest of Food to EMI in 1994 and retired, leaving Andy Ross as label head (Harris 2003: 139).

At the present time, many independent labels are distributed by major corporations, allowing the small independent company to make use of the corporations' financial muscle, distribution networks and economies of scale. Equally, major corporations occasionally distribute their records through independent distribution companies in order to foster an appeal with a fiercely independently minded indie-record-buying public (and to qualify for inclusion in indie charts). For example, the twenty-first-century indie band The Cooper Temple Clause have a record deal with RCA, part of the Bertelsmann corporation. This deal allows the band to release their records through a special subsidiary label, Morning Records. Morning Records' releases are distributed through an independent distributor, thus entitling the band's releases to be included in various national indie charts. Thus The Cooper Temple Clause are a good example of an indie band who partly adhere to indie's generic definition (The Cooper Temple Clause sound like Oasis might do, were the latter not fixated with the music of The Beatles), while only partly adhering to indie's belief in financial independence.

In summary, indie is a mode of production, a mode of distribution and a musical genre (a group of texts with stylistic similarities that are grouped together by music companies, retailers, broadcasters and fans alike). In the first two category are record companies such as Invicta HiFi, home to the successful Liverpool-based band Ladytron. Invicta HiFi is run from an office in Liverpool city centre by one person, distributing its records in the UK through Pinnacle, and abroad through the independent US record company Emperor Norton. In the third category are bands that rely upon the generic form of indie but are signed to, or distributed by, major labels.

Historical roots and antecedents

Early indie labels

Founded in 1946, Melodisc specialised in importing black music and selling it to the UK market. Adopting a methodology that would be successfully employed by 1990s' indie entrepreneurs, Melodisc founder Emil Shallit found that he was able to spot niche markets far quicker than the corporate majors and subsequently licensed for UK release jazz, blues, R&B and various African and Afro-Caribbean genres. In the 1960s, Melodisc also played a role in popularising Jamaican blues and ska in Britain with its subsidiary label Blue Beat. The singular popularity of Blue Beat in Britain led many ska fans to use the phrase Blue Beat to describe the genre itself (Bradley 2000: 127).

Another pre-punk indie, Island Records, also had roots in Jamaica.

Founded in Jamaica by the Jamaican-born Old Harrovian Chris Black-well, Blackwell soon realised there was an untapped market for Jamaican music in the UK, and moved to London in 1962 to market his Jamaican recordings and to license other recordings for UK release. By the late 1960s, the Island catalogue contained numerous Jamaican classics, including recordings by Jimmy Cliff, Derrick Harriot and Desmond Dekker, as well as tracks licensed from both Jamaican producers such as Duke Reid and Coxsone Dodd (see Chapter 6).

A partnership between Blackwell's Island and B&C, a music distribution company owned by Lee Gopthal, also led to the creation of Trojan Records, a massively successful UK-based label who made the most of the rocksteady and pop reggae boom of the late 1960s and early 1970s, selling over two million records on a range of sub-labels. In particular, Trojan/ B&C specialised in taking Jamaican tracks and adding strings and orchestral arrangements to ensure popularity with the British market (Bradley 2000: 232–59).

While Blackwell's Island was successful in the 1960s, nothing could prepare the company for the massive global success of Bob Marley and The Wailers. This success was built on Blackwell's suggestion that The Wailers could be marketed to Western audiences as a serious rock band. As such, the first Bob Marley and The Wailers album, *Catch A Fire*, is the first 'proper' reggae album in that it consists of more than a selection of previously released singles (Bradley 2000: 130). After a decade's worth of massive selling albums, Island finally had a number one single (with the new wave track Buggles' *Video Killed The Radio Star*), and despite Marley's death the label went from strength to strength, signing U2 in 1980. In 1989, Blackwell sold Island to Polygram, while retaining certain rights over the label's roster. After releasing a multi-million-selling U2 album in 1997, Island, along with the whole Polygram roster, was sold to the Canadian drinks giant Seagram in 1998. (Seagram's subsequently sold all their music interests to Universal, who now own Island.) In many respects, these deals, along with EMI purchasing 50 per cent of Chrysalis in 1988 and then buying out Virgin Music Group in 1992 for £560 million (Cavanagh 2001: 509), meant that the last of the pre-punk indies were dead, and that no matter how large an indie got, it could still be the target for a predatory bid by a major label (see also Napier-Bell 2002: 362).

A further example of a British indie reaping the rewards of small business efficiency and flexibility is the label Rak, founded by British music impresario Micky Most. The success of Rak was at least partly due to the label employing a different commercial strategy to the major labels. Whereas the major labels had a 'mud against the wall' approach (Laing

1985: 9), whereby the label would release a large number of records in the hope that a small percentage would be commercially successful, Rak released a far fewer number of records, relying upon Micky Most's intuition as to what would be a hit. As a result, whereas a label such as EMI released 145 singles between September 1974 and August 1975 and had ten hits, Rak released thirty-four singles and had twelve Top 20 hits. Bands signed to Rak included Peter Noone, Mud, Alexis Korner, Suzi Quatro and Kim Wilde (Kim Fowler).

Early musical influences

While the production and distribution methods of British independent labels such as Melodisc, Trojan, Island and Rak influenced the business practices of independent labels in the post-punk period and beyond, the musical influences of 1980s' indie were drawn equally from a range of avant-garde and pop artists from the 1960s who were signed to major labels in Britain and the United States. Dominant influences from Britain included the wistful balladeering, guitar playing and orchestral arrangements of Nick Drake, along with the classic pop of The Kinks, The Beatles, The Rolling Stones and The Who. Equally, punk's reinvigoration of rock had a lasting influence upon indie music. Dominant influences on indie from the United States included the dissonance and experimentation of The Velvet Underground, along with the psychedelic pop of a variety of 1960s' bands such as The Byrds, the Thirteenth Floor Elevators, The Seeds and The Chocolate Watch Band. What these British and American bands have in common is a belief in the efficacy of rock songwriting, an approach to performance that emphasises emotion and brevity over intellect and longevity, and a sense of amateurish enthusiasm, even if that enthusiasm was built upon the hard-won skills of dedicated musicians.

Social and political context

The social and political contexts of indie are dominated by the three dominant conjunctures[3] of British life in the second half of the twentieth century – the postwar social-democratic consensus, Thatcherism and New Labour Blairism. This section will deal with the relationship between the latter two conjunctures and the British indie scene.

The collapse of the postwar social-democratic consensus and the rise of the New Right

Come the 1970s, rising unemployment and an increase in industrial unrest following the miners' strike of 1974 marked the beginning of the end for the postwar social-democratic consensus. With Margaret Thatcher becoming Conservative leader in 1975 and going on to win the General Election of 1979, we see a marked shift in the economic, political, social and cultural terrain. Britain shifts sharply to the right, and politics is dominated by 'anti-collectivism' (Hall 1983: 27), privatisation, a free-market economics fostering a new form of entrepreneurialism, and a 'law and order' agenda that Stuart Hall refers to as 'authoritarian populism' (see Hall 1988).

From Thatcherism's rise in the 1970s through to the shift to New Labourism following the 1997 General Election, the structure and content of British indie is at least partially determined by its relationship to Thatcherism. Cavanagh notes that post-punk bands such as Magazine, Public Image Limited, The Pop Group, Joy Division and The Gang of Four produced music containing lyrics that 'would contemplate alienation, paranoia and morbidity' (Cavanagh 2001: 29). These tracks prefaced the national mood of the early 1980s, with rising unemployment, an increasing gap between rich and poor and increased social unrest (including riots in major British cities) dominating the nation's headlines throughout the decade. Indie took two approaches to countering the nation's malaise: either oblique or explicit protest (The Smiths, The Redskins and Billy Bragg), or escapism (Frankie Goes to Hollywood).

While it was difficult to find a musician in the 1980s prepared to espouse Conservative politics (Frith 1988: 202–3), it would be simplistic to suggest that all indie labels and indie bands opposed Thatcherism *en masse*. While it is true that Rough Trade appeared to be run along socialistic lines and 2-Tone released a range of left-leaning singles including The Specials' *Ghost Town* (a bleak commentary on the deleterious effects of unemployment), others took the words of Conservative politician Norman Tebbit to heart and 'got on their bikes and looked for work'. For example, Alan McGee was prepared to move from his native Glasgow in order to infiltrate the London indie scene. While McGee was later to become a key supporter of the Labour government of 1997–2001, he was still a well-motivated and ruthless businessman cut in the Thatcherite mould, and is quoted as saying 'I am absolutely a product of Thatcherism. She would have loved me' (Cavanagh 2001: 674).

In the 1980s, some saw the independent record scene as 'representing an emotional rejection, based on ethics and political beliefs, of everything the major labels stood for' (Cavanagh 2001: 38), yet it could also be suggested that 'indie' chimed more closely with the post-industrial entrepreneurial times than initial appearances suggested. Furthermore, while some labels might have been run according to non-commercial socialistic principles, the politics of indie were certainly muddied by the methods employed by Pinnacle, an independent record distributor that was run according to strict commercial principles and which some indie supporters claimed was 'a bastion of Thatcherism' (Cavanagh 2001: 241). Furthermore, to the horror of those who retained an adherence to indie as a generic style, Stock, Aitken and Waterman, the Fordist pop production line that dominated the charts in the late 1980s with hits by the likes of Kylie Minogue and Rick Astley, were also distributed by Pinnacle and qualified for inclusion in the indie charts as their record label, PWL, was entirely independent of the majors.

The collapse of Thatcherism and the rise of Britpop

While 1990 saw the resignation of Margaret Thatcher and the appointment of John Major as a successor, it was not until the General Election of 1997 that Thatcherism as a political discourse ceased to have a defining effect upon the political and cultural landscapes. During this intervening period, certain Britpop bands acted as harbingers of a new relationship between politics, pop and the British public. During the 1980s, indie had been a minority taste and earlier indie fans would have rejected the relentlessly populist approach employed in the 1990s. John Harris cites Menswear as a good example of a Britpop band prepared to jettison the shibboleths of the past, with Menswear's Simon White stating that 'at the end of the day vast financial gain has got to be your main motive. I want a helicopter' (quoted in Harris 2003: 208). Equally, the left-leaning indie fans of the 1980s would have also fought shy of Britpop's use of nationalistic images, including the use of the Union Jack in magazine photo shoots with Suede (*Select*, April 1993) and Oasis' Liam Gallagher and wife Patsy Kensit (*Vanity Fair*, February 1997).

During this period, Britpop also became inextricably connected to the collapse in support for the John Major-led Conservative government and the inevitability of a change of government in the General Election of 1997. In 1996, Oasis' Noel Gallagher expressed support for Blair at a British Phonogram Industry (BPI) awards ceremony, and Creation sponsored a Labour Party 'Youth Experience Rally' in Blackpool. A year later, Alan McGee made a £50,000 donation to the Labour Party, and was quoted extensively in an article in the *Daily Record* entitled 'Look back in anger: Labour man McGee puts his money where his mouth is' (25 March 1997). Not wishing to be outdone by his Britpop adversaries, Blur's Damon Albarn flirted with the Labour Party by having a series of meetings with its new leader Tony Blair, media guru Alistair Campbell and deputy leader John Prescott. Come the General Election of Thursday, 1 May 1997, Britpop luminaries such as Jarvis Cocker and McGee joined long-term Labour supporters such as George Michael and Simply Red's Mick Hucknall at an official party at the Royal Festival Hall in London.

Blairism, New Labour and 'Cool Britannia'[4]

Following the collapse of the Conservative vote in the 1997 election, there was less of a governmental emphasis on 'law and order' and a consequent softening of economic liberalism, with Labour's policies returning the country to near full employment (albeit according to figures that are heavily manipulated). While heavy industry and manufacturing industry were decimated during the three Conservative governments of 1979–97, the Labour government of 1997–2001 placed more of an emphasis on the role of the 'creative industries' in boosting Britain's economy. By 1997, the UK creative industries were beginning to be seen as a major future component of the UK economy.[5] This emphasis certainly chimed well with Labour's pre-election courting of Oasis and Blur. The elevated position of Oasis and McGee (Blur had turned against Labour by this point) was assured by Tony Blair's official Downing Street party of 30 July 1997. This prestigious occasion had a guest list that included the Pet Shop Boys, Noel Gallagher (along with his wife Meg Matthews), George Michael and Radio 1 DJ Simon Mayo, as well as television and film stars such as Michael Caine (Maurice Micklewhite) and Helen Mirren (Ilynea Lydia Mironoff).

Two months after the General Election of May 1997, the Labour government announced the formation of a 'Creative Industries Task Force'. In publicising this move Chris Smith, Secretary of State for the newly formed Department of Culture, Media and Sport, suggested that the members of the six-person task force, which included Alan McGee and Virgin's founder Richard Branson, understood 'how to build and develop creative businesses'. Nailing the flag of 'Cool Britannia' to this new economic project, Smith suggested that

> cultural and leisure activities are of growing significance. Not only to individuals; they are also of rapidly growing economic importance. They are the basic fuel of our hugely successful international tourist industry, and the heart of a series of activities in which Britain is genuinely a world leader. Cool Britannia is here to stay. (Quoted in Alberge and Midgley 1997)

The phrase 'Cool Britannia' and the 're-branding of Britain' thus became the most significant pseudo-political terms of the late 1990s. The latter term became connected to Foreign Secretary Robin Cook's formation of 'Panel 2000', a group of people 'chosen to help give Britain a "cool" image abroad' (quoted in Harris 2003: 355). Five years after this initiative began, the cultural historian Robert Hewison has suggested that the upper echelons of the Labour government 'see the arts instrumentally, as a means to help achieve social and urban regeneration. They are only interested in the arts insofar as they can see them achieving the New Labour vision' (quoted in Kettle 2002: 14). During this period, the Labour Party severed its relationship with McGee amid some acrimony, and the only legacy of this period is what Harris refers to as 'Britpop legislation' (Harris 2003: 360) that inaugurated the New Deal for Musicians (a government-funded scheme to encourage unemployed musicians) in October 1998.

The musical texts

Within this section, we move away from a categorisation of indie as a mode of production and/or distribution towards the categorisation of indie as a musical genre. Here we can draw a broad distinction between the 'indie pop' or 'shambling' bands of the 1980s, indie dance, and the more muscular sound of Britpop in the 1990s and beyond.

Shambling bands and indie pop
Generally, shambling bands subscribed to the following conventions:

- Band names often harked back to childhood or children's television.
- Songs were short, as the dominant mode of reception was the 45 rpm seven-inch single rather than the 45 rpm twelve-inch single, 33 rpm long player or compact disc. Some small indie labels also produced and distributed 'flexi-disks' – coloured and flexible round pieces of plastic with shallow grooves that emphasised treble rather than bass sounds. The flexi-disk offered the added advantage of being very cheap to produce and could easily be inserted into fanzines (the popularity of which dates back to the pioneering punk fanzine *Sniffin' Glue*).
- Songs conformed to a strict verse/chorus/verse/chorus format with a prominent middle eight.
- Dominant instruments were the electric guitar (often a twelve-string guitar, drawing influence from psychedelic pop from the 1960s), acoustic guitar, bass and drums.
- There was little in the way of electronic instrumentation on most indie pop singles.
- Vocals were as likely to be sung by a female lead singer or singers (the Shop Assistants and Tallulah Gosh) as they were by men.

- The lyrics of 'shambling' songs were dominated by themes of childhood and unrequited love.

Indie pop was a subgenre that emphasised innocence and amateurism, a kind of 'kiddy punk' that was heavily influenced by the sound and style of the singles of 1978 and 1979 by Buzzcocks. In his examination of shambling bands, the pop academic and music journalist Simon Frith draws upon the analysis of Simon Reynolds, suggesting that

> at a time when every sign of teenage rebellion since rock 'n' roll is part of some sales campaign, the only unpolluted source of non-conformity is childhood – the polymorphous perversity of pre-pubescence itself, and the infancy of British rock – the 1960s innocence embodied in the new groups' names: the Pastels, the Mighty Lemon Drops, the Woodentops, the Soap [sic] Dragons. For these groups, in Reynolds' words, 'the primal scene of consumption is the bedroom', and love is experienced as sensibility not sensuality. (Frith 1986)

Indie-dance and 'baggy'

The turn of the 1980s saw various 'traditional' indie bands begin to mix indie-pop melodies with dance grooves drawn from soul, funk, house and techno music. In particular, a musical renaissance in Manchester, briefly dubbed 'Madchester' after an EP by Happy Mondays, saw bands such as the Stone Roses, Inspiral Carpets, Charlatans and Northside enter both the indie charts and the mainstream. Notably creative examples of this hybrid form can be found on the first three Happy Mondays albums (*Squirrel and G-Man, Twenty Four Hour Party People Plastic Face Carnt Smile (White Out)*, *Bummed* and *Pills 'n' Thrills and Bellyaches*), and the Stone Roses' celebrated eponymous first album. Elsewhere bands such as Flowered Up (from London) managed to forge a distinct punk/funk identity with tracks such as *It's On*, *Egg Rush* and the celebrated *Weekender*, a track remixed and elongated by noted dance DJ Andy Weatherall.

Indie-dance/baggy lasted barely eighteen months. Scene leaders the Stone Roses found themselves in protracted legal battles with both management and their label Silvertone (a major subsidiary). These legal battles led to interminable delays in the release of their poorly received second album, while rampant drug abuse ensured that the Happy Mondays' career fell apart shortly after taking part in recording sessions in Barbados that were dominated by crack cocaine and other drug misuse. Flowered Up never achieved the nationwide acclaim that the indie-obsessed musical weeklies (*NME*, *Melody Maker*) predicted and promptly split up after an incendiary performance at the Glastonbury music festival in 1992, while The Inspiral Carpets split amid personal acrimony (although they subsequently re-formed for a lucrative farewell tour in 2002–3). In 1992, the collapse of Factory Records amid financial chaos ensured the death of Northside, and of the 'Madchester' scene only The Charlatans survived, releasing a number of hit singles and albums throughout the 1990s.

While indie-dance was seen as an attempt to meld American dance rhythms to the British pop aesthetic, its death left a vacuum in the British music scene. This void was filled, on the one hand, by house, techno and hardcore, and on the other hand, by American rock such as that produced by Soundgarden, Mudhoney and Nirvana (all signed to the Seattle indie label Sub Pop). However, the 1994 suicide of Nirvana's lead singer Kurt Cobain meant that the British indie scene began to look inwards towards notions of classic British pop.

Britpop

Dating back at least as far as Suede's attempted anti-American backlash of 1992 (see Maconie 1992), Britpop was born of both a frustration at the dominance of American bands in the British music scene of the early 1990s and an attempt to 'reclaim' and popularise a set of mythologically British traits within the development of popular music. As such, David Hesmondhalgh correctly suggests that Britpop was a musical discourse (Hesmondhalgh 2001) rather than a genre as such, although there were extra-discursive elements within Britpop. For example, Britpop was as likely to be released by a major conglomerate as a small label, and the Britpop boom of the mid-1990s saw the completion of the process whereby major labels released records aimed at the indie market. However, what interests us in this section is how the stylistic conventions of post-1980s' indie were shifted during the mid-1990s' Britpop phase. This all-encompassing shift led to the following musical changes:

- Whereas indie-pop favoured the stand-alone seven-inch 45 r.p.m. single, Britpop favoured singles that were used to promote full-length CDs and vinyl albums.
- Whereas indie-pop bands were as influenced by 1970s' punk as they were 1960s' rock, Britpop was influenced by a smaller range of 1960s' pop bands, especially the Small Faces, The Kinks and The Beatles (see Bennett 1997).
- Whereas indie-pop bands frequently sung in middle-class home counties' accents, Britpop favoured regional working-class accents (witness Oasis' 'Mancunianisms' and Blur's exaggerated cockney – a style borrowed from the Small Faces).
- Whereas indie-pop bands were as likely to be influenced by the underground American music of the 1960s and 1970s as they were British music from this period, Britpop saw a partial effacement of American influences.

- Whereas indie-pop lyrics most often dealt with issues around love and relationships, Britpop frequently focused upon issues of nationality and culture. For example, Cavanagh cites Blur's *Modern Life Is Rubbish* as the first Britpop record due to lyrics that 'pined for a traditional England of greasy spoons and Sunday roasts' and which rejected 'American life . . . [and] American music – not least the grunge movement that had been partly responsible for Blur's commercial decline' (Cavanagh 2001: 583).

The sum total of these stylistic distinctions was a music subgenre that seemed to include only a very narrow and almost exclusively 'white' set of musical influences. The pop commentator Jon Savage agreed:

> Welcome to the curiously hermetic, over-mediated world of Britpop. Initiated by Suede (who, during 1992, sang about 'the love and poison of London'), industrialized by BPI award-winners Blur on their 1994 album *Parklife* and fine-tuned by Elastica, this is a febrile, highly specific genre. Within a multicultural metropolis, where the dominant sounds are swingbeat, ragga or jungle, Britpop is a synthesis of white styles with any black influence bled out: the guitar-centricity of the late 80s indie rock, the social commentary of the Kinks, the laddish dandyism of the Small Faces, the smart-dumb spikiness of Wire, whose presence looms large over Elastica and latest music-press sensations Menswear. (Savage 1995: 413–14)

Other examples of Britpop bands include Pulp, Sleeper, Cast, Dodgy and Supergrass.

Post-Britpop indie

Following Blur's rejection of the light pastoral sounds of 1960s' British pop, the Britpop bubble burst, with the vast majority of late 1990s' bands rejecting the term and subgenre. Consequently, the late 1990s saw a fracturing of the indie sound. While many new indie bands can still be seen to be the inheritors of the generic form either of the shambling bands or of Britpop, there is now much more of a cross-generic influence of American and British dance musics. Whereas the dominant instrument of shambling bands and Britpop was the guitar, millennial indie is as likely to be dominated by soul, funk and rap breakbeats or the 'four-to-the-floor' crotchet beat of house and techno.

The Liverpool-based band Ladytron are a good example of this new indie eclecticism. Whereas previous Liverpool indie bands have traditionally relied upon psychedelia-tinged guitar pop, Ladytron draw influence from European electronic acts such as Kraftwerk and the synthpop of the 1980s. The European influence is emphasised by the deadpan delivery of Ladytron's vocals by both of their female vocalists, one from Glasgow and the other from Bulgaria. Elsewhere in Ladytron's sound, we find a fetishisation of primitive synthesisers, which deliver a harsher and less complex sound than contemporary samplers and sampling keyboards. It is interesting to note Ladytron's similarity to electronic pop acts from the early 1980s (ironic considering that many indie bands of the 1980s and 1990s often set themselves up as the heart felt guitar-led 'authentic' alternative to such 'synthetic' pop). In his article 'Against health and efficiency: independent music in the 1980s', Simon Reynolds puts forward the notion that alternative music (a near synonym of indie) acts as a home to 'oppositional meanings' and defines itself as 'pop's other' (Reynolds 1989: 246). It should therefore come as no surprise to us that once Britpop became the dominant pop mode of the mid-1990s the indie that followed the Britpop era should so readily reject the guitar in favour of other instruments.

Visual aesthetic

Shambling bands and indie pop

Elsewhere in his article, Reynolds points to a particular visual aesthetic for the indie pop of the mid-1980s. Whereas the mainstream pop and rock of the 1980s was viewed as being ever more professional and sophisticated (it was during this period that the phrase 'adult-oriented rock' or AOR was popularised), the overall aesthetic of shambling bands was one of amateurism and the innocence of childhood. While this is reflected in lyrics, vocal style and band names, it is also seen in record sleeves and the clothing of bands. As Reynolds states:

> A huge proportion of indie groups have pictures of children or childish things on their record sleeves . . . You can see this innocence in the way fanzines privilege naiveté and enthusiasm and mess, and use graphics from old annuals and children's books. (Reynolds 1989: 248)

As far as clothing was concerned, both male and female band members (and indie-pop fans) often favoured school-style anoraks and duffle coats, pastel, floral or polka-dot shirts, dungarees and school plimsolls. Even the haircuts of band members were seen to be connected to this desire for innocence, with floppy fringes or child-like short back and sides becoming briefly fashionable for young men, while female indie band members favoured bows and ribbons and/or ponytails. For female indie-pop followers the handbag was eschewed in favour of school satchels or duffle bags. Reynolds' explanation for this return to children's clothing is that

it conceals the signs of physical-maturity/sexual-difference . . . Against the mainstream image of a desirable body – vigorous, healthy, suntanned, muscled for men,
curvaceous for women, the indie ideal is slender, slight, pale of skin, childishly
androgynous . . . Both style and physical ideal seem to indicate a desire to distance
oneself from adult responsibility, to opt out of the material and sexual rat-race.
(Reynolds 1989: 251)

Here it can be seen how the indie scene offered an alternative to dominant
social and ideological values.

Britpop

Whereas the visual aesthetic of male and female indie pop followers
represented a desexualisation of style, Britpop certainly represented a
'remasculinisation' of male indie dress. For men and boys, Britpop
fashion harked back to the clothes worn by the same bands that Britpop
acts referred to in their music. The mod parka (as worn by Liam
Gallagher) was the favoured overcoat of the male (and occasionally
female) Britpop fan, and beneath it, Britpop fashion saw the return of
the Fred Perry tennis shirt (favoured by Blur's Damon Albarn and
Elastica's Justine Frischmann) and 'Sta-Prest' trousers. This is essentially
a mod-revival look that draws on the clothing style of the followers of
bands such as The Who (see Barnes 1991). While Britpop could not halt
the tide of mainstream fashion (which dictated that the trainer was the
default item of footwear for British teenagers and 'twenty somethings'),
Britpop did represent the last gasp of that 1980s' footwear staple, the
eight-hole Dr Marten's boot (worn by both male and female Britpop fans
and bands alike, with for example Elastica, Blur and Echobelly appearing
in 'Docs' in promotional photographs).

Elsewhere, on album-sleeve artwork, we see either references to
supposedly traditional elements of British life or to mod-influenced
British styles of the 1960s (greyhound racing on the cover of Blur's
Parklife, an English pier on Oasis' *Roll With It*, a mod scooter on Ocean
Colour Scene's *The Day We Caught The Train*, a peacock on the
Bluetones' *Expecting To Fly*). On promotional videos the story is largely
the same, with Andy Bennett singling out for attention Blur's video for
Parklife, where he suggests that there is a

stock of images which uphold the theme of Britishness – the row of terraced houses,
the ice cream van parked in the street and the individual members of Blur dressed
in casual clothes mimicking the typical stance of the British youth meeting up with
friends after school and playing out in the street. (Bennett 1997: n.p.)

As we can see in this video a narrator (Phil Daniels – star of the late 1970s cult mod film *Quadrophenia*) talks in an exaggerated cockney accent, whereas other videos by Pulp and Oasis are more likely to reference northern and central England. Bennett sees in this further references to a particularly English cultural form, namely the 'kitchen-sink' films of the early 1960s, including *Saturday Night and Sunday Morning* (set in Nottingham) and *A Taste of Honey* (set in Manchester) (Bennett 1997: n.p.).

A further visual movement connected with Britpop was the 'Britart' associated with PR guru turned art dealer Charles Saatchi. YBAs (Young British Artists) such as Sarah Lucas and Damien Hirst had met Blur's Graham Coxon and Alex James while studying at Goldsmiths College in London. British artists such Lucas, Hirst and Tracy Emin shared with bands such as Blur and Suede an aesthetic that was explicitly commercial, media-savvy, populist, yet conceptual and intellectual enough to appeal to key tastemakers.

Post-Britpop indie

In the earlier section on musical texts, we saw how, post-Britpop, the Liverpool-based but European-influenced indie band Ladytron rejected the guitar-centred nature of mid-1990s' indie while harking back to the electronic experimentalism of 1980s' 'new pop'. The visual aesthetic of Ladytron also followed suit. Whereas Britpop record covers and promotional materials were dominated unsurprisingly by images of Britishness, Ladytron's imagery is shot through with a European-like sophistication and coldness, while simultaneously fetishising new and old technology. For example, the cover of their 2001 album *604* featured a 'Speak and Maths' machine (an educational toy from the 1980s), and in the summer of 2002 Ladytron's website contained nothing other than a close-up photograph of one member of the band and a computerised image of two Apple Powerbook laptop computers. This not to suggest that all post-Britpop indie adheres to this aesthetic; however, Ladytron's imagery does nonetheless signal a complete rejection of Britpop's style, replacing authenticity with artifice, and replacing Britishness with a more European perspective.

Subsequent generic developments

The days when Britain was awash with medium-sized successful independent record companies such as Factory Records, Creation Records and Rough Trade seem to have passed. Many of the successful indie record companies of the 1980s were either purchased by major corporations (for example, EMI purchased Mute in 2002), weakened due to limited distribution opportunities or had collapsed due to a grasp of business sense that was outweighed by a penchant for philanthropic gestures. An example of the latter phenomenon can be found in the collapse of Factory Records. Factory's expansion into nightclub ownership was seen by Factory as a way of repaying the city of Manchester for its success. However, the purchase and maintenance of The Haçienda (along with the purchase of a new office block during the height of the boom in property prices (1989)) are now widely regarded as central reasons for Factory's financial collapse (see Wilson 2002).

In the 1990s, the commercial success of the 'Britpop' indie sound led major conglomerates to search out and sign similar bands. Notable successes include Mansun, signed to the EMI Group's Parlophone Records, and Stereophonics, signed to the V2 label. Following his sale of Virgin Records to Thorn EMI in 1992, Richard Branson founded the V2 label to provide an outlet for a roster of new bands. Significant financial losses in 2002 led Branson to sell a 47.5 per cent stake in the company to the investment bankers Morgan Stanley Dean Witter. At the time of this deal, Branson's 'corporate indie' was valued at £200 million, representing a halfway point between cottage industry labels such as Invicta HiFi and the five major conglomerates (http://news.bbc.co.uk/1/hi/entertainment/music/2158868.stm).

In the 1990s, the five major conglomerates that dominate music production and distribution consolidated their hold on the music industry through both horizontal integration (purchasing competitors and incorporating them within the corporation while retaining pseudo-independent label names for subsidiaries) and vertical integration (purchasing CD pressing plants or music retail outlets). The results of these processes are that we now have a fully globalised music industry. Yet, as we saw in the section on social and political context, this process of globalisation was happening at precisely the point that the UK government was placing an emphasis on the relevance of a specifically British music industry. The governmental emphasis on 'Cool Britannia' implied that there was a stable set of national creative industries, yet we can see that this was contrary to the increasingly globalised nature of the production of cultural texts. When Chris Smith was wooing the likes of Alan McGee (who in 1997 was a high-profile donor to Labour's coffers), other Labour ministers were relaxing their previously held antipathy to Rupert Murdoch, the controlling force behind News International (the publisher of, among other significant titles, *The Sun*, *The Times*, *News of the World*, and *The Sunday Times*) and British Sky Broadcasting. The latter company was the result of a takeover by Sky of British Satellite Broadcasting,[6] a failed UK-based enterprise. BSkyB has continued its rise to prominence following the collapse of ITV Digital (formerly Ondigital) in 2002, and at the time of writing BSkyB is the dominant player in the UK digital television market. Murdoch's empire dwarfs any UK-based concerns, and it is becoming clear that no matter how strongly the government attempts to promote UK-based cultural promotion, it will be the international conglomerates such as BSkyB, News International, AOL Time Warner, Sony, BMG and Universal that determine the nature of the relationship between culture and government in the future.

What this all means for indie is moot. Eighty per cent of recorded music is produced, distributed and sold by the five major record labels. The government's 'Cool Britannia' tag has proved to be as short lived as its musical predecessor Britpop, yet there is still a healthy independent music sector in the UK. Indeed, with the five major conglomerates worrying about the effects of Internet file sharing (a system that allows computer users to share and download each other's music purchases for free), and with the conglomerates struggling to mount their own successful online distribution networks, the independent sector could be well placed to bypass the major conglomerates' stranglehold of music distribution and market music direct to consumers. If the independent sector were to combine its low-cost niche marketing with the advantages of Internet distribution, their continued existence should be assured.

Notes

1. Major corporations frequently hide their status as conglomerates through the use of a myriad of 'imprints' and labels, many of which were independent prior to their purchase by the conglomerate concerned. At the time of writing, 'the majors' consist of AOL Time Warner, Bertelsmann, Universal, Sony, and Virgin EMI.

   The American entertainment giant AOL Time Warner trade under and run the following subsidiary music companies: Warner Bros. Records (Reprise Records, Maverick, WB Nashville, WB Jazzspace, Ruffnation), Elektra, Atlantic Records (these three label groups were at one time known as WEA – the Warner-Reprise, Elektra-Asylum, Atlantic group – which was formed by a merger in 1970, and AOL Time Warner still use the WEA imprint in Germany), Rhino (who also trade as Bright Night Records), Strictly Rhythm and Sub Pop.

   The privately-owned media corporation Bertelsmann has a 'corporate division' entitled the Bertelsmann Music Group (BMG) who trade as RCA, Ariola and Arista Records (which includes Bad Boy Entertainment and

BMG Funhouse). BMG also run the RCA Music Group's operating divisions including BMG Music Canada, BMG Special Products, RCA Records, RCA Label Group – Nashville and RCA Victor Group. The RCA Victor Group consists of Red Seal, RCA Victor, Windham Hill and Private Music. BMG also own the Zomba Label Group (Jive, Verity, Reunion, Silvertone, Jive-Electro and Brentwood), BMG Latin and Deconstruction.

Universal run the Universal Media Group (UMG), which includes the Decca Music Group (Decca, Decca Records, Phillips, the Britannia Music Club, Broadway and the iMusic Club), Deutsche Grammophon, Interscope Geffen A&M, the Island Def Jam Music Group (Def Jam Records, Def Soul Records, Island Records), MCA Records, MCA Nashville, Mercury Nashville, the Motown Record Company, Polydor, Universal Records (including Cash Money Records, Blackgound Records, The New No Limit Records, Republic Records), Universal Classics Group and the Verve Music Group (Verve, Impulse, GRP Records).

Sony Music Entertainment Incorporated is a wholly owned subsidiary of the giant Sony corporation and comprises four divisions: Sony Music (US), Sony Music International (all countries outside the US and Japan), Sony Classical (the worldwide classical music division) and Sony/ATV Music Publishing (the worldwide publishing company). Sony Music use the names of four wholly owned 'label groups': the Epic Records group (Crescent Moon, Darkchild, Epic Records, Hidden Beach, Independiente, Razor Sharp), the Columbia Records Group (American Recordings, Aware Records, Columbia Records and So So Def Recordings), Legacy Recordings and Sony Music Nashville (Columbia Records Nashville, Epic Records Nashville, Lucky Dog and Monument).

The company colloquially known as Virgin EMI has been renamed the EMI Group. This giant was created after Thorn EMI purchased Virgin Records from Richard Branson's Virgin Group in 1992. The EMI Group trade as Additive Records, Angel Records, Autonomy Records, Blue Note Records, Capitol Records, EMI: Chrysalis, Food Records, Grand Royal Records, Hemisphere Records, Hostile Records, Parlophone Records, Positiva Records, Priority Records, Real World, Source and Ultra-Lounge. Subsidiary and affiliated labels of Virgin include Astralwerks, Cheeba Sound, Higher Octave, Immortal, Luaka Bop, Narada, Pointblank and Rap-A-Lot.

(Sources: www.aoltimewarner.com, www.bmg.com, www.sony.com, www.vivendiuniversal.com, www.emigroup.com.)

2. Factory Records went further than Rough Trade and also allowed their bands to retain the rights to their own recordings.

3. In cultural studies the term 'conjuncture' refers to a period of economic, cultural, social and political life where social relations remain relatively stable. The term was popularised in cultural studies following the 'turn to Gramsci' that followed the publication of Antonio Gramsci's *Prison Notebooks* in 1971. See Hall (1988: 61–74) and Gramsci (1971: 177–80).

4. For an examination of 'Cool Britannia' and the 'Cultural Capitalism' of New Labour, see Bewes and Gilbert (2000).
5. At the time of writing, government figures put the total sector income at £112.5 billion (http://www.tradepartners.gov.uk).
6. The business deal which led to the creation of British Sky Broadcasting was originally dubbed a merger but takeover is more accurate, particularly as the new company traded as Sky, most BSB staff lost their jobs, BSB's unique satellite 'squarial' dishes were abandoned and the vast majority of BSB programming was cancelled.

Recommended reading

Cavanagh, D. (2001) *The Creation Records Story: My Magpie Eyes Are Hungry for the Prize*. London: Virgin.

Harris, J. (2003) *The Last Party: Britpop, Blair and the Demise of English Rock*. London: Fourth Estate.

Haslam, D. (1999) *Manchester England: The Story of the Pop Cult City*. London: Fourth Estate.

Larkin, C. (1998) *The Virgin Encyclopedia of Indie and New Wave*. London: Virgin.

Lazall, B. (1999) *Indie Hits: The Complete UK Singles and Albums Independent of Charts, 1980 to 1989*. London: Cherry Red Books.

Marshall, G. (1997) *The Two Tone Story*. Lockerbie: ST Publishing.

Muirhead, B. (1983) *Stiff: The Story of a Record Label, 1976–1982*. London: Blandford Press.

Rawlins, T. and Diggle, S. (2002) *Harmony in My Head: The Buzzcocks*. London: Helter Skelter

Reynolds, S. (1989) 'Against health and efficiency: independent music in the 1980s', in McRobbie, A. (ed.), *Zoot Suits and Second-Hand Dresses: An Anthology of Fashion and Music*. Boston: Unwin Hyman, pp. 245–55.

Strong, M. C. (1999) *The Great Alternative Indie Discography*. Edinburgh: Canongate Books.

Recommended listening

Antecedents

Buzzcocks (1977) *Spiral Scratch* [EP]. New Hormones.
Costello, Elvis (1977) *My Aim Is True*. Stiff.
Joy Division (1979) *Unknown Pleasures*. Factory Records.

Generic texts

Blur (1991) *Leisure*. Food.
The Cure (1986) *Standing On The Beach – The Singles*. Fiction.

Mansun (1997) *Attack of the Grey Lantern*. Parlophone.
Mighty Lemon Drops (1986) *Happy Head*. Chrysalis.
Oasis (1994) *Definitely Maybe*. Creation.
The Pastels (1987) *Up For A Bit With The Pastels*. Glass.
Primal Scream (1987) *Gentle Tuesday* [single]. Creation.
Shop Assistants (1986) *Shop Assistants*. Chrysalis.
The Smiths (2001) *The Very Best Of The Smiths*. WEA.
Soup Dragons (1990) *Love God*. Raw TV.
Stereophonics (1997) *Word Gets Around*. V2.
Stone Roses (1990) *The Stone Roses*. Silvertone.
Tallulah Gosh (1987) *Rock Legends: Volume 69*. 53rd and 3rd.
The Teardrop Explodes (1979) *Sleeping Gas* [EP]. Zoo.
Various (1988) *Doing it for The Kids*. Creation.
Various (1990) *C86*. Strange Fruit.
The Wedding Present (1987) *George Best*. Reception.

Subsequent generic developments

Various (1998) *Special Skool: The Best Of Invicta Hi-Fi*. Invicta Hi-Fi.

CHAPTER 11

Jungle: the breakbeat's revenge

An overview of the genre

Nomenclature in music has always been a controversial subject, and nowhere is this more so than with the 1990s' form of breakbeat dance music known as jungle. Within the context of the music discussed in this chapter, we need to examine two issues. Firstly, we must outline the etymological origins of the phrase 'jungle' and discuss the extent to which the term is pejorative or ideological. Secondly, we must investigate the distinctions between the terms 'jungle' and 'drum 'n' bass'.

There are broadly four suggested etymological origins of the use of the word 'jungle' within contemporary dance culture.

1. 'Junglist' is Jamaican patois. Within this definition, Push and Bush suggest that a junglist is a resident of Trenchtown in Jamaica (Push and Bush 1995: 90). MC Navigator of the London pirate radio station Kool-FM has a similar story:
   > The name jungle comes from this place in Kingston, Jamaica called Tivoli Gardens. The people who live there call it the Jungle, and the Junglists is the name of the local gang. The chant 'Alla the Junglists' was sampled from a sound system tape: the people over here started calling the music 'jungle'.
   > (Quoted in Reynolds 1995)
2. In much the same way that some African-Americans reappropriated certain racial epithets and used them as self-defined descriptions in the 1980s and 1990s, black music fans in London co-opted the phrase 'jungle' after British fascists termed late-1980s' rave music as 'jungle-bunny' music, due to its heavy black influence (see Push and Bush 1995: 90). It is for this latter reason that there is much controversy over the usage of the word. Some musicians (such as the breakbeat artists Shut Up and Dance) claim that the term is implicitly racist (see Verma 1999), while those who use the word suggest that it has lost all previous connotations.
3. A less controversial etymological origin of the phrase is its connections to the phrase 'concrete jungle' and the experience of living in the 'jungle' of inner-city life. Here the term is specifically connected to the economic recession of the early 1990s, yet it also draws upon the meanings of certain ska, rap and soul records from the past.[1]

4. Possibly connected to some of the suggested origins above is the connection between jazz music and the word 'jungle'. As Imruh Bakari suggests, the two terms were virtually synonymous during the first half of the twentieth century (Bakari 1999). Within this meaning of 'jungle', the *Oxford English Dictionary* talks of a style of jazz that is characterised by 'primitive sounds redolent of the jungle' (*Oxford English Dictionary Online*, 5 December 2002). For Bakari, a 'jazz aesthetic' is the central organising characteristic of jungle (Bakari 1999: 107). Perhaps the reappearance of the phrase 'jungle' can therefore be connected to the influence of jazz on the development of this genre.

Many who oppose the usage of the term 'jungle' often refer to this style of music as 'drum 'n' bass'. However, it should be noted that the phrase 'drum and bass' (or 'drum 'n' bass') only appeared several years after jungle had established itself as a successful music genre. In particular, the term 'drum 'n' bass' is used in the mid-to-late 1990s to described two very different breakbeat developments

'Drum 'n' bass' was used in the mid-1990s to describe a more melodic and 'ambient' style that saw jungle move out of raves and night clubs and into the UK album charts and review columns of broadsheet newspapers and music magazines. Key albums include Goldie's (Clifford Price) *Timeless*, A Guy Called Gerald's *Black Secret Technology* (both released in 1995) and Roni Size's (Ryan Williams) Mercury Music Award-winning album *New Forms* from 1997. Once jungle moved away from a ragga influence towards a jazz influence in 1993–4 (as witnessed by the release of 4 Hero's *Parallel Universe*), the usage of the term jungle declined.

The term 'drum 'n' bass' was also popularised at the point in the mid-1990s when a variety of musicians began to move away from the use of sampled breakbeats and towards the use of original drum patterns, composed and programmed entirely in the digital domain. The production of these 'second-generation' breakbeats led to the development of subgenres such as techstep (see below), which is a far more dissonant and 'angry' form of jungle than the ambient styles of Goldie, Roni Size and A Guy Called Gerald.

Although such a position is not without controversy, drum 'n' bass is essentially a near synonym for jungle,[2] although we accept that there *are* jungle subgenres, such as ragga jungle, which are generally not considered to be drum 'n' bass. As Martin James suggests, the drum 'n' bass/jungle split derives from a period in the mid-1990s when the subgenre of ragga jungle threatened to become hegemonic in breakbeat music. Within James' narrative, the formation of a shadowy collective of jungle musicians ('The Committee') led to a narrowing of the jungle sound and the decline of ragga jungle (see James 1997: 55–69). Whatever the reader's view on this debate (and there seem to be as many views on the 'jungle' versus 'drum 'n' bass' distinction as there are musicians working within the genre itself), we will be using the term 'jungle' to describe this genre of British dance music.

In summary, jungle is a form of electronic dance music that employs sampled, or more recently programmed, breakbeats that run at speeds in excess of 150 beats per minute. These breakbeats frequently originate from soul or funk records from the late 1960s and 1970s, although they may have been sampled and resampled since then (for example a modern jungle track might take a breakbeat from a rap record that had sampled a 1970s' soul record). The most famous of these is the breakbeat taken from The Winstons' track *Amen, Brother*. This breakbeat has formed the rhythmic bedrock of hundreds of different jungle tracks, and notable examples include LTJ Bukem's (Danny Williamson) *Music*, Ray Keith's *Terrorist*, Dillinja's (Carl Francis) *Ain't Seen Nothing*, Ganja Kru's *Bring The Horns*, DJ Hype's (Kevin Ford) *We Must Unite*, DJ Krust's (Keith Thompson) *Cloaking Device*, Lemon D's (Kevin King) *Why?*, Omni Trio's (Rob Haigh) *Together VIP* and The Ragga Twins and MC Navigator's (birth name unknown) *Lock Up*.

In contrast to these fast breakbeats are half-speed basslines, which often take the place of melody in the more minimalist jungle tracks. Occasionally, as on T Power vs. DJ Trace's (Mark Royal and Duncan Hutchison) track *Mutant Revisited*, this will be a 'rolling' bass where there is no space between each bass note. This extreme form of bass 'tenuto' is found almost exclusively in jungle and its hardcore predecessors (see below). Added to the drum and bass tracks are the following:

- horns (such as on Alex Reece's *Feel The Sunshine*);
- acoustic or electric guitar (such as on Squarepusher's (Tom Jenkinson) *Square-pusher Theme*);
- synthesised, sampled or 'real' strings (such as on Leviticus' *The Burial*);
- ambient 'pads' and washes (such as on a variety of tracks by LTJ Bukem, including *Demon's Theme* and *Horizons*);
- piano and keyboard melodies (such as on Roni Size's *It's A Jazz Thing*);
- sampled sounds (such as bird song – as found on LTJ Bukem's *Demon's Theme*);
- spoken vocals (such as on The Ganja Kru's *Super Sharp Shooter*);
- sung vocals (such as on Everything But The Girl's *Walking Wounded*); and
- sound effects.

Jungle is often augmented by the use of an MC. While ragga jungle saw the use of MCs on recorded works (for example on M Beat and General Levy's *Incredible* and UK Apache and Shy FX's *Original Nuttah*), come the etymological split between jungle and drum 'n' bass, the use of MCs was limited to clubs, soundsystems and the occasional mix CD or cassette. MCing is a form of rhythmic vocal improvisation that draws upon American rapping, Jamaican toasting and the African oral tradition. It is often the case that specific DJs (such as LTJ Bukem) only work with specific MCs (in Bukem's case MC Conrad) in order to present a unique combination of sounds and lyrics to the dancing audience.

The production, distribution and exchange of jungle music mirrors and extends the complex distribution methods of earlier forms of dance music in the UK. Throughout the 1990s, pirate radio stations particularly championed breakbeat music, and in the mid-1990s pirate radio became dominated by jungle (see Thompson 1998: 98–107). The popularity of pirate radio stations was at least partly derived from their ability to play jungle records many months before they were released 'legally'. On some occasions pirate radio DJs, along with their club and rave counterparts, played records that would never be released. This was because the tracks were not popular enough for a full commercial release or because they contained 'illegal' samples of recorded material for which the producer did not hold the intellectual property rights. Jungle DJs were able to do this through a distribution network that focused around the use of test pressings. Renamed 'dub plates' in tribute to their Jamaican reggae equivalents (see Chapter 6), these super-heavy twelve-inch records rapidly decreased in audibility and aural quality after repeated plays. However, this only accentuated the suggestion that jungle was dominated by a 'speed' aesthetic whereby the rapid obsolescence of a particular track was alleviated by a steady supply of new tracks, new dub plates and new twelve-inch mixes in specialist record shops. This trade in dub plates continued while jungle developed, even when new jungle singles and albums gained a prominent place in the high-street chains such as Virgin and HMV.

In terms of influence, jungle takes succour from a variety of previous musical genres. Within jungle we can hear breakbeats from soul, funk and, later, rap records. With certain jungle subgenres, such as ragga jungle, we can hear the influence of reggae. With the work of artists such as Roni Size, we can hear a significant jazz influence. With the more aggressive sounds of techstep, we can hear the influence of techno. In terms of its genesis, house and acid house figure prominently. In a sense, jungle is a hybrid genre that 'steals' sounds and rhythms from a range of earlier genres (sometimes quite literally).

Historical roots and antecedents

The roots of jungle music are to be found in the resurgence in the use of breakbeats within British dance music in the early 1990s. In order to understand the significance of this return to syncopation, we must first outline briefly the development of dance music in the 1980s.

American house, acid house and techno musics (see Glossary) had begun to arrive on British shores in the mid-1980s and were consumed by a small but fervent following of British fans. In particular, northern clubs such as The Haçienda played house music from 1986 onwards,[3] and come 1988, tabloid press coverage had ensured that acid house was the most notorious, and consequently most popular, musical phenomenon since punk. Early British house clubs and raves played either the metronomic rhythms of imported American house, acid house and techno, or adopted a so-called 'Balearic' style (named after eclectic Ibizan DJs such as DJ Alfredo). This latter style took in British house music such as that produced by M/A/R/R/S and Bomb the Bass, and rhythmic pop such as The Woodentops, U2, The Waterboys and Thrashing Doves (Reynolds 1998: 35–7).

By 1990 the grip that 'four-to-the-floor' house and techno held over the British rave scene was weakened by the brief appearance of a hybrid genre known as hip house and the development of a distinctively British dance genre which soon became known as hardcore. In particular, hip house used hip-hop breakbeats to provide a 'blacker' and 'funkier' feel than that provided by the Europhile sounds of 'four-to-the-floor' techno and house (which emphasised a precisely programmed crotchet beat). Considering the later genesis of jungle, it is ironic that it was late 1980s' American house producers, such as Royal House, Fast Eddie and Tyree, who had incorporated into their productions many of the soon-to-be-essential elements of jungle, namely breakbeats, James Brown samples and sound effects (Reynolds 1998: 32–3). However, this breakbeat house formula would require a few more mutations before what we now know as jungle became apparent.

By 1991, a range of UK-based artists were developing a form of hip house that took the American hip house formula and added deepened basslines drawn from Jamaican reggae. Whereas acts such as Shades of Rhythm and Shut Up and Dance experimented with breakbeat house, the first post-acid house dance records from Europe continued to employ a crotchet beat, but lacked the subtlety and refined minimalism of American house and techno, preferring to employ a far more aggressive and harsher style recorded at a higher tempo. Dutch, Belgian and German techno began to employ what became known as a 'Hoover' sound that was related to the drone-like sound of a vacuum cleaner.[4]

In 1990–1, the music played at British raves was moving further and further away from the austere minimalism of American techno, house, and acid house towards a more brutal fuller sound that drew upon the European techno outlined above. Tempi had risen from 120 beats per minute (the standard tempo of much 1980s' house and acid house) to 130–40 beats per minute. Basslines continued to become more prominent in the mix (with either the use of 'sub bass' or a more high-pitched bass drone), while the increasing dominance of the breakbeat meant that the last vestiges of the crotchet beat gradually faded into the background.

During 1991–2, this breakbeat dance music was incorporating aggressive keyboard 'stabs' or 'riffs' and sound effects designed to scare the listener. This music also employed a form of keyboard drone originally heard on Joey Beltram's *Mentasm*, alongside synthesised or sampled noise, and it was the nature of these final additions that led to this emerging British genre becoming known as hardcore (which differed from European-style techno in its reliance on breakbeats rather than 'four-to-the-floor' crotchets). It was during this period that fast breakbeat rhythms began to be called 'jungle' (as witnessed by the term's usage in the London listings magazine *City Limits*, 2 July 1992: 37). However, the generic form of jungle would not be fixed until two or three years later, and during 1992–3, the phrase 'darkcore' was prominent (Collin with Godfrey 1997: 252).

While this hardcore breakbeat sound developed, a schism appeared between the legal rave scene, which had developed following the effective criminalisation of illegal raves after the enactment of the Entertainments (Increased Penalties) Act 1990 (see Redhead 1993b: 20–2), and the 'indoor' club scene. Whereas European techno nightclubs, and, later, British hardcore- and jungle-dominated raves, nightclubs invariably favoured the allegedly more sophisticated sounds of house and techno. Elsewhere in the rave scene a further schism developed with many in the Scottish rave scene holding out against the re-emergence of the breakbeat and beginning to develop a style of music known colloquially as 'tartan techno' (which featured crotchet beats played at in excess of 140 beats per minute). In contrast, sampled breakbeats increasingly dominated DJ sets at English raves. What connected 'tartan techno' and English breakbeat hardcore was their increasing velocity and the effects this increase in velocity had on the rhythmic and non-rhythmic elements of the music. Tempi in excess of 140 beats per minute meant that the 'funky' syncopated quality of the original breakbeats were less noticeable than on the 1970s' funk records from which they had been sampled. Furthermore, in order to sync the non-rhythmic elements to the 140+ beats per minute of the sampled breakbeats, musicians began to record vocals and other sampled sounds at a higher pitch. This led to the use of what became known as 'chipmunk vocals', whereby sampled vocals were played at octaves higher than the original sample (see Reynolds 1998: 126).

Within the hardcore scene, a final schism was to develop which led to the beginnings of jungle, and the departure of what was known in the early-to-mid 1990s as 'happy hardcore'. Happy hardcore developed out of hardcore, but saw an expunging of the elements of hardcore that were seen as unsettling, 'dark' or aggressive. Happy hardcore eschewed the disturbing sound effects first seen in European techno, and also rejected the atonal noise, drone bass and minor-key chords that were beginning to dominate hardcore. These elements were rejected in favour of 'uplifting' melodies, 'bouncy' breakbeats and 'chipmunk' vocals frequently sampled from 1980s' chart hits (or more bizarrely soft rock records). Some happy hardcore continued to use breakbeats, while a variant known as '4-beat' reverted to the use of 'four-to-the-floor' crotchets. In contrast, 'non-happy hardcore', or as it was to be known during the autumn of 1992 and the early winter months of 1993 'darkcore', placed full emphasis on the most dissonant and unsettling elements of the hardcore formula, outlined by Simon Reynolds as 'metallic beats, murky modulated-bass, hideously warped vocals, [and] ectoplasmic smears of sample-texture' (Reynolds 1998: 196). Whereas happy hardcore employed vocals that focused on a traditional utopian rave message of 'peace, love, unity and respect' (or PLUR for the aficionados), darkcore occupied a far more dystopian position.

The final phase in the development of acid house into jungle involved a technological shift, an aesthetic shift and a continuation of the gradual increase in tempo that characterised the development of dance music from 1985–95. Firstly, the development of 'time-stretching' software and hardware in the mid-1990s meant that no longer would the breakbeat artist have to 'pitch up' non-rhythmic elements in order to match them to the frenetic rhythms of hardcore. Whereas early 1990s' hardcore and late 1990s' happy hardcore featured 'chipmunk' or 'helium' vocals, mid-1990s' jungle was dominated by vocals that were recorded at the same pitch as the original sample, but were distorted through early experiments in time-stretching (for an example of this, listen to the spoken vocals on DJ Hype's *Roll Da Beats*). Secondly, an aesthetic shift saw darkcore draw back from the apocalyptic density of its dystopian vision to encompass elements of lightness. Early jungle began to drop the excessive use of gloom-filled samples and dissonant chords, and began to focus on rhythmic experimentation and the micro editing of sampled breakbeats, a focus that would lead jungle to be dubbed 'breakbeat science' by some.[5] The music of jungle artist Omni Trio (the recording name of solo artist

Rob Haigh) emphasises this shift away from horror-filled sound effects to what Reynolds refers to as 'rhythmic psychedelia' (Reynolds 1998: 241). An early Omni Trio track entitled *Renegade Snares* captures early jungle's struggle between 'dark' and 'light', where militant and aggressive percussion is married to a sampled female voice that implores the listener to 'take me up'. Thirdly, the ever-increasing rhythmic tempo of dance music from 1985 onwards could not go on forever (although Dutch gabber, a form of ultra-fast techno, reached tempi in excess of 200 beats per minute by the mid-1990s). In Britain, once percussive speeds reached 160–80 beats per minute, jungle musicians began to look towards dub reggae basslines that matched jungle's hyper-rhythms because, at 80–90 beats per minute, these basslines were precisely half the speed of jungle breakbeats. This addition of slow basslines to fast breakbeats completed the transition and meant that jungle had far more 'funk' and 'groove' than those tracks that relied upon a 'four-to-the-floor' kick drum.

Social and political context

During the first years of the 1990s, the British economy suffered a recession that was deeper than the recession of ten years earlier. Inflation reached 10 per cent in 1990 and the country suffered a globally unprecedented drop in GDP from 1990 to 1991. The boom of the mid-to-late 1980s had encouraged a significant increase in house purchases and house prices which led to high rates of household debt. Bust followed boom, and a collapse in house prices, combined with a hike in interest rates (with base rates set at 15 per cent in 1990), left tens of thousands of homeowners in 'negative equity', where the mortgages on their property were valued at a much higher rate than the property's market worth. Unemployment peaked at 10.4 per cent in 1993, a figure that hid the 'real' level of unemployment, with the 'headline' figure artificially reduced by the Conservative government (all figures from Pope 1998).

Economists suggest that when we are denied work through involuntary unemployment, we seek out and complete other activities that provide us with social needs (see Jahoda 1982, and MacKay 1995). This certainly occurred with the rave generation, who, denied stable employment by corporate Britain, set up a loose network of musical micro-economies, with the first generation of jungle musicians inhabiting a space in between unemployment and the black economy. Many jungle musicians and fans organised illegal and semi-legal raves and produced music to be sold as white labels through a loose yet nationwide distribution network of small, independent music retailers. Like much DJing and MCing work, these paid tasks might not always have been declared to the authorities (Her Majesty's Inspector of Taxes, the Department of Employment, the Department of Social Security). As such, jungle musicians and rave and club organisers occupied a position in the grey economy that was equidistant between the opposing polarities of Thatcherite entrepreneurialism and left-wing collectivism and cooperativism. This rave economy mirrored the general economy's shift from manufacturing to service industries, one of the most prominent and significant economic developments of the 1990s.

No less than the semi-professional musicians, promoters and technicians of jungle, the music's audience were also affected by the deep recession of the early 1990s. However, whereas jungle musicians turned to different and non-official forms of unemployment, many unemployed rave fans saw their unemployment not in the terms of exclusion but in terms of choice. As MacKay suggests 'any reduction in employment involves compensation in leisure' (MacKay 1995). Whereas career employment requires dedication and attention to detail on a Monday morning, unemployment or employment in what have been termed 'McJobs' (Coupland 1992) allow rave and jungle fans to immerse themselves in a musical subculture. As a result, jungle flourished in the inner cities of London, Manchester and the West Midlands, and other areas of high unemployment.

Simon Reynolds sees the economic turmoil outlined above as being directly reflected in the music of hardcore, darkcore and jungle. For example, in his analysis of Nasty Habit's 1992 track *Here Come The Drumz*, Reynolds suggests that the track contains 'the sound of inner-city turmoil; the track samples a snatch of Public Enemy rabble-rousing, with Chuck D declaiming the title phrase stagefront and Flavor Flav barging in the blurt "Confusion!!"' (Reynolds 1998: 198). Label owner and musician Goldie, a colleague of Doc Scott (Scott McIlroy), who produced *Here Come The Drumz*, agrees that darkcore reflected British society's slide into economic depression: '"dark" came from the feeling of breakdown in society. It was winter, clubs were closing, the country was in decline. As an artist, I had to reflect it' (quoted in Reynolds 1998: 201–2).

However, there is a crucial difference between previous musical forms that reflected upon socio-economic forces and jungle, and that is that jungle is a predominantly vocal-free form (although, ironically, one of the most famous of jungle's few vocal phrases is the lyric 'inner-city life' found on Goldie's single of the same name). If we accept the semiotic maxim that all texts have meaning, then it is in the musical form of jungle that we find its meaning, rather than in its lyrical content. Reynolds clearly agrees when he suggests:

> Jungle's militant euphoria is fuelled by the desperation of the early nineties. Composed literally out of fracture ('breaks'), jungle paints a sound-picture of social disintegration and instability . . . Jungle contains a non-verbal response to troubled times, a kind of warrior-stance. The resistance is in the rhythms. (Reynolds 1998: 239)

Martin James agrees, describing T-Power's album *The Self Evident Truth Of An Intuitive Mind* as offering

> a foreboding dissonance, a bleak isolationist vision of a world under the intruding eye of surveillance cameras. If there was a sound of the concrete jungle facing up to the reality of life in the 1990s then it surely could be found on this album. (James 1997: 86–7)

As well as the above economic shifts, the 1990s also saw changes in the regulation of nightclubs and raves. The Entertainments (Increased Penalties) Act 1990 made unlicensed raves uneconomic through a massive increase in the level of fines that could be levied on organisers. This led to a split in the rave scene between unlicensed outdoor parties that evaded criminalisation through not charging an entrance fee, large legal outdoor raves (which became dominated by forms of breakbeat music) and nightclubs (which continued to play house and techno). Martin James suggests that rave's shift towards hardcore, darkcore and jungle was partly determined by this attempt at criminalisation, and that in a 'progression that seemed to reflect the anger surrounding the government's rave crackdown, the music took on a new intensity' (James 1997: 9). Four years after the enactment of this legislation, the Criminal Justice and Public Order Act 1994 made free unlicensed raves illegal, defining a rave as a 'gathering on land in the open air of 100 or more persons (whether or not trespassers) at which amplified music is played during the night' that consists of 'sounds wholly or predominantly characterised by the emission of a succession of repetitive beats' (Section 63, subsection 1).[6] This severely hampered the free party scene and forced many party organisers to hire appropriate indoor venues. As hardcore gave way to darkcore and jungle, the scene largely moved into traditional nightclubs, where it remains today (although there remains a market for occasional large spectaculars, such as the Fantasy Island rave for New Year's Eve 2002, where darkcore, jungle and happy hardcore featured prominently).

Whereas the above analysis focuses upon the relationship between music, economics, politics and legal regulation, jungle is also of importance when talking about the changing nature of British racial politics. Unlike many earlier forms of dance music, jungle draws equal influence from musical forms that have a broadly black parentage, such as rap music, as well as musical forms that have a broadly European genealogy, such as techno[7] and the ' "whiter-than-white" brutal bombast of the Euro-hardcore sound spawned in Belgium and Brooklyn' (Reynolds 1998: 247). While writers such as Jeremy Gilbert, Ewan Pearson, and Imruh Bakari talk of jungle as 'black music' and emphasise the influence of an African diasporic discourse on jungle (Bakari 1999: 107, Gilbert and Pearson 1999: 79–82), this neglects the equally important influence of British, Belgian and German techno on jungle. Jungle (like reggae) is a 'syncretic' form in that it combines previously incompatible musical discourses. The end result of this syncretism is that young people in England, Scotland and Wales feel they have an ownership of jungle irrespective of their ethnicity.

Bakari suggests that jungle occupies a position of 'underground' marginality that is distinct from the 'hegemonic' position of dominant Western culture. However, in a similar analysis offered by Norman Stolzoff with regard to reggae (Stolzoff 2000: 17), jungle is in a dominated economic position and is not able to flex its economic, political or cultural muscles over and above a dominating British culture. Jungle is not an exclusively black form (indeed its marginality is equally a matter of class rather than purely a matter of race or ethnicity). Jungle producers and the audience for jungle are racially and ethnically heterogeneous. It is clearly necessary to acknowledge Paul Gilroy's valuable work on the role of reggae, soul, funk, and rap in the lives of black Britons (see Gilroy 2002). It is also necessary to acknowledge that the black roots (and branches) of these musical forms gives them an explicitly anti-establishment and anti-capitalist politics (Gilroy 2002: 265–83). However, this does not mean that jungle can be described unproblematically as 'black music', merely that it draws upon musical and extra-musical discourses that have been seen as exclusively black in the past.[8]

This argument is influenced clearly by the work of Stuart Hall, in particular his argument that black cultural forms are already 'hybridized from a vernacular base', and that the 'necessary moment' of essentialism, where black music is seen to have an 'essential' set of characteristics (Hall 1992: 28), is gradually fading. If, as Hall suggests, 'blacks in the British diaspora must, at this historical moment, refuse the binary black *or* British' (Hall 1992: 29),[9] then the same is true of jungle music. We can talk of the relative influence of discourses of 'blackness' and 'whiteness' on certain musical forms, and we can certainly suggest that musical forms such as jungle are part of an African musical diaspora that also encompasses reggae and rap music. However, in the England, Scotland and Wales of the twenty-first century, we can no longer talk of specific genres of pop music as being *exclusively* 'white' or 'black'. Even the most Afrocentric of pop genres, such as reggae, are deeply influenced by European musical discourses, and there are certainly no European 'pop' forms that have not been influenced by African rhythms and the African vernacular tradition. While certain folk cultures (such as English Morris dancing or Ghanaian Atsiã) might retain their ethnic 'purity', newer dance music forms such as jungle, born and developed in a post-colonial world and 'connected to a network of global flows of culture' (Hesmondhalgh 2001: 275), are simultaneously black *and* white.

The musical texts

Hip house
Shades of Rhythm (1991) *Homicide* [single]. ZTT.
Unique 3 (1989) *The Theme* [single]. EMI.

A form of music popular at early raves, hip house attempted to mould the deep sounds of American techno and house to the sampled breakbeats of funk and soul music. Whereas house and techno generally employed the kick drums, hi-hats, snares and cymbals found on drum machines, hip house drew upon rap music's usage of fast breakbeats to provide a funkier feel to dancefloor rhythms.

Hardcore
Shut Up and Dance (1991) *£10 To Get in* [single]. Shut Up and Dance.
4 Hero (1991) *Mr Kirk's Nightmare* [single]. Reinforced.
SL2 (1992) *On A Ragga Tip* [single]. XL.

Whereas house and acid house were functionalist musics designed to facilitate dancing and little else, the shift from these genres to breakbeat hardcore marks a shift towards music designed to scare and frighten rather than merely 'uplift'. Spoken and sung vocals are invariably sampled (in the case of the 4 Hero track cited above from an episode of the TV drama *Star Trek*) rather than originally recorded. Hardcore was recorded on limited equipment, but it was in hardcore that we saw the sampler move stage forward (in particular those samplers produced by the Japanese electronics giant Akai), and this led to a relative decline in the popularity of drum machines. Unlike in other forms of dance music, hardcore makes use of a wide range of sound frequencies. Sub-bass and higher drone-like bass frequencies occupy the bottom end of the frequency range, vocals, keyboard-derived chords and simple 'sine wave' notes dominate mid-range frequencies, while cymbals, snares and hi-hats are tweaked and altered so that they sound particularly crisp at the top end of the frequency range.

'Toytown' rave
The Prodigy (1992) *Charly* [single]. XL.

Breakbeat hardcore enters the mainstream and exits shortly afterwards. Within such tracks the dark foreboding menace of hardcore is replaced by catchy choruses and melodic hooks placed alongside fast breakbeats and synthesiser stabs drawn from European techno. The Prodigy charted in 1991 with *Charly* (a breakbeat driven track that features a sample from a children's public information film produced to highlight the dangers of abduction) and *Everybody In The Place*. The Prodigy's success led to a rash of fast breakbeat tracks with catchy choruses that sampled children's television programmes and which featured none-too-subtle references to ecstasy consumption. Notable tracks included Urban Hype's *A Trip To Trumpton*, Shaft's *Roobarb & Custard* and Smart E's *Sesame's Treat*.

Darkcore
Doc Scott (1992) *Here Come the Drumz* [single]. Reinforced.
Goldie (1993) *Terminator* [single]. Synthetic.
Origin Unknown (1993) *Valley Of The Shadows* [single]. Ram.
DJ Ron (1993) *Crackman On The Line* [single]. Pure.

This marks the rave 'comedown' and the final iteration in the development of fast breakbeat before the generic form of jungle asserts itself. Here all the discursively 'happy' or 'uplifting' elements of acid house, house and hardcore are jettisoned and replaced by foreboding chords, murky mid-range breakbeats, booming 'tenuto' sub-bass, and spoken vocals and sound effects sampled from horror films and television documentaries.

Ragga jungle
Shy FX and UK Apache (1994) *Original Nuttah* [single]. DJ Only.
M Beat and General Levy (1994) *Incredible* [single]. Renk Records.

For a brief period during 1994, it looked as if ragga jungle would dominate the fast breakbeat scene. In Shy FX's (Andre Williams) chart hit *Original Nuttah* sampled spoken vocals from the film *Goodfellas* introduce the track. These vocals then segue into eerie strings and reggae-style toasting from UK Apache, which is then augmented by the arrival of a deep sub-bass bassline drawn from dub reggae. After seventy seconds, the bassline suddenly drops, the strings fade and for a few seconds the toasting continues a capella. Ten seconds later the bassline and strings return, this time complemented by an Amen-style breakbeat. This combination of dub reggae basslines, looped breakbeats and reggae chatter represents the basic formula of ragga jungle. Other elements are added to this formula including sound effects (such as the gun shots), single-note synthesised melodies and mid-range basslines (such as on Ragga Twins featuring Junior Reid's *Shine Eye*), while breakbeats are twisted, edited and treated with a variety of sound-enhancing filters and effects such as reverb, echo and frequency equalisation.

Ambient jungle/drum 'n' bass/artcore
LTJ Bukem (1992) *Demon's Theme* [single]. Good Looking.
LTJ Bukem (1995) *Horizons* [single]. Good Looking.
DJ Crystal (1994) *Sweet Dreams* [single]. Dee Jay Recordings.

The pendulum swings away from ragga-style aggression and darkcore-style dissonance towards the gentle sounds of filtered strings, 'found sounds' and melody. These elements then provide a strong contrast with the sampled breakbeats. Bukem's *Demon's Theme* remains an early example of the subgenre. Like many of Bukem's tracks, *Demon's Theme* begins with filtered strings. After 17 seconds, this is complemented by the sound of the sea, bird song and a deep resonant bassline. Two echoed cymbal hits make a brief appearance after 40 seconds, and at 53 seconds the breakbeat enters the sound frame. Throughout the track, the strings soar while the other elements fade in and out. After two minutes, a one-note and echoed melody is added to the mix, although this is by no means foregrounded. After two and a half minutes, a brief sampled female vocal signals the addition of an extra looped drum track which is heavily processed and at least partially reversed. Elsewhere in the track strings that are slightly more dissonant appear, while a horn is prominent during a middle section of the track. At 4 minutes 50 seconds, the track breaks down to a simple keyboard melody, bird song and strings. Lone cymbals gently crash, and after approximately 30 seconds the breakbeat returns, followed 10 seconds later by the bassline. Like many ambient jungle tracks, Bukem's *Demon's Theme* is somewhat longer than most other jungle tracks.

Intelligent jungle/drum 'n' bass
Various (1994) *Intelligent Minds of Jungle*. Reinforced.
4 Hero (1994) *Parallel Universe*. Reinforced.
Everything But The Girl (1996) *Walking Wounded* [single]. Virgin.

This marks the rise of album-focused breakbeat that sees the jungle tag dropped as the music is popularised outside its urban origins. The strings of ambient jungle remain and the breakbeat science is enhanced as drum loops are minutely edited and treated. Soulful vocals are added and basslines are at their deepest and warmest.

Jazz step
Alex Reece (1994) *Pulp Fiction* [single]. Metalheads.
DJ Krust (1995) *Jazz Note* [single]. V.
T-Power vs. MK Ultra (1995) *Mutant Jazz* [single]. SOUR.
Adam F (1996) *F-Jam* [single]. Positiva.
Roni Size (1998) *It's Jazzy* [single]. V.

This is a stripped-down subgenre of jungle that features crisp, 'trebly' breakbeats and mid-range kick drums, and which places an emphasis on the second and fourth beats in each bar. Soulful vocals, jazz horns and piano chords are also prominent. In many respects this form of jungle prefaced the late-1990s' popularity of two-step garage (see below).

Techstep
T-Power vs. MK Ultra (1996) *Mutant Revisited* [DJ Trace remix, single]. SOUR.
Various (1996) *Techsteppin'*. SOUR.
Ed Rush (1996) *Kilamanjaro/Subway* [single]. Prototype Recordings.
DJ Trace and Nico (1999) *Squadron* [single]. No U Turn.

Drum 'n' bass at its most dissonant and aggressive. Rather than the sampled breakbeats of early to mid-period jungle, techstep artists prefer to construct their own drum patterns through the use of computer-based sequencing software such as Steinberg's Cubase. Alongside fast 'industrial' beats we having a rolling bass, or what is known by many as the 'Reece bass', either sampled from or constructed to sound like the drone-like bassline used by the American techno artist Kevin Saunderson on records released under the name The Reece Project. In many respects, techstep is a hybrid genre that melds the most aggressive elements of European techno and jungle.

Jump up
DJ Hype (1996) *Original Foundation* [EP]. Ganja Records.
Ganja Kru (1996) *Super Sharp Shooter* [EP]. Parousia.

This is a form of jungle where the influence of rap and hip-hop culture is at its highest. As well as using sampled breakbeats, much jump up also features MCing that is more clearly derived from rapping than the more African-Caribbean MCing of ragga jungle. Many see the popularity of jump up in the late 1990s and early 2000s as signalling a return to 'the dark side' after the dominance of ambient and jazz jungle styles.

Drill 'n' bass

Aphex Twin (1995) *Hangable Auto Bulb* [EP]. Warp.
Squarepusher (1996) *Conumber* [EP]. Spymania.
U-ziq (1997) *Urmer Bile Trax* [EP]. Astralwerks.

This is drum 'n' bass without the funk or soul influences. Drill 'n' bass also makes use of non-musical sounds ('found sounds') in place of drums and other traditional rhythmic instruments. Often produced by musicians that are more easily classifiable as indie musicians, drill 'n' bass includes breakbeat tracks by Squarepusher (Tom Jenkinsen), U-ziq (Mike Paradinas) and the Aphex Twin (Richard D. James). The latter two artists also produce music that draws upon ambient, but aims to upset rather than soothe. Such 'illbient' music has a similar relationship to ambient that drill 'n' bass has with drum 'n' bass.

Visual aesthetic

While the visual aesthetics of other genres examined in this book are obvious, jungle's style is much less apparent. In its early development there was a dominant theme, and from the moment hardcore gave way to darkcore (itself often referred to simply as 'dark'), jungle preferred a murky, gloomy and sinister visual style within record sleeves, artwork and club decor. In many respects, this was an attempt to reflect literally the sense of darkness, danger and illegality enveloping the rave scene in the early to mid-1990s. Deleterious drug use had increased, and the increased criminalisation of the rave scene led to the arrival of criminal gangs who controlled the door policies and consequently controlled the distribution and sale of drugs at many raves and clubs. Martin James notes an early example of this dark aesthetic:

> The very first Jungle Fever [an early jungle rave held in August 1993] was almost a statement of intent to the whole scene. The venue was decorated like a graveyard with tombstones, coffins and Gothic statues in a move which attempted to exaggerate the dark mood of the times. (James 1997: 39)

Jungle raving. Out of the darkside and into the light.

While the preference of early jungle promoters and musicians might have been for a dark aesthetic, the audience for jungle had different ideas. Whereas the usual baggy rave apparel of bright or 'day-glo' clothes, plain T-shirts and 'beanie' hats was not replicated in jungle, neither was the 'gothic' nature of the music. If the darkness of jungle music was a clear reflection of the economic mood of the country, the clothes of jungle fans could not be so easily 'read off' from a set of economic determinants. However, there is still a connection between economics and aesthetic. Rather than thrift-shop recession chic, jungle fans chose to rise out of the national mood of depression through the display of the more exclusive 'diffusion' lines of the world's leading *haute-couture* designers.

Although there was an early attempt at literalism during the ragga jungle period, with jungle fans wearing jungle camouflage trousers and jackets, green string vests and the occasional piece of safari wear, the later sartorial style of jungle featured clothes designed by Versace, Moschino and Armani. This obsession with major-label fashion was also seen on both sides of jungle's gender divide. Whereas the male junglists wore fashion-house trousers and labelled shoes or trainers beneath padded flight jackets, early female jungle fans were influenced by Jamaican dancehall fashions that veered towards minimalism (micro-skirts, hot pants, bras), and this continued into the late 1990s with boutique clothing and sexy club wear (as opposed to the unisex fashions of 1980s' acid house).

In many respects, jungle's upmarket clothing reflects a trend within the American hip-hop scene that has been referred to as 'ghetto fabulous'. While hip-hop journalist Nelson George traces this style back to the rap videos released by the Uptown record label, including videos for Heavy D, Mary J. Blige, Jodeci and Soul for Real (George 1998: 119), Boston journalist Amy Alexander suggests that

> to be 'ghetto fabulous' is to engage in a lifestyle, expressed primarily through one's fashion choices, that celebrates new money, personal independence, and a distinct lack of interest in whatever the mainstream style mavens identify as 'good taste.' It suggests a kind of 'hood-bred reverence for flashy, Mack Daddy-Superfly-type clothing . . . and a fashion agenda based on the earliest dreams of an inner-city youngster who longs for what he imagines is a plush lifestyle, a world in which the champagne flows freely, all the cars have shiny rims, and the only thing thicker than the platinum chain around his neck is the wad of cash in his pocket. (Alexander 2001: n.p.)

While minor amendments need to be made before applying the term to jungle (for example the limited incomes of jungle fans would preclude the wearing of thick platinum chains), the effect of jungle glamour is pretty much the same. Jungle fashion 'cocks a snook' at the traditional British discourses of thriftiness and modesty, while also asserting a pride in appearances that has been the root of many music-based fashions. The fact that jungle glamour arose at the tail end of an economic recession also asserts a flagrant disregard for the country's reduced financial circumstances and an unwillingness to be cowed by economic forces that the 'fashionista' is unable to control. Reynolds notes further stylistic excesses during the early years of jungle where 'for a while there was fashion among the more chic black junglists to carry handkerchiefs, in order to dab away every last drop of perspiration and preserve the aura of aloof coolness' (Reynolds 1998: 250). This coolness in the midst of chaos is the very essence of the early jungle sartorial aesthetic. While jungle glamour was dominant in most jungle clubs in the early-to-mid 1990s, an influx of students who preferred a more low-key style in the late 1990s and beyond has led to a dilution of the more acutely fashion-conscious trends. Nowadays, jungle fashion is more or less the same as smart British club wear.

Subsequent generic developments

Interestingly, the sartorial developments outlined above also help to partly explain subsequent developments. In the late 1990s, jungle had seemed to run out of creative steam, with many jungle fans wondering what lay ahead for the scene. Attendance at the more ostentatious jungle clubs, such as London's Roast and Thunder & Joy, had declined. In a reverse development, there was a marked increase in smaller clubs, and a diffusion of the drum 'n' bass scene away from the large cities towards smaller cities and towns. In particular, Britain's large student population, which had previously ignored jungle in favour of indie, techno and 'big beat' (a breakbeat-driven hybrid of old-school rap and techno with some junglist flavourings), began to attend drum 'n' bass nights in considerable numbers.[10] This process was at least partly accentuated by the arrival of techstep, which was a form of jungle that saw a lessening of importance in the 'blacker' elements of jungle's melting pot of sounds.

During 1996–7 the more elegantly dressed fans of jungle, along with a wide range of black jungle musicians, jumped ship into the nascent 'speed garage' scene. Late 1990s' speed garage was, like jungle, a particularly British hybrid of a variety of sources. The basis of the sound was drawn from pirate radio, where some disillusioned junglists turned to American garage but played the music at an increased tempo through the use of pitch-adjusting Technics turntables. The tempo increases of up to 8 per cent meant that 120–30 beats per minute garage was played at 130–40 beats per minute. Using this basic garage template pirate radio DJs and their club counterparts would 'work' the mixer, altering the relative frequencies of a track (more often than not to deepen the bass sounds and remove mid-range frequencies) while also adding special effects such as echo and reverb. This fast 'dubbed' garage sound would then be mixed by the DJ in the same way as jungle. Whereas the dominant form of mixing house, techno and American garage would be the slow fade, where the beats of two records would be synchronised and the DJ set would flow from record to record with minimal disruption, jungle DJs followed their rap counterparts by scratching, rhythmically chopping and cutting between records. Jungle added to the rap repertoire of mixing techniques through its distinctive use of the 'rewind', whereby the DJ would manually rewind a copy of a particular track so that, for a minute or so, the track was played backwards at an accelerating tempo. Once the stylus had reached the beginning of the track, the record would then be replayed. This process was completed for the most popular club tracks, with jungle fans shouting for a 'rewind' if they felt a particular track merited this special treatment. (This approach is similar to the Jamaican selector's 'forward' manoeuvre, see Stolzoff 2000: 207.) Emerging garage DJs took these DJing techniques and applied them to garage. This, combined with a pirate radio or club MC, meant that the garage played in the UK by disaffected junglists began to sound qualitatively different to the garage as played by more traditional garage DJs.

The inevitable next step was the recording of British garage tracks at a faster tempo than American garage, and which featured the sound manipulation of the jungle DJ and the sound-effect motifs of jungle music. One final shift led to speed garage, as for the first time since the demise of hip house fast breakbeats began to augment crotchet beats. In many respects, the high levels of hybridity in British dance music in the 1990s meant that a breakbeat/crotchet hybrid was almost inevitable. Speed garage basslines were drawn from Jamaican reggae and filtered through jungle's sub-bass sensibility. Jungle and ragga-style sound effects, such as the rash of gun shot volleys heard on popular speed garage tracks such as Strictly Dub's *Small Step* and 187 Lockdown's *Gunman*, were also added to the mix.

Soon after speed garage settled into a generic formula it mutated into a slightly different form and continues to mutate today. In 1998, there was a rash of speed garage remixes of jungle and house tracks, and this was accompanied by the rise of a range of chart-bound speed garage acts such as 187 Lockdown and Tuff Jam. Once speed garage had charted, it appeared that the sound had run its natural full course and would require further development if UK garage was to maintain a longevity. This came through the expunging of the warped 'junglist' basslines of speed garage, the gradual fading out of the breakbeat and the emphasis on two beats in the bar of the 4 : 4 time signature. This later beat structure, originally developed in hardstep drum 'n' bass, led this form of garage to be renamed two-step garage. Overall, two-step garage had a smoother, more soulful feel than speed garage (particularly with regard to its use of soulful vocals that avoided the time-stretched spoken vocals of speed garage), relied less on the dub sound effects and abrupt rhythmic disruptions of speed garage. As such, it was closer to the original 1980s' New York garage sound, although it retained a British sensibility through the 'breakbeat science' incorporated within the minutiae of its rhythm structure.

Come 2000–3, the two-step rhythm structure became less and less popular, and as such, the name UK garage came to the fore. Expunged largely of jungle influences, with few reggae basslines or 'breakbeat science', UK garage in 2003 is far less of an experimental and avant-garde form than jungle and is now far closer to American garage than any of its predecessors. The less avant-garde the garage track, the more potential it has for chart success, and recent years have seen acts from the garage scene have significant chart success, as witnessed by the continuing popularity of the So Solid Crew for the teenage market and Ms Dynamite

(Niomi McLean-Daley), winner of the 2002 Mercury Music Award. Jungle continues to fluctuate in popularity, and the nightlife of most cities and towns will feature at least one weekly or monthly jungle night. Within the jungle scene, no particular faction or subgenre is hegemonic, with individual jungle clubs now booking a wide range of DJs rather than sticking to one specific sound.

Notes

1. Here we refer to Bob Marley's *Concrete Jungle* and the Specials' track of the same name. Bob Marley was the leading figure in 1970s' reggae, and his inclusive style had a deep influence upon a variety of British musical movements, including jungle. Reggae basslines and drum patterns and Jamaican vocal styles are all to be found within jungle. Equally, the Specials were dominant figures in the British ska revival of the late 1970s, and jungle was certainly influenced by the multiracial nature of the bands signed to the Specials' 2-Tone record label. Elsewhere in jungle's antecedents is the chorus from Grandmaster Flash and the Furious Five's 1982 rap *The Message*, which suggests that 'it's like a jungle, sometimes it makes me wonder how I keep from goin' under'. Grandmaster Flash and the Furious Five's track began a discourse of urban commentary that is still prevalent within rap music, and the phrase 'concrete jungle' also appears in a variety of more recent rap tracks including Cash Money Millionaires' *Undisputed*, R. Kelly and Crucial Conflict's *Ghetto Queen*, Nas' *Undying Love* and Skee-Lo's *I Wish*. Other writers also point to the naming of James Brown's 1986 album *In The Jungle Groove* as being of importance (Collin with Godfrey 1997: 253–4), and it is certainly the case that breakbeats from Brown's soul classics form the bedrock of much jungle.
2. Even the *Oxford English Dictionary* has a view on this debate, stating that 'drum and bass' is

   > a style of popular dance music originating in Britain in the early 1990s, variously thought of as derived from or identical to jungle, and characterized primarily by a fast drum track and a heavy, usually slower, bass track, but often also featuring synthesized or sampled strings, piano, or other instrumentation. (*Oxford English Dictionary Online*, 5 December 2002)

   Furthermore, the *OED* comes down firmly on the side of the mooted Jamaican etymology outlined above, although it does suggest that 'the precise origin of the usage is disputed'.
3. The Haçienda is probably the most written about nightclub of recent times. For an examination of its central importance to the development of a distinctly British club culture, see Savage (1992). For an examination of the relationship between the authorities, the press and The Haçienda's

218 POPULAR MUSIC GENRES: AN INTRODUCTION

clientele and management, see Redhead (1993b). For an examination of the club from the point of view of an academic, a DJ and a journalist, see Rietveld (1998), Haslam (1999) and Muddles (2002).

4. Ironically, this style of European techno was at least partly derived from the experimentations of those American artists who were outside the more restrained Chicago/Detroit axis, with New York's Joey Beltram a particular influence with *Energy Flash* in 1990 and *Mentasm* in 1991 (see Reynolds 1998: 108–13).

5. Reynolds puts it well:

> Sampled and fed into the computer, beats were chopped up, rese-quenced and processed with ever-increasing degrees of complexity. Effects like 'time-stretching/compression', pitchshifting, 'ghosting' and psychedelia-style reverse gave the percussion an eerie, chromatic quality that blurred the line between melody, rhythm and timbre. Separate drum 'hits' within a single breakbeat could be subjected to different degrees of echo and reverb, so that each percussive accent seems to occur in a different acoustic space . . . The term 'breakbeat science' fits because the process of building up jungle rhythm tracks is incredibly time-consuming and tricky, involving a near-surgical pre-cision. (Reynolds 1998: 241)

6. Interestingly, the phrasing of the 1994 Act appears to let jungle 'off the hook' so to speak, since it is, to paraphrase the Act, defined by a *lack* of repetitive beats. By this we mean that the syncopation of jungle breakbeats, combined with the 'breakbeat science' that sees breakbeats dismembered, edited, chopped, changed and reconstituted, often resists characterisation as 're-petitive' (unlike the 4 : 4 programmed beats of house and techno). However, we fear that, without the aid of a defence barrister who is also a musicologist, such an argument would receive short shrift from the police and the courts. Therefore, perhaps Hillegonda Rietveld is correct in her suggestion that the notion of 'repetitive beats', along with

> the concepts of 'night' and 'dance', are ill-defined in both existing and proposed British laws and seem to be motivated by an attempt to curb particular lifestyles and cultural expressions which do not belong to the 'dominant' classes, who make desperate attempts to hold on to their dispersing power. (Rietveld 1998: 60)

7. While the authors acknowledge that those Detroit musicians who fixed the generic boundaries of techno in the 1980s were largely African-Americans, it nonetheless remains a fact that these musicians were 'Europhiles' in that they were most heavily influenced by the avant-garde and modernist electronic musical movements of the twentieth century and the synthpop artists of the 1970s and 1980s. Confirmation of this can be found in John McCready's interview with Depeche Mode in Detroit in 1989 (McCready 1989). While some of the early techno pioneers (such as Derrick May) talk of the influence of funk and jazz (two musical forms that draw heavily on

discourses of blackness) on their music, this is less noticeable than the ostensibly 'white' European influences.

8. Simon Reynolds goes further, and suggests that jungle disrupts the binary opposition between the discourses of African diasporic music and Western music:

> Jungle's radicalism resides in the way it upturns Western music's hierarchy of melody/harmony over rhythm/timbre. In jungle, the rhythm is the melody; the drum patterns are as hooky as the vocal samples or keyboard refrains. In Omni Trio's classic *Renegade Snares*, the snare tattoo is the mnemonic, even more than the three-note, one-finger piano motif. (Reynolds 1998: 242)

9. Original emphasis.

10. Nowhere was this more obvious than in Liverpool. Despite its large black population, Liverpool had not sustained a jungle club until the late 1990s. In the early 1990s there were some breakbeat hardcore events held at venues such as The Hard Dock and the 051, but the switch from hardcore to jungle saw a decline in popularity in fast breakbeat music. In 1996, Liverpool 'superclub' Cream booked LTJ Bukem's Logical Progression team for a monthly residency in a newly built third room known as The Courtyard. While Bukem et al.'s monthly appearances were deemed successful and led to a decline in the popularity of the house music being played on Cream's main dancefloor at the time, the residency finished amid acrimony as Bukem began to leave the DJing duties to his team rather than playing on a monthly basis himself. This left a gap in the Liverpool music scene that was not filled until the rise of two new jungle promoters, Chrome and X, both of which had a predominantly white student audience. Interestingly, the late 1990s' influx of students also led to a rise in the popularity of rap music in the city centre. By 1999–2000, the dye had been set and jungle and rap in Liverpool remained a largely student-oriented affair, with some support in the black community for garage and R&B nights. The reasons for the relative unpopularity of jungle are unclear, but they cannot have been helped by a history of racist door policies in Liverpool's clubland and a relatively high level of racial segregation in Liverpool itself, with Liverpool's black community being based largely in Toxteth and other areas of south Liverpool.

Recommended reading

Collin, M. with Godfrey, J. (1997) *Altered State: The Story of Ecstasy Culture and Acid House*, London: Serpent's Tail.

Gilbert, J. and Pearson, E. (1999) *Discographies: Dance Music, Culture and the Politics of Sound*. London: Routledge.

Gilroy, P. (2002) *There Ain't No Black in the Union Jack*, 2nd edn. London: Routledge.

James, M. (1997) *State of Bass: Jungle: The Story So Far*. Basingstoke: Boxtree.

Redhead, S. (1990) *The End-of-the-Century Party: Youth and Pop towards 2000.* Manchester: Manchester University Press.

Redhead, S. (ed.) (1993) *Rave Off: Politics and Deviance in Contemporary Youth Culture.* Aldershot: Avebury.

Reynolds, S. (1998) *Energy Flash: A Journey through Rave Music and Dance Culture.* London: Picador.

Recommended listening

Antecedents

4 Hero (1991) *Mr Kirk's Nightmare* [single]. Reinforced.

Joey Beltram (1991) *Mentasm* [single]. R&S.

Origin Unknown (1993) *Valley of the Shadows* [single]. Ram.

Generic texts

A Guy Called Gerald (1995) *Black Secret Technology.* Juice Box.

Adam F (1996) *F-Jam* [single]. Positiva.

Alex Reece (1996) *So Far.* 4th and Broadway.

Everything But The Girl (1996) *Walking Wounded.* Virgin.

4 Hero (1994) *Parallel Universe.* Reinforced.

Ganja Kru (1996) *Super Sharp Shooter* [EP]. Parousia.

Goldie (1995) *Timeless.* FFRR.

M Beat and General Levy (1994) *Incredible* [single]. Renk Records.

Roni Size (1997) *New Forms.* Talkin' Loud.

Shy FX and UK Apache (1994) *Original Nuttah* [single]. DJ Only.

Squarepusher (1996) *Feed Me Weird Things.* Rephlex.

T-Power (1995) *The Self-Evident Truth Of An Intuitive Mind.* SOUR.

T-Power vs. MK Ultra (1996) *Mutant Revisited* [DJ Trace remix, single]. SOUR.

Various (1994) *Intelligent Minds Of Jungle.* Reinforced.

Various (1995) *Artcore Vol.1: Ambient Jungle.* React.

Various (1996) *LTJ Bukem Presents Logical Progression Vol. 1.* FFRR.

Subsequent generic developments

187 Lockdown (1998) *187 Lockdown* [single]. East West.

Shanks and Bigfoot (2000) *Swings And Roundabouts.* Pepper.

So Solid Crew (2001) *They Don't Know.* Independiente.

Glossary

AABA form. This is the traditional form of much pre-rock era popular music, particularly in fields such as vaudeville, music hall, stage show tunes and songs within film musicals. The form is one of the two main pop song structures, along with the folk and blues pattern built upon a single repeated verse and refrain. It consists of a 32-bar pattern comprising an eight-bar verse/chorus (A) repeated twice, then followed by a bridge or middle eight (B), sometimes in a changed key, before the return of the A pattern, which could lead to a fade out or another repetition of one of the two patterns in some cases. Many of the 'classic' song composers of the twentieth century, such as George Gershwin, Cole Porter, Hoagy Carmichael and Rodgers and Hart made great use of the form. The AABA form, although very standardised, did offer a model for the pop singles market that has proven durable to the present day.

Acid house. A highly synthesised form of house music. Acid house is characterised by its four-to-the-floor beats, linear structure, lack of lyrics (other than the occasional spoken word), and the undulating frequencies produced by sound sources such as the Roland TB-303 bass squencer. Whereas house music has a narrative emphasis on notions of love and unity, acid house is more self-reflexive in its emphasis on artificially and mechanisation.

Auteur. *Auteur* and *auteur* theory are terms associated with French film theory, in particular the critical journal *Cahiers du Cinéma*. Auteur theory argued for the re-evaluation of so-called 'commercial' films and 'journeyman' directors such as John Ford and Alfred Hitchcock, stating that such directors' work carried a 'personal' and artistic imprint not inferior to more critically lauded works or 'creative' genres. This theory is equally applicable to popular music, particularly to those with creative input in more than one area (production, musicianship, composition, performance). However, as well as doing much to help elevate 'low' forms of culture, *auteur* theory can have problematic consequences, particularly relating to the establishment of a 'canon' of worth and the denial of the collaborative nature of music. The theory has value but should not be used in a deterministic or qualitative manner.

Authenticity paradigm. This applies to schools of criticism and individual critics who set up a binary divide between forms of music seen as honest, creative or real, and those seen as commercially compromised, standardised or more about profit. As Shuker suggests, it is 'a central concept in the discourses surrounding popular music' (Shuker 1998: 20–1). Although discredited by many in recent analyses, the paradigm is still widespread and is useful in enabling the ideological assumptions of the analyst to be exposed.

Belle époque/art nouveau. These terms refer to art and artefacts produced in the *fin-de-siècle* period around 1900, particularly in France and the UK. Such products drew heavily upon oriental design for their inspiration and were often seen to be decadent, overly decorative or controversial by the staid establishment of the period. Much of the stimulus for the appropriation of this style within the UK psychedelic scene came following the Aubrey Beardsley exhibition at London's Victoria & Albert Museum in 1966 (Gilbert 2003: 50).

Black Panthers. A radical black power organisation in the US that rose to prominence in the late 1960s. Revolutionary in aim and militant in its support for the right of black people to defend themselves against attack, the Black Panthers hit the headlines in the late 1960s due to their support for the North Vietnamese in the fight against 'the common enemy' of the United States government. Attacked and undermined by the FBI, the Black Panther Party survived into the 1970s but came to an end amid internal disputes at the end of the decade.

Bricolage. The construction of a text from a variety of fragments found elsewhere. The term is used within the structuralist anthropology of Claude Lévi-Strauss to describe the way that social myths are constructed from historical fragments of folk memory.

Canon/canonic. A canon is a body of work that a usually bourgeois elite decides is of transcendent worth or value. So, for example, within drama Shakespeare would be canonic, and within painting Rubens. Popular music studies has wrestled with the concept of a canon for many years; obvious candidates for inclusion would be The Beatles, Bob Dylan and Aretha Franklin, or whole genres such as blues or folk. Because of the 'high art' tendencies resulting from establishing a canon, many within the field would be wary of its widespread or unproblematic adoption. In this book, we have sought to argue for worth in popular music to be negotiated between elements rather than imposed from above.

Carnivalesque. A term popularised in cultural studies by the Soviet academic Mikhail Bakhtin (Bakhtin 1984) who developed the theories of Rabelais concerning the importance of the medieval carnival. These theorists emphasised the carnival as a symbolic site allowing for a reversal of social roles and status, allowing for the disenfranchised to become 'king' or 'queen' for a day. This reversal was allowed for the status quo to be maintained for all but these specific events, providing a 'safe' social outlet for potentially subversive political tendencies. The parallels within metal concerts in particular, and popular music as a whole, are self-evident.

Concept album. In general terms, an album consisting of tracks or ideas linked across several compositions. The identification of the first concept album is difficult. Some would say that the idea pre-dates prog rock, but certainly this genre did make great use of it. Concept albums could take many forms, but were often concerned with somewhat overblown and weighty philosophical or metaphysical issues. Sometimes concept works consisted of tracks lasting a complete side of an album. Indeed, on Yes' *Tales From Topographic Oceans*, each side of a double album consists of one track. The album as a whole was based upon the issues raised in Paramahansa Yoganda's *Autobiography of a Yogi* (Holm-Hudson 2002: 14). The concept album form became one of the most vilified aspects of prog rock when the genre was critically discredited during the punk era.

Conjunctural analysis. This concept argues against the 'big-bang' theory of history in stating that things do not emerge out of a vacuum but are encouraged to do so by varied and contingent factors. Shepherd argues for a conjunctural analysis in helping us to understand the reasons for the emergence of rock 'n' roll in the mid-1950s, rather than adopting the mythologising model relating to it all being due to Elvis, for example (see Shepherd 1991).

Contextualism. An approach to the study of media texts and cultural practices that relates texts and practices to their social, cultural, political and economic contexts.

Creolisation. The linguistic term 'creolisation' refers to the process whereby a grammatically simplified form of an imported language (such as English) fuses with a local language and gradually becomes the mother tongue of a specific people. This is the case with the patois spoken by most Jamaicans (as opposed to the allegedly more 'literate' standard English spoken elsewhere).

Crossover. A term usually applied to music produced by black or marginalised communities which is either created or promoted to cross over into a white or mainstream market. For many commentators, this inevitably results in a 'dilution' of the 'essence' of the original message (see George 1988). Because of the inherent inequalities between races in Western communities and the historical appropriation of so-called black genres by white audiences, crossover is typically a one-way process. In marketing terms, there is less of an imperative for 'white' music to crossover into the black community. Some of the biggest selling albums in popular music, such as Michael Jackson's *Thriller* and Prince's *Purple Rain*, have been classic examples of the crossover phenomenon.

Dialectical relationships. A dialectical relationship between two different cultural phenomenon (texts or practices) is one where the central 'meaning' of each phenomena is informed and reinforced through reference to the other phenomenon.

Dionysian. Often set up as a binary opposition against the Apollonian tendency in art and affect. Dionysian, based upon the Greek god Dionysus (or Bacchus), represents excess, hedonism, intoxication, bodily response and ecstatic states, whereas Apollonian, from the Greek god Apollo, represents order, rationality and a cerebral state of mind.

Ethnicity.   An ethnic group can be defined as a distinct social group that shares a specific origin and specific cultural, historical, racial, religious or linguistic features. Ethnic groups can be contrasted with classes (which are generally defined by wealth or occupation) and races (which are defined by genetic and physical attributes).

Five Percent Nation.   Also known as the Nation of Gods and Earths, the Five Percenters are a US-based Islamic organisation founded on the premise of self-government and black supremacy in the arts and sciences.

Fordism and post-Fordism.   Named after Henry Ford, Fordism is a period of industrial development where production of both material and cultural goods is organised according to an assembly line model that produces standardised goods at low prices. Fordist plants reward workers with a relatively high income to encourage them to spend their money on consumer goods that are themselves produced by Fordist methods. Fordism is connected to Taylorism, a pseudo-scientific way of ensuring efficient management of human resources. Post-Fordism refers to the more recent rise in small-scale production aimed at niche rather than mass markets. Post-Fordism is also associated with increased consumer choice, 'just-in-time' production methods, 'labour flexibility' (a.k.a. short-term contracts, part-time working and decreases in job security) and de-unionised workplaces.

Four-to-the-floor.   A crotchet beat perfectly sequenced on each beat of the bar.

Funk/funky.   The etymological roots of these terms are varied, but often surprisingly apt in symbolising the ethos and affect of funk music. They have been historically employed to describe a musty or a sexual smell, a mean mood, a loss of control, or a bad temper or situation. Within the recent popular music era, funk/funky stand as connoting syncopation, groove, energy, rhythmic intensity, 'danceability' and usually black ethnicity.

Genre/metagenre/subgenre.   Genre is defined by Shuker as 'a category, or a type . . . widely used to analyse popular music texts' (Shuker 1998: 145–9). Genre-based analysis – long established in disciplines such as film studies – allows for both textual and contextual characteristics to be considered when categorising a musical example. Associated terms such as metagenre or subgenre can also be used to broaden the critical frame or narrow it. Thus soul could be considered a genre definable within broad parameters but itself included within the broader metagenre of R&B or 'black music'. Within the genre of soul, we could divide the form into subgenres such as Motown or southern soul. Of course, the use of such terms is contestable, subjective and not without controversy. Nevertheless, put simply, genre analysis allows texts to be interpreted and demythologised in the light of a broad range of critical criteria.

Gesamkunsterwerk. For the composer Richard Wagner, this term related to the concept of the unified art work: 'music, visual motifs and verbal expression are inextricably intertwined to convey a coherent artistic vision' (Macan 1997: 11).

Globalisation. A term used to describe the apparent creation of a global culture and economics. Globalisation is the result of, among other factors, the internationalisation of capital, the creation of a global 'information economy', digitisation and computerisation, the decreasing importance of nation states within a variety of transnational bodies such as the European Union, international media conglomeration, Westernisation of non-Western cultures, economic liberalisation and consequent decreases in trade tariffs, and the increased importance of international law.

Gothic. A term originally used to describe a style of architecture, later extended to cover literature and art in general. Gothic art tends to deal with concepts such as the sublime and the uncanny, and psychic states of disturbance, dread and hysteria. Within popular music the term was first widely adopted to describe both the music and appearance of certain post-punk groups such as Siouxsie and the Banshees, The Cure and Joy Division and their devotees. In terms of subject matter, imbued atmosphere and the black, theatrically extreme forms of dress, there were clear connections between post-punk and metal tendencies such as black metal and thrash metal. The gothic dimension and look has remained a strong component in metal music and subculture for over twenty years.

Homology. Within academic analysis, a homology is a precise structural fit between subjectivity, cultural texts and cultural practices. Homology is a broadly Marxist term, originally adapted by Paul Willis to describe the relationship within biker culture between motor bikes, rock 'n' roll and alcohol consumption, and the relationship within hippie culture between progressive rock, LSD and the mind-set of hippies themselves (Willis 1978). In particular, homology theory emphasises structural similarities, so, for example, Willis suggests that hippie notions of time are structurally related to the distorted perceptions of time experienced by LSD users and the disruptions of musical time found within tracks such as *A Day In The Life* by The Beatles.

House. An electronic dance music based on a strict 4 : 4 time signature, with a sequenced kick drum on all four crotchets of each bar, at speeds of around 120–30 beats per minute. Melody and vocals are used to break up repetition. House music was originally developed in the early 1980s by American musicians and DJs such as Frankie Knuckles, Farley Keith, DJ Pierre and Chip-E. Initially house drew influence from up-tempo R&B and Salsoul. In particular house DJs took records from these genres and 'remixed' them, re-editing them for dancefloor consumption and adding percussion from newly developed drum machines. The term house itself is an abbreviation of the name of The Warehouse club in Chicago, and was used by local record shops to describe the music played there.

Interdisciplinarity.   An approach to study that relies upon methodological and theoretical principles drawn from two or more academic disciplines.

Intertextuality.   A belief that the meaning of a specific media text is at least partly derived through reference to other texts.

Major/indie.   In the contemporary music scene, major record companies are thought of as having a global reach and influence. Majors also often own several linked elements in the production chain – such as publishing rights, recording studios and Internet interests. This allows them to 'synergise' sales and maximise profits. Indie, or independent, labels can be wholly separate from the majors or reliant on them for aspects of the distribution or marketing process, and many mythologies relating to the 'integrity' of indie labels as opposed to the 'uncaring' nature of the majors have been expressed. Since the late 1970s, the term indie has also been applied generically to styles of music seen as 'underground' or uncompromised by the constraints of global capital and large-scale marketing and promotion.

The Merry Pranksters.   A loosely knit group of alternative/beatnik artists who toured the US in the early years of psychedelia and distributed drugs as part of a 'Kool-Aid Acid Test'. The events were said to have closely resembled the subsequent hippie 'rave' or 'freak out'. Bands such as the Grateful Dead would sometimes perform.

Metre.   A succession of beats, and associated gaps between beats, that make up the basic rhythmic structure of a piece of music. Forms of metre are often expressed as a time signature, for example '4 : 4', which refers to four equally emphasised beats to the bar.

Musical avant-garde.   A very nebulous term relating to any music or performers attempting to stretch the boundaries in conceptual, compositional or performance terms. Historically, the term has been generally applied to bourgeois art movements of the early twentieth century, such as Modernism, Dada and Futurism, or individuals such as Schoenberg, Varèse, Cage and Stockhausen (see Prendergast 2000, and Toop 1995). The work of the musical *avant-garde* usually alienates the critical mainstream, at least initially, before being partially co-opted at a later point. This can clearly be seen to have happened within popular music genres such as psychedelia and progressive rock.

Musicology.   A form of scholarly study of music that concentrates on analysing musical texts and often focuses its attentions upon transcribed forms of the music itself (for example musical scores and notation).

Musique concrète.   A term closely associated with certain aspects of the musical *avant-garde*. *Musique concrète* utilised non-musical and 'found elements' in order to produce sound or adapted conventional instruments in order to distort their tonal qualities. For instance, Stockhausen would produce a performance piece based on players retuning short-wave radios. Such experimentation had an impact upon groups such as Pink Floyd and Roxy Music, who made great use of tape loops and non-musical timbres within their compositions.

Nation of Islam. A US-based black separatist organisation founded in 1985 by the Muslim preacher Louis Farrakhan. Farrakhan has often courted controversy, particularly with regard to his alleged anti-semitism, and is currently banned from entering both the United Kingdom and Israel.

Negotiation. This concept, influenced by structuralist and reader-response theories of interpretation (see Barthes 1977), argues that there is no inherent meaning or value in any work or text. In simple terms, 'readers write texts'. For the purposes of our book, we take the position that although different texts do encourage certain interpretative strategies or provide 'preferred readings', the ultimate responsibility for constructing meaning lies in the negotiation between the text and the reader's own values, experiences and cultural identity. Equally important is the role of the individual's 'reading community' or peer group. Within this philosophy, a hierarchical set of beliefs and values is replaced by a reader-centred model wherein the most important aspect of interpretation is what the text reveals about the interpreter rather than about the text itself.

Nihilism. A total rejection of both religious belief and existing social values and morals.

Postmodernism/postmodernity. These two closely linked concepts have proven fundamental to the understanding of shifts in critical thinking, cultural production and textual analysis for more than twenty years. The term postmodernity usually refers to tendencies in late-capitalist society related to notions of hybridity and identity, globalisation and post-Fordist production processes. Postmodernism usually refers to such textual approaches that emphasise irony, playfulness, parody, pastiche, depthlessness and a creative sense of schizophrenia that denies unity, faith in absolutes and profundity. Readers are advised to undertake additional reading of texts that specifically deal with these concepts and their applications in popular music and cultural studies in general (see Harvey 1989, and Lipsitz 1996).

Powerchord. Instead of the more common chord built upon triads (1–3–5 in semitonal terms), the metal powerchord often dropped the 'comforting' middle interval and built upon the diminished chord of a root note plus a 4th or 5th. As well as being easy to play, this chord allowed for more 'spaces' to be filled with overtones or harmonics, made hugely significant by both distortion and overdriven amplification. These chords could be 'hammered' or damped to give a rapid 'chugging' sound so beloved of up-tempo metal.

Rhizome. Originally an agricultural term used to describe an underground stem which develops separate roots and shoots, the term is used here to describe the development of different offshoots of a specific genre.

Riff. Typically, a cyclical musical phrase or pattern. Historically associated with styles such as jazz and instruments such as the trumpet or saxophone, the term riff became widely adopted in pop circles and is most closely associated with styles built upon guitar distortion such as metal. Metal riffs could be played by a solo instrument or a whole rhythm section. Although widespread in metal, riffs, as opposed to blues-based guitar lines or 'licks', are more central to European metal than American modes of expression. Bands such as Black Sabbath fashioned tracks around often three or four riffs, with one pattern underpinning the verse, the chorus, the change and the intro/fade. The distorted guitar riff is the most important single element in metal. As long as the riff is memorable, almost any other sonic shortcoming is excusable to fans of the genre.

Situationism.   The Situationist International was an art movement formed in 1957 by French writer Guy Debord. Drawing equal amounts of theoretical sustenance from Marxism and anarchism, situationism was initially a Utopian art movement that rejected the growing consumerism of the twentieth century while also placing emphasis on *détournement*, usually translated as 'diversion'. While debate rages over the precise nature of situationism (the work of Stewart Home contains a particularly punk twist on this debate – see Home 1995), it is often taken to mean an interest in the creation of specific 'situations'. The intention of such situations is to shock people out of their complacency so that 'spectators' can begin to see the ideological nature of their consumer fetishism and the extent to which they are enslaved by an all-encompassing capitalist machine.

Subculture.   A term generally applied in the analysis of young people that suggests that certain groups of individuals have interests and beliefs that they share with each other but do not necessarily share with the rest of society. Subcultural definitions can focus upon modes of speech, political or ethical values, symbolic allegiances, cultural mores or modes of dress. Within cultural studies, subcultural theory is often presented with a Marxist twist. Within such analyses, members of a subculture share a 'biographical' allegiance with each other that might be cultural, sartorial, musical or attitudinal, while also sharing 'focal concerns' with a 'parent' culture (the phrase used to describe either working-class culture or middle-class culture) that are broadly economic and structural (see Hall and Jefferson 1975). Thus, while skinheads are young people who share a particular style of dress and an attitude, they also share with their 'parent' working-class culture a celebration of manual labour and a suspicion of anything considered *effete* or elitist.

Syncretic.   Strictly speaking, a syncretism is an amalgamation of different religions or schools of thought (*The Concise Oxford Dictionary*, Judy Pearsall (ed.), Oxford University Press, 2001). However, the term is used by academics such as Stolzoff (2000) and Gilroy (1994) to refer to the 'creolisation' of a culture, whereby cultural texts and practices are the result of a power struggle between those of African descent and the ruling elite of European descent. In applying the term to reggae, we should note that despite its trenchant Afrocentricism, reggae still incorporates lyrical and musical elements of European origin.

Techno.   A form of electronic dance music that has its origins in house music. While the gay club scene of Chicago developed the distinctive 4 : 4 beat of house music, it was Detroit which took this blueprint and developed a more minimal yet aggressive form that emphasises synthesis and artificiality rather than the 'authenticist' electronic soul of house.

Tenuto. A note held at its full value or longer. Tenuto or 'rolling' bass is found in drum 'n' bass records where there is no gap between individual bass notes.

Textualism. An approach to the study of media forms that focuses upon the study of the organisation, content and structure of texts.

Verisimilitude. An appearance of truth or reality.

Zeitgeist. A German term meaning literally 'spirit of the times'. It can be applied to many aspects of popular music in its social context. Thus the wearing of bells and Kaftans by the hippie subculture could be said to relate to the fascination with Eastern dress and philosophy in the late-1960s' *Zeitgeist*, or the classic punk song subjects of boredom, alienation, or unemployment could relate to the social conditions in Britain in the late 1970s' *Zeitgeist*.

Bibliography

Abbott, K. (ed.) (2001) *Calling Out Around The World: A Motown Reader*. London: Helter-Skelter.

Alberge, D. and Midgley, C. (1997) 'Task force of the talents will seek culture of success', *The Times*, 15 July.

Alexanders, A. (2001) ' "Ghetto fabulous"?', available from http://www.africa-na.com/columns/Alexander/bl_lines_14.asp, 14 February.

Arnett, J. (1996) *Metalheads: Heavy Metal Music and Adolescent Alienation*. Boulder, CO: Westview.

Bakari, I. (1999) 'Exploding silence: African-Caribbean and African-American music in British culture towards 2000', in Blake, A. (ed.), *Living Through Pop*. London: Routledge.

Baker, H. (1984) *Blues, Ideology, and Afro-American Literature: A Vernacular Theory*. Chicago: University of Chicago Press.

Bakhtin, M. (1984) *Rabelais and His World*, trans. H. Iswolsky. Bloomington, IN: Indiana University Press.

Barnard, S. (2000) *On the Radio*. Milton Keynes: Open University Press.

Barnes, R. (1991) *Mods!* London: Plexus.

Barrett, L. E., Sr (1997) *The Rastafarians*. Boston, MA: Beacon Press.

Barthes, R. (1977) 'The death of the author', in *Image, Music, Text*. London: Fontana.

Barthes, R. [1967] (1985) *Système de la Mode [The Fashion System]*. London: Jonathan Cape.

Bennett, A. (1997) ' "*Village greens and terraced streets*" ": *Britpop and representations of "Britishness"*'. Paper presented at 'Britpop: Towards a Musicological Assessment' conference, Leeds, April.

Bennett, A. (2000) *Popular Music and Youth Culture: Music, Identity and Place*. London: Macmillan Press.

Bennett, A. (2001) *Cultures of Popular Music*. Buckingham: Open University Press.

Bennett, T. (1981) 'Popular culture and hegemony in post-war Britain', in *U203 Popular Culture*, coursebook, Milton Keynes: Open University Press.

Berkeley, H. (1977) *The Odyssey of Enoch: A Political Memoir*. London: Hamish Hamilton.

Bewes, T. and Gilbert, J. (2000) *Cultural Capitalism*. London: Lawrence & Wishart.

Bilby, K. (1995) 'Jamaica', in Manuel, P. (ed.), *Caribbean Currents: Caribbean Music from Rumba to Reggae*. Philadelphia: Temple University Press.

Birch, W. (2000) *No Sleep Till Canvey Island*. London: Virgin.

Blake, A. (1997) *The Land without Music: An Archaeology of Sound in Britain*. Manchester: Manchester University Press.

Bogdanor, V. and Skidelsky, R. (1970) *The Age of Affluence, 1951–1964*. London: Macmillan Press.

Booth, A. (2001) *The British Economy in the Twentieth Century*. Basingstoke: Palgrave.

Bowman, D. (2002) ' "Let them all make their own music": individualism, Rush and the progressive/hard rock alloy', in Holm-Hudson, K. (ed.) *Progressive Rock Reconsidered*. London: Routledge

Brackett, D. (2000) *Interpreting Popular Music*. Berkeley, CA: University of California Press.

Bradley, L. (2000) *Bass Culture: When Reggae Was King*. London: Penguin

Brathwaite, E. K. (1970) *Folk Culture of the Slaves in Jamaica*. London: New Beacon Books.

Brown, A. (1982) 'Tamla hits the top', *History of Rock*, 36: 701.

Brown, G. (2001) *Otis Redding: Try a Little Tenderness*. Edinburgh: Mojo.

Buckley, D. (1999) *Strange Fascination: David Bowie, the Definitive Story*. London: Virgin.

Burgess, P. and Parker, A. (1999) *Satellite*. London: Abstract Sounds Publishing.

Burns, L. & Lafrance, M. (2000) *Disruptive Divas: Feminism, Identity & Popular Music*. London: Routledge.

Burrows, T. (1998) *The Complete Encyclopedia of the Guitar*. London: Schirmer.

Carroll, P. N. (1990) *It Seemed Like Nothing Happened: America in the 1970s*. New Brunswick, NJ: Rutgers University Press.

Castleman, C. (1982) *Getting Up: Subway Graffiti in New York*. Massachusetts: M.I.T. Press.

Cavanagh, D. (2001) *The Creation Records Story: My Magpie Eyes Are Hungry for the Prize*. London: Virgin.

Cavanagh, D. (2002) 'Run for your lives', *Mojo*, May: 56–64.

Chapman, R. (1992) *Selling the Sixties: The Pirates and Pop Music Radio*. London: Routledge.

Childs, D. (1984) *Britain Since 1945: A Political History*. London: Methuen.

Christie, I. (2003) *Sound of the Beast: The Complete Headbanging History of Heavy Metal*. London: HarperEntertainment.

Collin, M. with Godfrey, J. (1997) *Altered State: The Story of Ecstasy Culture and Acid House*. London: Serpent's Tail.

Condry, I. (1999) 'The social production of difference: imitation and authenticity in Japanese rap music', in Fehrenbach, H. and Poiger, U. (eds), *Transactions,*

Transgressions, Transformations: American Culture in Western Europe and Japan. Providence, RI: Berghahn.

Conefrey, M. (dir.) (1996) *Hang On To Yourself*, from the TV documentary series *Dancing in the Street*. London: BBC.

Cooper, M. (1982) *Liverpool Explodes.* London: Sidgwick & Jackson.

Cooper, M. and Chalfant, H. (1984) *Subway Art.* New York: Holt, Rinehart & Winston.

Corbett, J. (1994) *Extended Play: Sounding Off from John Cage to Dr Funkenstein.* London: Duke University Press.

Cosgrove, S. (1988) Sleeve notes to accompany *Techno! – The New Dance Sound of Detroit* [album]. Virgin.

Coupland, D. (1992) *Generation X: Tales for an Accelerated Culture.* London: Abacus.

Coxall, B. and Robins, L. (1998) *British Politics since the War.* Basingstoke: Macmillan Press.

Cunningham, M. (1999) *Good Vibrations: A History of Record Production.* London: Sanctuary.

Davis, S. (1985) *Hammer of the Gods: The Led Zeppelin Saga.* New York: William Morrow.

Donnelly, K. (2001) *Film Music: Critical Approaches.* Continuum International.

Du Noyer, P. (2002) 'Contact', *Mojo.* July: 74–82.

Dyson, M. E. (1996) *Between God and Gangsta Rap: Bearing Witness to Black Culture.* Oxford: Oxford University Press.

Edmonds, B. (2002) 'No Exit', *Mojo*, June: 58–62.

Eshun, K. (1998) *More Brilliant than the Sun, Adventures in Sonic Fiction.* London: Quartet Books.

Everett, W. (1999) *The Beatles as Musicians: Revolver through the Anthology.* Oxford: Oxford University Press.

Fielder, H. (1984) *The Book of Genesis.* London: Sidgwick & Jackson.

Flur, W. (2000) *Kraftwerk: I Was a Robot.* London: Sanctuary.

Fowler, P. (1982) 'The mod generation', in *History of Rock*, 41, London: Orbis, pp. 801–3.

Francis-Jackson, C. (1995) *The Official Dancehall Dictionary: A Guide to Jamaican Dialect and Dancehall Slang.* Kingston: Kingston Publishers.

Fricke, D. (1996) Album sleevenotes to accompany the CD reissue of the Byrds' *Younger Than Yesterday.*

Frith, S. (1980) 'The Coventry Sound', *New Society*, republished in Frith, S. (1988) *Music for Pleasure.* Cambridge: Polity Press, pp. 77–80.

Frith, S. (1982) 'The year it all came together', in *History of Rock*, 1, London: Orbis, pp. 2–20.

Frith, S. (1983) *Sound Effects: Youth, Leisure and the Politics of Rock 'n' Roll.* London: Constable.

Frith, S. (1986) 'The revenge of the nerds', republished in Frith, S. (1988) *Music for Pleasure.* Cambridge: Polity Press, pp. 200–1.

Frith, S. (1988) *Music for Pleasure*. Cambridge: Polity Press.

Frith, S. (1996) *Performing Rites: Evaluating Popular Music*. Oxford: Oxford University Press.

Frith, S. and Home, H. (1987) *Art into Pop*. London: Methuen.

Frith, S. and McRobbie, A. (2000) 'Rock and sexuality' in Frith, S. and Goodwin, A. (eds), *On Record: Rock, Pop and the Written Word*, London: Routledge.

Fukuyama, F. (1993) *The End of History and the Last Man*. New York: Avon Books.

Garofalo, R. (1997) *Rockin' Out: Popular Music in the USA*. Boston: Allyn & Bacon.

George, N. (1986) *Where Did Our Love Go?* London: Omnibus.

George, N. (1988) *The Death of Rhythm & Blues*. London: Omnibus.

George, N. (1998) *Hip Hop America*. London: Penguin Books.

Gilbert, J. and Pearson, E. (1999) *Discographies: Dance Music, Culture and the Politics of Sound*. London: Routledge.

Gilbert, P. (2003) 'Out of our heads', *Mojo*. September: 44–51.

Gillett, C. (1983) *The Sound of the City: The Rise of Rock and Roll*. New York: Pantheon.

Gilroy, P. (1993) *Small Acts: Thoughts on the Politics of Black Cultures*. London: Serpent's Tail.

Gilroy, P. (1994) ' "After the love has gone": bio politics and the ethno-poetics in the black public sphere', *Public Culture*, 7 (1): 49–76.

Gilroy, P. (2002) *There Ain't No Black in the Union Jack*, 2nd edn. London: Routledge.

Goodman, S. (2002) *Inside the Greesleeves Riddimachine*, http://www.hyperdub.-com/softwar/greensleeves.cfm, September.

Gorman, P. (2001a) *The Look: Adventures in Rock and Pop Fashion*. London: Sanctuary.

Gorman, P. (2001b) *In Their Own Write: Adventures in the Music Press*. London: Sanctuary.

Gramsci, A. (1971) *Selections from the Prison Notebooks of Antonio Gramsci*, trans. Q. Hoare and G. Nowell Smith. London: Lawrence & Wishart.

Gray, O. (1991) *Radicalism and Social Change in Jamaica, 1960–1972*. Knoxville, TN: University of Tennessee Press.

Grossberg, L. (1986) 'Is there rock after punk?', *Critical Studies in Mass Communication* (1).

Gunst, L. (1995) *Born Fi' Dead: A Journey Through the Jamaican Posse Underworld*. New York: Henry Holt.

Guralnick, P. (1986) *Sweet Soul Music*. London: HarperCollins.

Hall, S. (1980) 'Popular-democratic vs authoritarian populism: two ways of "taking democracy seriously" ', in Hunt, A. (ed.), *Marxism and Democracy*. New Jersey: Humanities Press

Hall, S. (1983) 'The great moving right show', in Hall, S. and Jacques, M. (eds), *The Politics of Thatcherism*. London: Lawrence & Wishart, pp. 19–39.

Hall, S. (1988) *The Hard Road to Renewal: Thatcherism and the Crisis of the Left*. London: Verso.

Hall, S. (1992) 'What is this "Black" in Black popular culture', in Wallace, M. (ed.), *Black Popular Culture*. New York: Dia Center for the Arts.

Hall, S. and Jacques, M. (eds) (1983) *The Politics of Thatcherism*. London: Lawrence & Wishart.

Hall, S. and Jacques, M. (eds) (1989) *New Times: The Changing Face of Politics in the 1990s*. London: Lawrence & Wishart.

Hall, S. and Jefferson, T. (eds) (1975) *Resistance Through Rituals: Youth Subcultures in Post-war Britain*. Hutchinson: London.

Hall, S., Critcher, T., Jefferson, T., Clarke, T. and Roberts, B. (1978) *Policing the Crisis: Mugging, the State and Law and Order*. Basingstoke: Macmillan Press.

Handelman, D. (1989) 'Money for nothing and the chicks are free: on the road with Mötley Crüe', *Rolling Stone*, 13 August: 34.

Harris, J. (2003) *The Last Party: Britpop, Blair and the Demise of English Rock*. London: Fourth Estate.

Hartley, J. (1994) 'Discourse', in O'Sullivan, T., Hartley, J. Saunders, D. Montgomery, M. and Fiske, J. (eds), *Key Concepts in Communication and Cultural Studies*, 2nd edn. London: Routledge.

Haslam, D. (1999) *Manchester England: The Story of the Pop Cult City*. London: Fourth Estate.

Hebdige, D. (1987) *Cut 'n' Mix: Culture, Identity and Caribbean Music*. London: Comedia.

Hennessy, P. (1993) *Never Again*. London: Vintage.

Hesmondhalgh, D. (2001) 'British popular music and national identity', in Morley, D. and Robins, K. (eds), *British Cultural Studies*. Oxford: Oxford University Press.

Heylin, C. (1993) *From the Velvets to the Voidoids: A Pre-Punk History for a Post-Punk World*. London: Penguin.

Heylin, C. (1998) *Never Mind The Bollocks, Here's the Sex Pistols*. New York: Schirmer Books.

Hicks, M. (1999) *Sixties Rock: Garage, Psychedelic and Other Satisfactions*. Urbana, IL, and Chicago: University of Illinois Press.

Hill, D. (1986) *Designer Boys and Material Girls*. London: Blandford Press.

Hirshey, G. (1985) *Nowhere to Run*. London: Pan.

Hodkinson, P. (2002) *Goth: Identity, Style and Subculture*. London: Berg.

Holm-Hudson, K. (ed.) (2002) *Progressive Rock Reconsidered*. London: Routledge.

Home, S. (1995) *Cranked Up Really High: Genre Theory and Punk Rock*. Hove: Codex.

Ingham, C. (2000) 'The Don', *Mojo*, April.

Iveson, K. (1997) 'Partying, politics and getting paid – hip hop and national identity in Australia', *Overland*, 147: 39–47.

Jahoda, M. (1982) *Employment and Unemployment: A Social-Psychological Analysis*. Cambridge: Cambridge University Press.

James, M. (1997) *State of Bass: Jungle: The Story So Far*. Basingstoke: Boxtree.

Johnson, R. (1927) 'Fitting gramophone records: how the Panotrope accompanies the film', *Kinematograph Weekly*, 10 November: 81.

Jones, S. (1988) *Black Culture, White Youth: The Reggae Tradition from JA to UK*. London: Macmillan.

Kelly, R. D. G. (1997) *Yo' Mama's Disfunktional: Fighting the Culture Wars in Urban America*. Boston, MA: Beacon Press.

Kettle, M. (2002) 'Things can only get better', *The Guardian*, G2 supplement, 11 July: 14–15.

Knight, N. (1982) *Skinhead*. London: Omnibus Press.

Krims, A. (2000) *Rap Music and the Poetics of Identity*. Cambridge: Cambridge University Press.

Laing, D. (1985) *One Chord Wonders: Power and Meaning in Punk Rock*. Milton Keynes: Open University Press.

Larkin, C. (1998) *The Virgin Encyclopedia of Indie and New Wave*. London: Virgin.

Lazall, B. (1999) *Indie Hits: The Complete UK Singles and Albums Independent of Charts, 1980 to 1989*. London: Cherry Red Books.

Lee, S. (1995) 'Re-examining the concept of the "independent" record company: the case of Wax Trax! Records', *Popular Music*, 14: 13–31.

Lester, P. (2002) 'Wild Boy', *The Guardian*, Review section, 23 August: 6–7.

Light, A. (ed.) (1999) *The Vibe History of Hip Hop*. London: Plexus Publishing.

Lipsitz, G. (1994) *Dangerous Crossroads: Popular Music, Postmodernism and the Poetics of Place*. London: Verso.

Lista, G. (2001) *Futurism*. Paris: Pierre Travail.

Logan, N. and Woffinden, B. (1982) *Illustrated Encyclopedia of Rock*. London: Salamander/Hamlyn.

Longhurst, B. (1995) *Popular Music and Society*. London: Polity Press.

Lyotard, J. F. (1984) *The Postmodern Condition: A Report on Knowledge*, trans. Geoff Bennington and Brian Massumi. Minneapolis, MN: University of Minnesota Press.

Macan, E. (1997) *Rocking the Classics: English Progressive Rock and the Counter-culture*. Oxford: Oxford University Press.

McCready, J. (1989) 'Modus operandum: Depeche Mode in Detroit', *The Face*, April.

MacDonald, I. (1998) *Revolution in the Head: The Beatles Recordings and the Sixties*. London: Pimlico.

Macdonald, N. (2001) *The Graffiti Subculture: Youth, Masculinity and Identity in London and New York*. Basingstoke: Palgrave/Macmillan Press.

McGartland, T. (1995) *Buzzcocks*. London: Omnibus.

McInnes, C. (1961) *Absolute Beginners*. London: Allison & Busby.

McIver, J. (2000) *Extreme Metal*. London: Omnibus.

MacKay, R. R. (1995) 'Unemployment as Exclusion: Unemployment as Choice'. Paper presented to the Regional Studies Association Conference, Bangor: University of Wales.

MacMillan, M. (2001) *The New Wave of British Heavy Metal Encyclopedia*. Berlin: Verlag Jeske.

Maconie, S. (1992) 'The Bretttish Movement', *New Musical Express*, 14 September.

Malins, S. (2001) *Depeche Mode: A Biography*. London: André Deutsch.

Manuel, P. (1995) *Caribbean Currents: Caribbean Music from Rumba to Reggae*. Philadelphia: Temple University Press.

Marcus, G. (1989) *Lipstick Traces: A Secret History of the 20th Century*. New York: Secker & Warberg.

Marshall, G. (1997) *The Two Tone Story*. Lockerbie: ST Publishing.

Marwick, A. (1982) *British Society Since 1945*. London: Penguin.

Marwick, A. (1991) *Culture in Britain Since 1945*. London: Blackwell.

Masouri, J. (2002) 'Catcha more fire', *Mojo*, August: 21.

Maxwell, I. (1997) 'Phat Beat, Dope Rhymes – Hip Hop Down Under Comin' Upper.' PhD thesis, Sydney: Centre for Performance Studies, University of Sydney.

Maycock, J. (2002) 'Loud and proud', *Guardian Weekend*, 20 July: 30–5.

Maycock, J. (2003) 'Death or glory' *Mojo*, July: 66–74.

Meeks, B. (1996) *Radical Caribbean: From Black Power to Abu Bakr*. Kingston, Jamaica: University of West Indies Press.

Middleton, R. (1990) *Studying Popular Music*. Milton Keynes: Open University Press.

Middleton, R., and Muncie, J. (1981) 'Pop culture, pop music and post-war youth: counter-cultures', in *U203 Popular Culture*, coursebook. Milton Keynes: Open University Press.

Mitchell, T. (1998) 'Australian hip hop as a 'glocal' subculture'. Paper presented to the Ultimo Series Seminar, Sydney, University of Technology Sydney.

Moore, A. (1993) *Rock: The Primary Text*. Buckingham: Open University Press.

Morgan, K. O. (1990) *The People's Peace: British History, 1945–1989*. Oxford: Oxford University Press.

Morrow, C. (1999) *Stir It Up: Reggae Album Cover Art*. San Francisco: Chronicle Books.

Morse, D. (1982) 'Black and proud', *History of Rock*, 36: 781–3.

Moynihan, M. and Soderlind, D. (1998) *Lords of Chaos: The Bloody Rise of the Satanic Metal Underground*. Los Angeles: Feral House.

Muddles, M. (2002) *From Joy Division to New Order: The True Story of Anthony H. Wilson and Factory Records*. London: Virgin.

Muirhead, B. (1983) *Stiff: The Story of a Record Label, 1976–1982*. London: Blandford Press.

Mulholland, M. (2002) *The Longest War: Northern Ireland's Troubled History*. Oxford: Oxford University Press.

Murray, C.-S. (1989) *Crosstown Traffic: Jimi Hendrix and Post-war Pop*. London: Faber & Faber.

Napier-Bell, S. (2002) *Black Vinyl White Powder*. London: Ebury Press.

Negus, K. (1996) *Popular Music in Theory: An Introduction*. London: Polity Press.

Nuttall, J. (1970) *Bomb Culture*. London: Paladin.

Osgerby, B. (1999) ' "Chewing out a rhythm on my bubble-gum": the teenage aesthetic and genealogies of American punk', in Sabin, R. (ed.), *Punk Rock: So What?* London: Routledge, pp. 154–69.

Palmer, R. (1995) *Rock and Roll: An Unruly History*. New York: Harmony.

Patterson, A. (1996) Sleeve notes accompanying *Supernatural Fairy Tales: The Progressive Rock Era*. Rhino, pp. 10–40.

Payne, A. and Sutton, P. (eds) (1993) *Modern Caribbean Politics*. Baltimore, MD: Johns Hopkins University Press.

Platt, J. (1982) 'Street life: how love went sour on Haight Ashbury', *History of Rock*, 46.

Platt, J. (1983) 'Psychedelic wallflowers', *History of Rock*, 70.

Pope, R. (1998) *The British Economy Since 1914: A Study in Decline*. London: Longman.

Porter, D. (2002) *Rapcore: The Nu-Metal Rap Fusion* London: Plexus.

Potter, R. (1995) *Spectacular Vernaculars: Hip-Hop and the Politics of Post-modernism*. New York: State University of New York Press.

Prendergast, M. (2000) *The Ambient Century*. London: Bloomsbury.

Push and Bush (1995) 'Word to the wise', *Muzik*, 3, August: 90.

Rawlins, T. and Diggle, S. (2002) *Harmony in My Head, The Buzzcocks*. London: Helter Skelter.

Redhead, S. (1990) *The End-of-the-Century Party: Youth and Pop Towards 2000*. Manchester: Manchester University Press.

Redhead, S. (ed.) (1993a) *Rave Off: Politics and Deviance in Contemporary Youth Culture*. Aldershot: Avebury.

Redhead, S. (1993b) 'The politics of ecstasy', in Redhead, S. (ed.), *Rave Off: Politics and Deviance in Contemporary Youth Culture*. Aldershot: Avebury, pp. 7–28.

Reynolds, S. (1985) 'New pop and its aftermath', *Monitor*, 4.

Reynolds, S. (1989) 'Against health and efficiency: independent music in the 1980s', in McRobbie, A. (ed.), *Zoot Suits and Second-Hand Dresses: An Anthology of Fashion and Music*. Basingstoke: Macmillan Education, pp. 245–55.

Reynolds, S. (1995) 'Jungle Fever: London's hottest dance scene spikes techno music with a reggae flavor', *Details* (US edition), January.

Reynolds, S. (1998) *Energy Flash: A Journey through Rave Music and Dance Culture*. London: Picador.

Rietveld, H. (1998) *This Is Our House: House Music, Cultural Spaces and Technologies*. Aldershot: Ashgate.

Rimmer, D. (1985) *Like Punk Never Happened: Culture Club and the New Pop.* London: Faber & Faber.

Rimmer, D. (2001) 'Northern Soul and Motown', in Abbott, K. (ed.) *Calling out Around the World: A Motown Reader.* London: Helta-Skelter.

Rimmer, D. (2003) *New Romantics: The Look.* London: Omnibus Press.

Ritzer, G. (1993) *The McDonaldization of Society.* Thousand Oaks, CA: Pine Forge Press.

Robertson, R. (1995) 'Glocalization: time-space and homogeneity-heterogeneity', in Featherstone, M., Lash, S. and Robertson, R. (eds), *Global Modernities.* London: Sage.

Rose, T. (1994) *Black Noise: Rap Music and Black Culture in Contemporary America.* Middleton, NH: Weslyan University Press.

Sabin, R. (ed.) (1999a) *Punk Rock: So What?* London: Routledge.

Sabin, R. (1999b) 'Introduction', in Sabin, R. (ed.), *Punk Rock: So What?* London: Routledge, pp. 1–14.

Sabin, R. (1999c) ' "I won't let that dago by": Rethinking punk and racism', in Sabin, R. (ed.), *Punk Rock: So What?* London: Routledge, pp. 199–218.

Savage, J. (1977) 'New musick', *Sounds* 26 November.

Savage, J. (1979) 'Gary Numan: in every dream car, a Heart-throb', *Melody Maker*, 20 October.

Savage, J. (1981) 'An enclosed world: the New Romantics', *Time Out*, 30 January–5 February.

Savage, J. (1982) 'Soft Cell: the whip hand', *The Face*, January.

Savage, J. (1983) 'Androgyny: confused chromosomes and camp followers', *The Face*, June.

Savage, J. (1985) 'Humpty Dumpty and the new authenticity', *The Face*, July.

Savage, J. (ed.) (1992) *The Haçienda Must Be Built.* London: International Music Publications.

Savage, J. (1994a) *England's Dreaming: Anarchy, Sex Pistols, Punk Rock and Beyond.* London: Faber & Faber.

Savage, J. (1994b) 'Psychedelia', booklet accompanying *Mojo*, July.

Savage, J. (1997) *Time Travel: From the Sex Pistols to Nirvana: Pop, Media and Sexuality, 1977–96.* London: Vintage.

Schoen, D. E. (1977) *Enoch Powell and the Powellites.* London and Basingstoke: Macmillan Press.

Selvin, J. (2001) 'Lucifer rising', *Mojo*, August: 80–90.

Sheinbaum, J. (2002) 'Progressive rock and the inversion of musical values', in Holm-Hudson, K. (ed.), *Progressive Rock Reconsidered.* London: Routledge, pp. 21–42.

Shepherd, J. (1991) *Music as Social Text.* Cambridge: Polity.

Shuker, R. (1994) *Understanding Popular Music.* London: Routledge.

Shuker, R. (1998) *Key Concepts in Popular Music.* London: Routledge.

Sked, A. and Cook, C. (1979) *Post-war Britain.* Brighton: Harvester Press.

Stevens, J. (1989) *Storming Heaven: LSD and the American Dream*. London: Paladin.

Stolzoff, N. C. (2000) *Wake the Town and Tell the People: Dancehall Culture in Jamaica*. Durham, NC, and London: Duke University Press.

Strong, M. C. (1999) *The Great Alternative Indie Discography*. Edinburgh: Canongate Books.

Stump, P. (1998) *The Music's All That Matters: A History of Progressive Rock*. London: Quartet.

Tamm, E. (1989) *Brian Eno, his Music and the Vertical Color of Sound*. London: Faber & Faber.

Thompson, B. (1998) *Seven Years of Plenty: A Handbook of Irrefutable Pop greatness, 1991–1998*. London: Phoenix.

Thorgerson, S. and Powell, A. (1999) *One Hundred Best Album Covers*. London: Dorling-Kindersley.

Toop, D. (1995) *Ocean of Sound: Aether Talk, Ambient Sound and Imaginary Worlds*. London: Serpent's Tail.

Toop, D. (1999) *Rap Attack #3: African Rap to Global Hip Hop*. London: Serpent's Tail.

Verma, R. (1999) 'Shut Up and Dance', in *Knowledge Magazine*, available at http://195.82.125.20/shutupanddance.shtml.

Vickers, T. (1995) *Mothership Connection*, album sleevenotes to accompany *The Best of Parliament: Give Up the Funk*. Casablanca.

Vincent, R. (1996) *Funk: the Music, the People & the Rhythm of the One*. New York: St Martin's.

Walser, R. (1993) *Running with the Devil: Power, Gender and Madness in Heavy Metal Music*. Hanover, NY: Wesleyan University Press.

Ward, B. (1998) *Just My Soul Responding: Rhythm and Blues, Black Consciousness and Race Relations*. London: UCL Press.

Ward, B. (2001) 'Just my soul responding', in Abbott, K. (ed.) *Calling Out Around the World: A Motown Reader*. London: Helter-Skelter.

Waters, A. M. (1985) *Race, Class, and Political Symbols: Rastafari and Reggae in Jamaican Politics*. Oxford: Transaction Books.

Weinger, H. and Leeds, A. (1996) *It's A New Day*, album sleevenotes to accompany *Foundations of Funk: A Brand New Bag, 1964–1969*. Polydor.

Weinstein, D. (2000) *Heavy Metal: The Music and Its Culture*. Cambridge, MA: Da Capo Press.

Werner, C. (1999) *A Change is Gonna Come: Music, Race and the Soul of America*. New York: Plume.

West, C. (1997) 'Interview', in Storey (ed.), *Cultural Theory and Popular Culture: A Reader*. London: Prentice Hall.

Widgery, D. (1986) *Beating Time: Riot 'n' Race 'n' Rock 'n' Roll*. London: Chatto & Windus.

Williams, R. (1993) 'The trip', *Mojo*, November: 40–60.

Willis, P. (1978) *Profane Culture*. London: Routledge & Kegan Paul.
Wilson, T. (2002) *24 Hour Party People*. London: Channel 4 Books.
Whitehead, P. (1985) *The Writing on the Wall: Britain in the Seventies*. London: Michael Joseph.
Whiteley, S. (1992) *The Space Between the Notes: Rock and the Counter-culture*. London: Routledge.
York, P. (1980) *Style Wars*. London: Sidgwick & Jackson.
York, P. and Jennings, C. (1995) *Peter York's Eighties*. London: BBC Books.

Index